LIVING WAGES
AND THE WELFARE STATE
The Anglo-American Social Model
in Transition

Shaun Wilson

P

First published in Great Britain in 2021 by

Policy Press, an imprint of
Bristol University Press
University of Bristol
1-9 Old Park Hill
Bristol
BS2 8BB
UK
t: +44 (0)117 954 5940
e: bup-info@bristol.ac.uk

Details of international sales and distribution partners are available at
policy.bristoluniversitypress.co.uk

British Library Cataloguing in Publication Data
A catalogue record for this book is available from the British Library

ISBN 978-1-4473-4118-5 hardcover
ISBN 978-1-4473-4120-8 paperback
ISBN 978-1-4473-4121-5 ePub
ISBN 978-1-4473-4119-2 ePdf

Cover design: Clifford Hayes
Front cover image: Alamy ETXX2G

For my Dad,
Geoffrey Raymond Wilson

Contents

List of tables

Preface and acknowledgements

Times have been tough for progressives in the so-called 'liberal welfare state' countries, which are the focus of this book. Thankfully, there has been a great flourishing of new ideas in recent times and they hold promise, over time and with the backing of an electoral and social coalition, of influencing the foundations of employment and welfare. This contribution does not focus solely on the 'big ideas' for reform. Rather, it tries to account for *actual* signs of transformation that have taken place as a result of minimum wage reforms and living wage campaigns in many countries, perhaps most spectacularly in the conservative liberal welfare state of the US. These changes are starting to accumulate into something significant, challenging the orthodoxy about the 'necessity' of low minimum wages in an era of globalisation and technological change. As many have observed, on their own, higher minimum wage floors do not – and will not – resolve the failings of labour markets that are not regulated for 21st-century workplace organisation, the dynamics of household organisation, and the opportunities to exploit workers. Still, it is an open question whether improved minimums will spark greater mobilisation for broader progressive reforms that will benefit ordinary workers and revitalise the labour movement on which the health of democracy and broad potential for greater equality depend. The COVID-19 crisis has been a painful reminder of the fragility of life on our planet, of democratic institutions, and of the situation faced by many frontline and essential workers who have worked to keep societies going. As a colleague suggested, the pandemic is a reminder for everyone that the world only functions because of the daily activities of millions of people who are poorly paid.

Writing a book is both a solitary and collective exercise, the result of the assistance and insights of many others whose research in the areas of social policy, political science, and industrial relations have helped me greatly. I would like to acknowledge the wisdom and advice of the following people. Particular thanks go to Honorary Professor Joc Pixley of Macquarie University for her support and advice. I also greatly benefited from conversation with Professor John Miles of the University of Toronto when this project first began, and extend my gratitude to Associate Professor Rod Haddow and the Department of Political Science of the University of Toronto for hosting my stay in 2017. Thanks also go to Professor Jim Stanford (Centre for Future Work), Professor John Buchanan (University of Sydney), Professor

Ian McAllister (ANU), Associate Professor Sarah Kaine (University of Technology, Sydney), Professor Alan Morris (University of Technology, Sydney), Professor Gabrielle Meagher (Macquarie University), and Professor Peter Saunders (University of NSW). I am also grateful to the Organisation for Economic Co-operation and Development and the International Social Survey Programme for the wealth of data they make readily available to the academic community. Finally, I express deep gratitude to both my parents for their ongoing love and support.

Introduction: the challenge of a living wage

This book addresses one important way of dealing with minimum claims to justice through decent minimum or living wages. These claims have come at a time when widening inequalities have become an unavoidable fact (Nolan and Valenzuela 2019), one made worse by the COVID-19 pandemic and economic crisis that started in 2020. Even before then, the steady flow of reports documenting rising inequality in the rich 'liberal' world, coming from reputable and technically minded agencies, was not surprising, given that a decades-long push to return to 'business rule' in the economy and the labour market was designed to expand the profit share. As French social scientist Thomas Piketty (2013) has persuasively shown in his *Capital in the Twenty-First Century*, the concentration of wealth and its tendency to produce higher returns than the general growth rate mean that the present century risks seeing rising income and wealth inequality, a problem only reversed after World War Two with massive government intervention (see also Cassidy 2014).

The countries that form the particular focus of this book are the six English-speaking 'liberal' welfare states of Australia, Canada, Ireland, New Zealand, the United Kingdom, and the United States. They form a distinct cluster in analyses of welfare states and work relations, and although there are important differences between these countries and their politics and policies, they have followed policies antithetical to the remedies for runaway inequality that Piketty has identified. The consequences have been widening inequality, particularly in the UK and the US (Piketty 2013, Figure 9.2). These two countries have been completely transformed by rising inequality. High and rising inequality causes social and political malaise, evident in crime, mistrust, unhealthy individualism, and deteriorating public health (Wilkinson and Pickett 2009). These problems are mostly worse in the English-speaking cluster among the rich democracies, with the US and the UK ranking first and third on Wilkinson and Pickett's (2009, Figure 1, p 497) widely referenced indicators. Apart from generally lean welfare systems, these countries have all institutionalised pro-employer labour markets, with policy deliberately pushing their populations to depend on overextended labour markets. This dependence is further promoted by sociological processes common to many countries as inequalities related to gender and employment change. But rising dependence

1

on overextended labour markets is also the result of difficult times. Households are working more, partly to offset stagnant living standards made worse by policy. Moreover, 'work activation' social policies, particularly in Australia, the UK and the US, have made dependence on low-paid work the only escape route from harsher and more inadequate social assistance systems.

It is hardly a surprise, then, that the battle for living wages over the past decade or so has emerged in the pro-employer, lean welfare Anglo welfare states. Engineered reliance on low-wage and pro-employer labour markets have centred claims for justice and redistribution on low-paid work. When conservatives say that the best form of welfare is work (Jackson 2019), they implicitly acknowledge this reality. Justice claims for adequate resources more than ever now depend on the quality and security of low-wage employment. Somewhat contradictorily, the battle for living wages has taken off at a time when public discussion about paid employment casts major doubt about the future of work. Commentators are telling their readers and listeners of a coming 'end of work' – automation and artificial technologies are apparently gathering such pace that traditional jobs and industries will be swept away (Ford 2015; Yang et al 2019). Such predictions are not new. They started with the 19th-century technological revolutions and gathered pace again in the 1950s with predictions of high unemployment from pervasive automation. And such predictions have kept coming in waves, renewed practically every decade (Arendt [1958] 1998; Gorz 1982; Rifkin 2000; Standing 2015).

For workers and businesses confronted by technological change, these predictions have a real and often painful significance. Moreover, with threats of faster technical innovation, stories of displacement will define the experiences of more people and their communities. One study has suggested that Donald Trump's margin of victory in the Electoral College in the 2016 US presidential elections was extended by the impact of rising voter exposure to robots at work in electorally crucial counties (Frey et al 2018, p 437).

Anxieties about paid employment shove public discourse in two directions. The first presses new demands – from above – for workers to lower their expectations and accept belt-tightening. The second urges a transformation of jobs misery through the embrace of new utopias. The utopia of our times is the universal basic income. This idea is not new by any means. But it is more actively pursued now than at any other time except perhaps the 1970s. Its prominence is a direct response to the faltering union-led social democratic project of full employment and an encompassing welfare state (Habermas 1986). Basic income prospects are boosted by a loose and broad alliance of typically opposed interests. The political right sees basic income as a progressively more realistic path to achieving economist Milton Friedman's paradise of a small state and a marketplace that spans social as well as economic institutions. These advocates make no prediction of an end to work (far from it), but rather seek an end to the churn of 'tax-and-spend' redistribution, labour markets regulated for the industrial era, and interfering welfare bureaucracy.

By contrast, the left grounds a basic income on rising technological unemployment that further adds to the insecurity of workers already stressed by low-paid jobs, personal debt, and hardline welfare. Moreover, recent anthropological critiques add to long-standing arguments about the utility of many jobs. For Graeber (2018), the apparent preponderance of 'bullshit jobs' is a sign of the status and power of bosses to keep people busy in pointless ways (see Thompson and Pitts 2018 for a refutation). Pessimistic about weakened unions and apparently declining future employment, the left is now joined by a pro-business liberalism that sees a basic income as the social foundation of a new 'risk society' based on entrepreneurialism and gig employment. At times, the basic income left has unwittingly added to cultural and class contempt for low-paid workers and their jobs. Many of these workers perform essential services. And the COVID-19 pandemic brought their plight to attention of the public, and for some in the community, perhaps for the first time.

Yet some workers are fighting back and defending the integrity of their work. And policy institutions, seen as inflexibly committed to neoliberalism and austerity for the working class, have been responsive – at least to some extent. The 'Fight for $15' movement in the US represents a major challenge to low-wage orthodoxy in economics and the corporate control enforcing low wages in the food, care, and cleaning industries. In the UK, a policy designed as a minimal concession to trade unions that had barely survived Thatcherism – Prime Minister Blair's National Minimum Wage of 1998 – became *the* major social reform of post-millennial Britain. Waltman (2008, p 206) recalls that

> As Mr Blair was preparing to leave office, the public was asked 'Which three of the following would you judge to have been the greatest successes of Tony Blair's time as prime minister?' Introducing the minimum wage stood way out in front, winning the nod of 54%.

Similar improvements in minimum wages in NZ, and institutional innovations in Ireland and Canada's provinces, indicated that, prior to COVID-19, an unexpected challenge to the Anglo-American model of deregulated labour markets and low wages was under way. In the UK, NZ, and Canada, the Kaitz index – a simple measure that tracks the relative value of the minimum wage compared to the median wage – had risen by at least 10% between 2000 and 2020 (OECD 2020a).

Are these claims for 'living wages' – delivered through improved statutory minimum wages – last-gasp struggles for an outmoded form of economic justice? Crafting a satisfactory response to this question is the aim of this book. What is clear from the outset is that the success of the living wages movement offers counterfactuals to claims by an economic orthodoxy that has defended low-wage work and to the pessimism of a political left doubting any revival of the struggle over work and full employment.

The first of these counterfactuals addresses viable alternatives. Living wage campaigns have produced greater success than limited or stalled experiments with basic income in countries like Canada, Switzerland, Finland, and Italy. Despite pervasive gloom, working-class movements are still generating collective action, either through unions or in alliance with community organisations and political parties, to improve living standards. And they do so with widespread support from voters. The second counterfactual challenges the end of work thesis. Curiously, given the zeitgeist, the *volume* of paid employment produced by rich nation labour markets has remained stable, even as new waves of technology enter workplaces. True, workers are committing fewer paid hours in an average week. But the number of people in paid work continued to reach new records before the COVID-19 crisis. Even though rising dependence on paid employment has complex and occasionally problematic causes, it also continues to open up opportunities for women and other marginalised workers. And, as Pixley (1993) argues, employment remains a central arena for social struggle. Moreover, there is surprisingly little evidence – contrary to orthodox predictions – that improved minimum wages are driving up unemployment or that technology is finally tipping aggregate employment into secular decline. The third counterfactual questions whether low-wage jobs are miserable – beyond reform. Workers in 'unskilled' jobs paid at or near minimum wages continue to tell social researchers they like their jobs. And these workers are 'voting with their feet' in seeking to improve them.

All three counterfactuals are contestable. They may turn out to be wrong or only partial signals of likely trends. Technology, for example, may finally win out against organisational demands for human labour. What's left of paid work may result in the normalisation of temporary contracts for the many – and in ways that weaken workplace solidarity. And, future political conflicts may only further marginalise worker struggles as liberals move centre stage in their battles with populists over democracy.

This book develops a perspective fully aware of the fragility of these premises. But it also offers an alternative perspective to currently popular narratives, one that chronicles modest but real achievements of low-wage workers and their representatives in the two decades leading up to 2020. At the same time, it is guided by hope that the social justice and democratic energy achieved through workplaces is not a fading story left over from the struggles of the 19th and 20th centuries.

Valuing an hour's work

This book intentionally straddles related fields – the sociology of work, industrial relations, and social policy – which have become separated by academic conventions reflecting the institutional development of welfare states. The living wages movement in the liberal welfare states of the six English-speaking countries helps bring them back together. Bonoli (2003) observes that the regulation of employment plays a critical though often hidden role in the functioning of welfare states. That observation makes sense to Australians, for example, where the welfarist function of the 'basic' award wage since early federation (Castles 1985) has kept industrial relations research and social policy analysis more united.

Elsewhere in the liberal world, Bonoli's observation is gaining prescience by the day. The separation of social policy from wage-earner realities that occurred after World War Two became plausible because wage-earner institutions developed their own solid foundations, at least for most male breadwinners. Minimum wage-setting institutions started to matter less where collective bargaining spread the benefits of capitalist growth widely and where the number of minimum wage workers was either small or tiny. Writing on changes in the UK, Waltman (2008) notes that earlier preoccupations with minimum wages boards faded as a more ambitious and encompassing system of wage-earner bargaining and benefits developed. Something similar happened in the US when the Roosevelt era is compared to the decades that followed.

The revival of minimum wage and living wage politics underlines the seriousness of faltering wage-earner institutions, especially in the liberal world. At the same time, these failures point to the painful political limits of redistributive strategies of 'tax and spend' to further contain rising inequality. New efforts to construct wage-earner institutions from below are a reminder that employment matters to how welfare states develop and change – and most importantly, how they develop durable foundations. It is thus no surprise that minimum wage laws continue to expand on a global scale. Since 1990, a further nine Organisation for Economic Co-operation and Development (OECD) countries introduced a minimum wage, mainly in Eastern Europe (ACTU 2016, p 91; see also Dube et al 2020). Minimum wages are usually statutory devices, enforced, however inadequately, through law or, more directly, through workers' agency.

In some jurisdictions, including the six countries studied here, minimum wages directly influence the pay and job quality of over 10% of the workforce. Moreover, minimum wages indirectly benefit many more low-wage workers as well as middle-income households. This benefit is the indirect impact of minimums on the pay of non-minimum wage workers through what economists call 'spillover' effects. Only in a few rich country jurisdictions is the statutory minimum wage alien to the functioning of the social aspects of labour markets. For example, Nordic countries have used their strong collective bargaining institutions as an alternative way of protecting low-paid workers (Alsos et al 2019).

The terms 'minimum' and 'living' wages carry obvious and vital distinctions. Minimum wages, as enforceable standards, make no tangible reference to the life situations, living costs, or life chances of workers. By contrast, a living wage involves direct considerations of the socioeconomic situations of workers. The idea invokes *normative* considerations about wage rates in a positive, progressive sense (Anker 2006, p 315). Living wages – understood as a decent minimum that could support a male breadwinner family – found their earliest and most extensive expression in Australia's wage-earners' welfare state. This normative standard was set in motion by reformist judge Henry B. Higgins in the first decade of the 20th century (see Chapter 2). As Castles and Mitchell (1993) point out, Australia and NZ remained so distinct in this respect that the antipodean wage-earner approach departed in institutionally significant ways from the Anglo-American approach, producing in Castles and Mitchell's formulation a distinct type of welfare state.

Living wage movements in the 21st century have once again gained momentum because of the heavy dependence of low-income workers, more frequently women and migrants, on minimum or near-minimum wage employment. In the US, which has the most business-controlled labour market of the rich democracies, there are reports that most jobs now rate as either poor or mediocre on a multidimensional quality measure (Rothwell and Crabtree 2020). At the same time, urbanisation presses on living costs. Globalised cities like London, Sydney, Vancouver, San Francisco, Auckland, and Dublin put pressure on new generations of urban residents, especially on workers like cleaners, gardeners, care workers, and hospitality staff who confront steep housing costs.

To assess genuine need, advocacy organisations and academic outfits are now determining minimum requirements of a living wage with increasing sophistication and technical detail. One example is MIT's living wage calculator in the US (Ross and Bateman 2020); another is the Resolution Foundation's research in the UK. These tools build on global efforts in social policy research and development studies to better estimate the actual living costs of low-income communities, including low-income workers. The most global of these exercises is the living wage methodology and framework fashioned by Richard Anker (2006), whose insights inform this book.

This book makes reference to both *minimum* and *living* wage campaigns when describing the politics and policy of minimum wage reforms. Often it makes sense to use both terms to describe the same campaigns and reform efforts. Living wage campaigns frequently yield improvements to minimum wages that fall well short of genuinely living wages – and that is not a surprise given that living wages are the peak claim of this new generation workers' movement. Nonetheless, higher minimums still mean welfare improvements for workers and for the economy and society. And the idea of living wages rallies workers and activists through what social movement scholars call 'consensus mobilisation' around a valued common cause (Klandermans 1988).

The notion of a living wage encounters foreseeable problems, both definitional and practical. How are living standards measured to assess the wages needed to cover the basic costs of diverse households? Should a living wage vary by regional living costs? Is it meaningful to celebrate the achievement of even major improvements in hourly wage rates without addressing underemployment, or job strain, or employer repression in workplaces? In starting out to write this book, it became clear that the concept of living wages was more than a struggle over the worth of an hour's paid work.

Table I.1 helps capture the full dimension of the problem. It is a framework for discussing living wages in a scaffolded way. Definition I – the most typical aspiration – refers to the hourly wage, paid full time, that would support ordinary workers to avoid relative poverty. Most of the legislative and campaigning goals discussed in this book aim at producing wage rates that reduce relative poverty among workers. But these goals assume workers have routinely sufficient hours of work and that wage rates cover the living costs of dependants. As Anker (2006, pp 314–15) makes clear, minimum wage improvements that aim to be *living* wages (definition II) must consider not only the complexity of the 'needs of workers and their families' and 'the cost of living', but also the value of social security benefits. Anker is right. And his claim provides solid grounds for bringing the living wage problem into a welfare frame of analysis – the central task of this book. Across the liberal welfare states, greater welfare paternalism combined with benefit cutbacks have made working-age populations dependent on paid employment. Accordingly, wages are obliged to play a larger role in the social security of low-income households. Seeking living wages is now central to reducing insecurity.

Even where wages are lifted to prevent poverty in most scenarios (across family types and hours worked), living wage campaigns raise questions about the quality of jobs. Living wage employment implies that jobs should have greater quality. Employment must not only ensure a measure of income security but produce 'labour market security' (that is, hours, tenure) and offer workers intrinsic benefits, that is, 'a quality working environment' (Cazes et al 2015; also see Rothwell and Crabtree 2020). Definition III describes welfare states that pursue these conditions for jobs – work often described as unskilled occupations. Low-wage work, of course, becomes that way through long-standing processes of social devaluation. But COVID-19 has, at least temporarily, forced a major social revaluation of ordinary, essential jobs and the workers who perform them (Bavel et al 2020). Many essential jobs during the pandemic – cleaning jobs, supermarket work, childcare – are low-paid or minimum wage employment.

Definition IV describes a final step, describing a social security regime committed to a living wage welfare state. It necessarily entails the transformation of poor quality, poverty-level employment. This aspiration is something that liberal welfare states have not even come close to achieving. Such an ambition for a 'post-liberal' welfare state would not only ensure minimum standards in the labour market, it would also deploy state capacity to reduce pressure on working families in the increasingly privatised worlds of the liberal countries. Money makes a huge difference to poorer working families. But it does not overcome the deficiencies and high costs associated with privatised basic services in housing, education, health, and childcare.

Table I.1: Definitional scope of minimum and living wages

	Definition
I Minimum wages	Statutory or regulatory minimum wage rates that bind employers. Typically, legally enforceable. Decision processes vary by jurisdiction; can vary by parliament, ministerial decree, ballot, or court decision. Minimum wage rates are not typically determined in a 'living wage' standards framework; may vary according to perceived market conditions or ideological perspectives of decision-makers
II Living wages	Statutory or regulatory minimum wage rates that bind employers and are determined by a fair measure of actual living costs faced by workers and their families
III Living wage employment	Employment policies that ensure a fair rate of hourly pay and protect other aspects of job quality: sufficient hours of work, reasonable degree of job security, access to other benefits, and access to representation
IV Living wage welfare state	A social security regime that builds broader wage-earner and welfare institutions based on principles of definitions II and III above. Social contract involves public goods intervention to lower living costs and provide social security

Labour markets and welfare futures

Social science explanations for the development of the welfare state have variously emphasised class mobilisation, the strains of war, the advance of administration and industry, and finally, the demands emanating from richer, more diverse, and older populations. Progressive liberals and their allies fought for public pensions, while unions and socialists also fought for protection against unemployment, collective bargaining, and job security. The disruption and turmoil of two world wars and a world depression put democratising states under tremendous pressure. Organised working classes combined with progressive parties and elites to do something about unemployment and the disruptive impact of mass insecurity on health, family life, and communities. Welfare state expansion meant that, by the first few decades of the 21st century, affluent democratic nations had built social protection regimes accounting for somewhere between 15% and 30% of GDP. One way or another, the middle classes have been incorporated into the welfare state compact. In Nordic countries, universalist programmes have achieved this. In countries like the US and Australia, the middle class benefits from the 'hidden' welfare state of extensive tax expenditures set up to insulate privileges for the better-off and wealthy (Howard 1997). All these states will be even larger in the post–COVID-19 period, given the expansion of government and the partial collapse of private sector employment.

High-quality analysis suggests that the patterns of growth and change in welfare states have become less dependent on class conflict and institutional politics over time (Brady and Lee 2014). Twenty-first-century welfare states appear to be growing through the forces of passive change. Population ageing, to take the most obvious example, is adding to higher healthcare costs as well as greater expenditures on pensions (OECD 2016). Do these trends suggest that the power resources approach of Walter Korpi (1980) and others has lost explanatory force? The answer is no. Power resources remain central, perhaps most convincingly illustrated by power resources on the other side: corporate and political resistance to universal healthcare in the US, for example. Although the partisan character and extent of welfare state retrenchment are subjects of a long, ongoing debate in the literature (Starke 2006), evidence suggests that welfare state expenditures are still subject to partisan retrenchment (Amable et al 2006). Of course, austerity politics has spread across the political divide. Moreover, long-term privatisation processes that do not necessarily reduce expenditures, but may affect quality, add further to the story. Contract processes in welfare sectors involving private and non-profit actors continue to underline the ability of market power to influence the direction of social policy. 'Marketisation' is now a major feature of liberal state social service provision (Meagher and Wilson 2015), although these developments are also significant in Nordic countries like Sweden (Meagher and Szebehely 2019).

What is *really* meant when scholars talk about the decline of power resources is the fading capacity of trade unions and the political left to further institutionalise encompassing welfare states. Declining strike rates and union membership, as well as weak performances by labour parties in Australia and the UK, and the exclusion of the political left from power in countries like Canada, Ireland, and the US give credibility to this account. But are the English-speaking democracies reaching a significant turning point? True, declines in working-class mobilisation over the past few decades have been especially pronounced in the liberal world. Australia, the UK, and the US stand out even further in this respect. The result has been pro-employer labour market deregulation and even repression and harassment of organised labour. But the problems that unions once effectively addressed have only become more pronounced. Before the pandemic, the failure of wage-earner institutions to protect working-class communities was showing up in a wide range of indicators: growth in poor-quality jobs, wage theft and worker abuse, and declines in living standards added to by expensive housing, education, and healthcare. The OECD's *Under Pressure: The Squeezed Middle Class* report (2019a, p 135) made it clear that the wages crisis was far from affecting only poorer workers, stating that 'slow wage growth is the prime reason for stagnant middle-class incomes', and it was increasingly difficult for working families to preserve middle-income status.

Stressed working- and middle-class households produce consequences for politics. Attempts to address the 'new normal' of the faltering opportunity structures of the labour market are now central. Donald Trump's 2016 appeal to angry blue-collar America was a populist political economy that hid its enrichment of the wealthy while promising struggling voters that tariffs and tax cuts would save jobs and protect living standards. Likewise, the radical reform of a universal basic income addresses the apparent new normal of labour markets, this time by giving up on their distributional potential. For that reason, basic income has attracted a far wider audience on the left and right – precariously employed students are now joined by elite policymakers seeking remedies to failing labour markets in ways that do not rely on unions or the institutions of full employment.

My argument is that redistributive projects, either of the conservative/populist right or the postindustrial left, will eventually falter without addressing the deeper 'predistributive' crisis generating inequality in labour markets. Campaigns for higher minimum or living wages are part of a broader recognition of this reality, even though the distributional problems of labour markets require institutional redress beyond that of the most expansive visions of the living wage movement. Still, arguments for a significantly higher wages floor are foundational to a pro-labour refurbishment of liberal labour markets. Moreover, there is potential for a broader consensus in this respect. As we shall see next, some liberals and conservatives have made the case for supporting higher minimums as well.

Three cases for a living wage

Social science projects, especially ones dealing with inequality, demand that the researcher balance the normative case for reform – including the role of advocacy – with dispassionate analysis. For the most part in this project, these two goals reinforce each other. However, it is also clear the progressive reforms have unintended consequences or carry risks. With higher minimum wages, several possibilities are obvious. Employers can retaliate by sacking workers, intensifying work, or automating low-skill jobs out of existence. Alternatively, they can ignore generous minimums, setting lower 'market' wages with trivial legal consequence. Politicians can strategically address the policy demands of the living wage movements as a way of blocking more powerful challenges. Higher and fairer minimum wages can also exacerbate 'free rider' problems for unions where improved state protections make it harder to recruit workers to the cause of more ambitious but necessary reforms.

The successes of the living wage movement rest in part on the wide normative appeal of a fair and decent minimum wage. This may particularly true in the liberal countries where minimum wages seem set to play a larger social and political function in the future. It is thus important to understand these normative claims, and to show how they intertwine with strategy and calculation for the dominant actors in this field of conflict.

The liberal case

Since this book focuses on six liberal welfare states, the *liberal* case for living wages carries obviously heightened significance. Tensions within liberalism that date back well over a century mean that unifying liberal positions on questions of economic justice and public policy are now uncommon. Market utilitarians and political liberals are, for the most part, fiercely divided on distributional questions. For instance, the policy liberalism of neoclassical economists who write on labour markets today tends to overlap with neoliberal or libertarian policy prescriptions that disregard most forms of progressive labour market interventions. In fact, as Chapter 3 outlines, the policy framework insisted upon by labour market economists has remained hostile to minimum wages aimed at high and rising wage floors. This hostility has been confirmed by recent survey results from the US (Corder 2019). The report finds that of the 197 economists who responded to the survey: 'Two-in-five (39%) think the minimum wage should remain at $7.25 or be lowered, with two-thirds in total (66%) believing the minimum wage should be $10 an hour or less' (Corder 2019, p 4).

Of course, policy norms have their own political economy. Low minimum wages suit influential employers in particular sectors of the economy. They suit policymakers convinced about wage-induced unemployment and its impact on unaffordable welfare expenditures and frustration at government for not resolving joblessness. Indeed, a tough-minded liberalism gained greater policy force given the rising unemployment from the 1970s onwards and the social and fiscal misery it entailed. Squeezing wages at the bottom, economists proposed, could underwrite job creation in much tougher times, ones where globalisation and technology would eat away at job creation in entry-level positions, for young people, or for those with fewer or dated skills. Although most neoclassical economists recognise that minimum wages have *some* social policy or welfare role, most see the remedy for poverty in buoyant employment conditions, a competitive struggle for skills and improvement, and, where necessary, 'non-distorting' transfers like the Earned Income Tax Credit (EITC) in the US (Corder 2019, p 10).

An older social liberalism, however, had come to see the political economy of low wages differently. This included, for example, the liberalism of Australia's far-sighted Henry B. Higgins, who was central to the construction of the wage-earner welfare state in Australia and whose influence extended to progressives in America and the rest of the 'Anglo' world (Lake 2019). In noting that late 19th-century social liberalism had travelled from 'freedom of contract to critique of contract', Sawer (2012, p 72) notes:

> the economic argument was only one of a battery of arguments for redistribution. Justice arguments were also central: it was society rather than individuals that provided the social and legal infrastructure and the market for products that enabled the accumulation of wealth. Society had a corresponding right to a share in the social value it helped to create.

Later in the 20th century, John Rawls' political liberalism, also concerned with the durable foundations of justice, broke just as decisively with market utilitarianism; 'unlimited' market freedoms (that is, property rights) had to give way to the priority of institutions that form the 'social bases of self respect' (Rogers 2019, p 1553; see also Freeman 2007). Rawls' well-known difference principle, with its focus on justice for the least advantaged, inevitably called attention to the quality of public policy-making around the incomes and resources available to poor people and workers. Although Rawls appears to offer a preference for the kind of welfare policies of progressive neoclassical thinkers today (that is, tax and transfer policies to distribute justice), Rogers (2019, p 1555) argues that Rawls did not exclude minimum wage provisions as a form of social justice and that a case can be made that they provide formal entitlements granting 'self-respect' to workers.

Indeed, one might view any new liberal interest in higher minimum or living wages as not far beyond the current compromise that combines ultra-liberalised labour markets with poverty-alleviating cash payments to working families. After all, a liberal defence of strong minimum wages might also have an interest in defending broader labour market deregulation, keeping individualised private contracts for the remainder of the workforce. Some US liberals, for instance, now wary of corporate excess and cognisant of the benign effects of higher minimum wages, may consider moderate living wage policies as progressively pragmatic reforms to unstable and unfair labour markets. This is especially the case, as we shall see, now that the econometric evidence undermines long-held insistences that higher minimums are bad for jobs. Economist Paul Krugman (2016) is a leading example of a liberal progressive who has absorbed the emerging econometric evidence about the impact of higher minimum wages and adapted his thinking about the functioning of labour markets accordingly.

The conservative case

The contemporary liberal case for higher minimum wages blends new empirical evidence, a Rawlsian-style commitment to direct the benefits of policy to the poorest, and perhaps a shrewd motivation to protect employers from even greater intervention down the track. As it turns out, the pressure for improved minimum wages is an indirect consequence of a successful policy alliance forged between pro-business neoliberals and pro-work, pro-family neoconservatives. Neoliberal reform, when it weakens worker rights, cuts welfare, and raises taxes on workers to fund tax cuts for the rich, is tremendously unpopular. This is especially true when worker or citizen mobilisations have articulated these threats to disengaged or distracted publics. By contrast, neoconservative ideas promoting hard work and family values have solid foundations within the electorate. Political elites, accordingly, have drawn heavily on neoconservative rhetoric about work and family to bolster unpopular neoliberal goals in the areas of workfare, reducing union rights, and labour market policy. To illustrate – neoliberal proposals for 'market-clearing' minimum wages have zero appeal to workers or voters. But claims about promoting paid work as the cornerstone of personal responsibility, dignity, family support, and initiative are neoconservative buttresses for harsh agendas.

Neoconservative arguments, for example, have boosted the appeal of efforts to dismantle 'passive' welfare programmes, particularly in countries like the US, the UK, and Australia. They have also helped to revise public expectations about how – and how much – welfare states should shield poor communities. Welfare state retrenchment is designed to rely on the market for paid employment. In the US, where these reforms have been most far-reaching, previously welfare-dependent households have indeed either transitioned into jobs (mostly poorly paid) or become dependent on cashless forms of welfare like food stamps or reliant on informal economies (see Edin and Shaefer 2016; Shaefer and Edin 2018).

However, an expanding dependence on low-wage labour markets across the English-speaking countries has, in turn, put pressure on a neoconservative ideology promoting the discipline of work and the centrality of family. In his influential *The New Paternalism*, Lawrence Mead (1997) acknowledged that workfare policies would result in more voter pressure for decently paid jobs. Conservative voters across the liberal countries strongly endorse tough welfare policies. But they are considerably less comfortable with low wages for full-time workers, expressing support for higher minimums in opinion polls in Australia, the UK, and the US (Dahlgreen 2014; Gartrell 2017; Ingraham 2019). Working for very low wages contradicts a conservative social contract leaning heavily on paid work in promoting enterprise and family. Not surprisingly, revisionist conservatism in the US is starting to look at the country's semi-trashed labour market institutions as a national economic hazard. Proposals to bring wage-earners into a neoconservative wage-earner model are now surfacing among pro-Republican intellectuals (Cass 2018; Naidu 2020). Emerging support for wage subsidies among conservatives, for example, highlights uneasiness about the consequences of an economy and society built on poor-quality, low-paid jobs. Still, few US Republican politicians and governments support claims for higher minimum wages, such as those promoted by Fight for $15. Indeed, a rear-guard Republican action to stop city-level campaigns legislating for local living wages in some so-called 'red states' has gathered force (Huizar and Lathrop 2019).

However, a refurbishing of 'compassionate conservatism' has been under way in the UK as Conservatives have targeted working-class voters. In 2015, then Conservative Chancellor of the Exchequer George Osborne provided critical support to living wages by legislating a series of significant yearly increases to the National Minimum Wage. Several objectives underpinned this policy about-face from the political party that had abolished minimum wages two decades earlier. The Conservatives after 2010 had wanted to cut income support to working families and other benefits as part of their quest for smaller government as well as to appease neoconservative resentment at the 'big state' approach of New Labour. The government came to recognise that profit-hoarding employers would need to do more heavy lifting if the UK was to avoid ever-worsening poverty resulting from its own neo-Thatcherite welfare policies. The government also calculated that a living wage policy would assist in bringing disaffected blue-collar voters across to the Conservatives on polling day. In 2015, the hyper-liberal *Economist* magazine was predictably critical of Osborne's commitment to a national living wage.[1] But it applauded the underlying logic of the Conservatives' move:

> Mr Osborne's rebranding of the Tories as the party of working people, chasing poor, northern votes that Labour has long taken for granted, is welcome and impressive. So is the alchemy by which he has turned fiscal rectitude into a vote-winner – other European countries should take note.

As I have suggested, normative claims in politics have their roots in a set of interests in the political economy. Liberals who see the value of and evidence in favour of decent minimum wages and neoconservatives who see living wages as essential to a 'work and family' social contract still listen to the corporate sector that dominates the networks, resources, and ideas generation on their side of politics. The corporate sector is motivated by rising profits so any 'normalisation' of widely enforced and high minimum wages will alarm corporations and their political allies. Eventually this push will invigorate business resistance in the coming decade. However, there is more to the story. Some business organisations, for ethical and strategic reasons, have voluntarily committed to hourly rates closer to living wages, such as firms in high-cost London. Community-led campaigns by the Living Wage Foundation add credibility to corporates: 'many employers [in London] adopt the Living Wage largely for reputational gains and/or out of a sense of moral duty' (Johnson et al 2019, p 331). Perhaps even more significantly, large and profitable corporations can also exercise monopolistic power in paying higher minimum wages. Apart from any reputational gains, dominant employers will see advantage in squeezing competitors by paying higher minimum wages that smaller capital cannot. Moreover, higher minimums can reduce staff turnover that unwittingly frustrates tough-minded and profit-hungry managements. Matsakis (2018) illustrates this point: US retailer Amazon raised its minimum wage to $15 when it faced additional pressures to keep seasonal employees at a time when the official US unemployment rate was below 4%. These pressures have subsided in the post-COVID world but they underline strategic corporate interest in higher minimums over time.

Labour movements and the socialist case

Liberal and conservative cases for supporting higher minimum wages rest on a mix of moral claims, revised econometric evidence, and political calculation. They can however border on conditional defences, dependent on the preservation of other policy objectives. Most observers would associate the revival of living wage ambitions with trade union activism or a renewed social democratic claim-making, adapted for neoliberal times. Although history presents a more complex and equivocating picture, unions have clear reasons to support living wages in the contemporary context. This is even the case where most low-wage workers remain non-union and where generous statutory minimums only further promote the 'free rider' tendencies among hard-to-recruit workers that frustrate union organising. Ultimately, Anglo-American union movements have a strong interest in a new centre-left ascendancy, one that builds or defends a system of collective bargaining where unions have ready and greater capacity to organise the workforce. But conditions across the six liberal welfare states, with the possible exceptions of Canada and NZ, are far from these.

Labour movements have maintained a commitment to the moral dignity and the democratic rights of wage-earners in an uncomplicated and vital way, free from the agonising over 'market freedoms' preoccupying liberals. But union emphasis on statutory minimums has varied across contexts and time, with collective agreements often preferred institutional arrangements. However, union movements may now have clearer interests in a strong set of statutory minimum wages, given the difficulties union organisations continue to encounter. Labour market and jobs transformation, combined with pro-business rules, has seen the bottom third or more of the workforce experience poor growth in pay in the context of fragmenting working life. The strains of multiple job holding, short-hours contracts, poor leave arrangements, and weakened entitlements only add to the stresses contributed by poor hourly pay rates. Significant pay increases for minimum wage workers have spillover impacts that amount to more than higher wages. And some of these impacts assist union recruitment and organising. Higher minimum wage floors engender greater job commitment and less labour market churn – two factors that impede union organising in low-wage sectors. Likewise, where living wage claims involve grassroots activism, they expand opportunities for union organising in hard-to-unionise sectors. Larger benefits may follow. Minimum wage struggles emanating from unionised workers offer one possible path to bolder claims such as for collective contracts or political campaigns for industry-wide agreements.

Living wage campaigns may even represent important 'green shoots' for social democratic renewal. The campaigning success of Fight for $15 and the growing mass of evidence that higher minimum wages are not adding to unemployment has given the under-threat moderate factions of centre-left parties greater confidence to embrace predistributive politics. Centre-left leaders face strong challenges from democratic socialists with ambitious agendas for employment – and who see living wages as part of programmatic reform. The centre-left establishment's embrace of living wages politics in the US and in Australia, NZ, Ireland, and Canada is a step towards dealing with the injustices of ultra-liberalised labour markets without dismantling that model altogether. Both democratic socialist and centre-left political projects embrace living wage predistribution for another reason they share in common. They need revenue to finance other parts of their programmes. With hard times and austerity producing tax-resistant electorates, both sides of the political left have an interest in predistribution to achieve greater equality.

Revenue and tax problems aside, centre-left parties are chasing voters. This is especially the case as conservative populists across the liberal world forge electoral coalitions that include disaffected older and blue-collar workers. These voters contributed to Trump's 2016 victory in the US, Prime Minister Morrison's upset Coalition win in Australia in 2019, and Prime Minister Johnson's landslide in the UK later the same year. Pundits, however, tell an exaggerated story when they conclude that the working classes have deserted labour parties in Australia, the UK and NZ, and the Democrats in the US. Working-class voters have higher rates of non-voting. Moreover, a younger and more multicultural working class votes differently to an older white, blue-collar working class whose defections from labour and progressive parties dominate the media. Living wage policies appeal to women, younger workers, and migrants who represent the low-wage working class, even if it is still unclear how important the politics of minimum wages will be to voter choices.

The English-speaking liberal world

The political economy of minimum wages is relevant to a much wider group of countries than the six liberal welfare states that are our focus here. In discussing the dynamics of minimum wage reform, one could defend a much broader or plainly different country selection.

In the past few years, Germany has introduced a minimum wage to deal with emergent institutional gaps that have opened up in its collectivist system (Bosch 2018), President Moon of South Korea boldly increased minimum wages as part of government efforts at reflation and promoting justice at work, and socialist-led governments in Spain and Portugal have made similarly bold moves. Casting around further, it is even clearer that the institutionalisation or significant improvement in minimum wages is part of a global trend (Boeri 2012; ACTU 2016; Dube et al 2020).

What grounds are there for focusing on the six English-speaking or 'liberal' countries? There are three main reasons that justify such a focus. The first relates to remarkable developments across the liberal countries in recent years (see Table I.2). In New Zealand, minimum wage policies developed by two Labour-led governments of Helen Clark (1999–2008) and Jacinda Ardern (2017–) have pushed the minimum to 66% of median wages in 2019. This is now the highest Kaitz score of the rich OECD nations in 2019 (OECD 2020a).[2] The UK has moved closer to consensus about a living wage with the Conservative government's successive minimum wage increases since it announced a national living wage policy in 2015. A Kaitz index of 60% promised for 2020 (McKnight 2020) would represent a staggering increase of 19% since 2000. In the US, the Fight for $15 movement has produced some of most successful working-class mobilisations of recent decades. They are beginning to have a transformative influence on US wages policy. And, three big Canadian provinces – Alberta, British Columbia and Ontario – have also made bold reforms in recent years, enough to push up the overall Kaitz index quite sharply between 2017 and 2020 to a record 51% of the median. My estimate is that the Kaitz scores for these three provinces sit in the mid-50s range.

Among very high-income OECD nations, two of the liberal countries emerge in the top three improvements in the Kaitz index since 2000 (OECD 2020a). Among these countries, by far the largest change in the Kaitz score between 2000 and 2019 was recorded for South Korea (+34%). However, New Zealand and the UK are next (with improvements of +13% and +11% respectively) and Canada's improvement is also large but contained by the failure of all provinces to make similarly bold moves. Large movements were also recorded among countries with lower GDP per capita incomes. Here, I am referring particularly to Portugal, under a leftwing coalition led by Prime Minister Antonio Costa, and the Eastern European states of Hungary, Latvia, and Poland. Spain has joined this group with large improvements under the socialist-led government of Pedro Sánchez.

However, the remaining three liberal countries – the US, Ireland, and Australia – do not rank well when it comes to Kaitz score improvements. There are reasons for these lagging performances that need to be mentioned. The US Kaitz score reported by the OECD (2020a) is extremely low, reflecting a national minimum wage deliberately suppressed by Republicans. A *New York Times* analysis better reveals emerging improvements: 'To put the growth in perspective: It took the 19 years ending in 2013 for the Kaitz index to rise four percentage points. In the six years since 2013, it has risen 13 percentage points' (Tedeschi 2019). Moreover, US states with $15 minimum wages will achieve Kaitz index scores of around or above 60% of median wages, a common goal for reformist movements. Large cities like Los Angeles, Chicago and New York have already achieved Kaitz scores above 60%, benefiting large numbers of workers (Table 0.2).

Ireland's situation has reversed course from its disastrous cut to the minimum wage following the global financial crisis, with institution building through the 2010s under a Fine-Gael and Labour coalition. By 2020, its Kaitz score was estimated to be in the high 40s. Finally, Australia, once the OECD leader, has fallen back on this measure. This is because of a conservative shift in its national politics and wage-setting institutions since the late 1990s, suggesting that its commission-determined wage decisions are now inferior to partisan parliamentary battles over the minimum wage evident elsewhere. That is fascinating, reversing a long-standing trend that disfavoured parliamentary control.

Table I.2: Kaitz scores for minimum wages, selected countries, 2020

Score	City/state or province/country
Above 70	Los Angeles
60–69	New Zealand, UK* Seattle, Phoenix, Chicago, New York City, San Diego France, Portugal, South Korea
50–59	Australia, Canada** Alberta, Ontario, British Columbia
40–49	Ireland Belgium, Germany, Japan, Netherlands, Spain
30–39	USA Dallas, Philadelphia

Notes: * UK estimate for 2020 from McKnight (2020); ** Estimates for Canadian provinces based on Statistics Canada earnings data.

Sources: OECD (2020a); Eichel (2020); Statistics Canada (2020); McKnight (2020)

Taking account of measurement issues and the most recent changes, there is strong evidence of a significant policy shift in the liberal countries. Adjustments to a post-COVID-19 world may shift the politics of minimum wages in unpredictable directions. But, on present trends, the 2020s may see sustained, significant improvements in Kaitz index scores for four or even five of the six English-speaking states. This likelihood brings us to the second reason for focusing on the six English-speaking welfare states: the *patterned* nature of adjustments to minimum wage settings. Not without controversy, industrial relations and welfare state scholars have emphasised policy consistencies that suggest an English-speaking 'family' (Francis Castles' term). In the sphere of industrial relations, Freeman et al (2007) point to the common 'Anglo' legal heritage and contractual labour institutions of these countries. These foundations have made minimum wages central to current conflicts over the direction of labour market policy. Similarly, across the domain of welfare states, Castles (2010, p 642) argues that a 'distinct English-speaking world of welfare is apparent in respect of spending patterns and redistributive outcomes as well as of policy outcomes in the realm of the personal'. A similar characterisation of the liberal English-speaking countries is central to the regime-level analysis of Gøsta Esping-Andersen (1990).

Even more compelling evidence of family-level developments is any direct sign that the English-speaking countries benefit from policy diffusion, that is, the broad tendency of states within the liberal cluster to learn from each other, adapting policy to domestic circumstances. That learning is not only state-driven but rather involves a wider range of actors and activist forces. Evidence in this book identifies the US case as significant, given the visible struggles over minimum wages there as well as its intellectual hegemony. However, other influences on cross-national policy development matter too. These include the award wages model of Australia as a model for emulation, and the large minimum wage improvements in NZ and the UK to 60% or more of the median wage. The latter serve as broader encouragement to activists and policymakers that higher minimum wages do not generate significant job losses and that they can be used as a vehicle for wage-earner welfare.

The third reason for a focus on the English-speaking world relates to the strength of the 'low minimum wage' and anti-welfare orthodoxy across English-speaking welfare states. Neoliberal ideas and policies have spread globally with varying impact. But, in the rich democratic world, their impact has been greatest on the liberal countries. Here, the pursuit of deregulated labour markets reinforced by tough and increasingly marketised welfare has gone furthest. My argument is that the emerging 'disruption' to the low minimum wage policy consensus can be partly traced to long-term deficiencies emerging in income support available to people in the working-age population. Not surprisingly, pressure for 'compensation' has started to build up elsewhere, particularly given the state of low wages.

The goal of this book is not to dogmatically assert that the revival of the politics and policy in favour higher minimum wages has uniquely Anglo-American foundations. There are clear signs that predistributive wages strategies are emerging elsewhere for similar reasons, ones that relate to the dilemmas confronted by redistributive strategies in liberal states. Rather, the goal is to identify the constellation of social, political, and economic forces that have led to a mobilisation for living wages across the liberal countries. These comparisons are mindful of the limits of a 'family'-level analysis. For one, these countries have geographical, historical, and policy differences. Indeed, minimum wage policy responses reflect these differences as well as common paths. US exceptionalism, as Castles (2010) points out, is a further significant qualification to analysis to the so-called 'liberal cluster'. At the other end, Australia's award wages system, preserving a more generous scaffolding of effective minimums, distinguishes it from the uniform minimums that apply in the other five countries.

At another level, a policy focus on common trends in a particular cluster of nations risks ignoring the impact of policy convergence across regimes, often produced by global and supranational influences (Schmitt and Starke 2011). One useful illustration of this problem is the introduction of a statutory minimum wage in Germany in 2015. A legal minimum wage now features in the once archetypal 'coordinated' labour market, previously dominated by collective bargaining (Mabbett 2016; Marx and Starke 2017). However, as Bosch (2018) shows, the German minimum wage serves a different institutional function than the liberal country minimum wages do.

A final word on the country-level comparisons made in this book. The overall approach is argument driven and does not attempt a comprehensive comparison of these six cases. I have drawn on case-level policy trends, developments, conflicts and data selectively – largely with the aim of developing an overall perspective on the shifting role and controversies of the minimum wage in the lean welfare states of the liberal countries. In essence, liberal countries are dealing with the headache of ultra-liberalised labour markets and minimum wage reforms are playing a fascinating corrective role. In the post-COVID-19 world, the gains of the living wages movement will need to be defended against a resurgent orthodoxy that will insist on 'market clearing' minimums to resolve historic unemployment. The stage seems set for a new battle between higher minimums and public sector-led employment policies, perhaps in the form of a jobs guarantee, and a renewed market-driven project of a low wage economy driven by political patronage and worker exploitation.

Intellectual declarations

This book is written to address themes and problems in several intersecting literatures. The first literature is comparative social policy. My perspective is that low-wage labour markets are becoming central to understanding welfare state dynamics. Labour markets matter particularly to the liberal welfare states where social policy debates have a long history of fights over the morals and efforts of poor people and, related, the central focus of paid employment as the sole legitimate means for securing a livelihood. The second literature is the sociology of labour markets. Economists have dominated labour market discussions, especially about minimum wages, and their enormous efforts to quantify the impact of wages on employment inform this book. At another level, economists have dominated advice to government so much that a 'policy monopoly' (Meyer 2003) in favour of deregulation and wage restraint has formed. That has insisted strongly that permanent wage restraint at the 'bottom' of the labour market is necessary to preserve routine jobs in a postindustrial economy confronting technological change and globalisation.

This book documents the weakening of that monopoly through a combination of worker mobilisation, intellectual discovery, and legislative action. These developments allow for the sociology of low-wage labour markets to also inform policymakers. Minimum wages tell us about the quality of working life, the experience of social stress, the health and responsiveness of democratic institutions, and broader ways to address poverty. Two other literatures assist in the intellectual game plan of this book. From policy sciences we draw heavily on the concepts of 'policy monopolies' and 'advocacy coalitions'. These concepts help explain how social forces can act on, and significantly change, a policy consensus. From the study of social movements, I draw on the concept of 'political opportunity structure'. This concept is a useful umbrella term for cataloguing the factors that help press new forms of minimum wage policy and politics on established institutions.

Finally, some influences on the approach taken in this book should be noted. The relationship between welfare policies and low-wage labour markets – particularly in the 'Anglosphere' – has been a persistent theme in the literature, taken up in classics (Polanyi [1944] 2001), applied generally to modern welfare states (Bonoli 2003) and to Australia's historic wage-earner model (Castles 1985), and made central to analyses such as Myles and Pierson (1997). This book builds on these legacies, reminding readers that the interplay between bad jobs and harsh welfare endures as a problem of the liberal model. Understanding the dynamics of capitalist organisation and state policies at an overarching level is also important for the entire project. Insights from Wright (2015) on class and Tilly (1999) on inequality and organisation inform my thinking in diffuse ways. Burawoy (2018) captures my own normative commitments when he states: 'the central feature of sociology is indeed to contest the overextension of the market and the overextension of the state'. Those two problems apply here. Ultra-liberalised labour markets overextend when they apply the organisation of profits and low-wage labour to every corner of social life. And state power is overextended when welfare policies become so supervisory that they intrude into people's lives or deter the community from obtaining the necessary social support.

Organisation of this book

This book proceeds across five chapters and a conclusion. The most logical place to start our exploration is with the key features and problems of low-wage labour markets of the liberal countries now disrupted by the consequences of COVID-19. This exploration, in Chapter 1, presents International Social Survey Programme (ISSP) Work Orientations survey research as well as analysis of secondary data sources and commentary. The aim is to develop a better understanding of the political economy and social experience of low-wage labour markets. Here, a focus on the bottom *third* of wage-earners is justified, given that minimum wage reforms have an impact on a larger number of workers than those directly subject to legal minimums. Once a stronger perspective on who works in low-wage jobs, and the problems these workers encounter on the job (low pay, multiple job holding, and more frequent job changes) is developed, I can describe the factors driving the crisis in working-class living standards in Chapter 2. My argument is that pressure for a living wage becomes even sharper when intersecting problems of housing insecurity, household debt, and workfare are made evident.

Low minimum wages in liberal countries like Canada, the UK, and the US do not fully account for the slowdown in wages growth. This decline in the rich world is so large that it features in Branko Milanovic's (2016) 'elephant curve' pattern of changes in global incomes growth. Although the institutional hiatus producing low wages has wider causes, I argue in Chapter 3 that the low minimum wage consensus has been an important feature of a policy monopoly over labour markets (Meyer 2003) defended by orthodox policymakers. This monopoly has insisted on low minimum wages as a necessary response to global and technological forces, one that would underwrite employment growth for young, entry-level workers, and low-skilled workers respectively. Chapter 3 provides further background to the breakdown in this consensus over the past few decades, one that curiously starts from within the technically minded economics profession but has since been bolstered by the results of large-scale 'natural experiments' produced by legislated minimum wage rises. This challenge has not (yet) reconstituted itself as 'high wages' policy consensus. But it may well provide the intellectual foundations for what Dube (2019a), in his report to the UK Conservative government, called more 'ambitious wages policies' in the future.

The policy monopoly enforcing the low minimums orthodoxy has two sociopolitical variants. One is categorically *neoliberal*, buttressed by neoconservative welfare reform. It sides with employer power, rationalising away the social problems caused by low wages by pointing to the welfare and business losses incurred by counterproductive labour market interference. The second might be called a *social liberal* compromise, influential across both centre-left and centre-right politics in the English-speaking world. Low minimums have been garrisoned as a chief means of defending employment, but social liberals do accept the need for policy to address the poverty problem through social protection. The consensus has promoted negative income tax-style arrangements such as the EITC in the US or tax credits for working families such as in the UK and NZ. A mix of family supplements and low taxes on low earners operate with similar ambitions and effects elsewhere. These targeted measures have been somewhat successful. But on their own, they have not been able to contain rising earnings inequalities. Their limitations as policy tools, reinforced by pressure on budgets, help explain renewed pressure for better minimums.

The living wage movement has been, until recently, based on the mobilisation of hope and aspirations of a fairer deal at the bottom of the labour market. But now, there are real achievements across all six countries that can be chronicled and compared. This is the main task of Chapter 4. A key distinction can be discerned between reforms involving political parties responsive to unions and those challenges that have been exerted from below. Reforms in NZ and the UK since the late 1990s, for example, responded to union pressures on their respective labour parties and the emergence of institutional deficits, with new or revived institutions forging consensus on improved minimum wages. Pressure for living wages has also emerged from below, particularly in the US. Grassroots union mobilisation, sometimes in coalition with community organisations, has energised battles with employers or legislatures. Other times, local or national efforts have focused on extracting voluntary living wage commitments from employers.

In documenting rising pressures for reform, Chapter 4 identifies resources for change in shifting political opportunity structures. The new political economy of low-wage work depends on gradually building constituencies for greater union and grassroots mobilisation. Moreover, COVID-19 has focused the public mind on the dependence of societies on low-paid workers for its essential functions. Yet liberal labour markets, on a range of measures, are not only underperforming against the well-known success stories of Scandinavia, but they also underperform against those of Continental Europe typically criticised for high unemployment. These problems are now grinding against institutional structures that protect employer power and low wages. Weakened intellectual resistance to wage increases from economists, policy elites, and business think-tanks has forced open a powerfully defended policy monopoly. Moreover, centre-left politics across the English-speaking welfare states has begun to endorse higher minimum wages, in part to defend against leftwing challengers and in part to meet redistributive goals without encountering the tax resistance entailed in fiscal expansion.

The reform movement has achieved considerable successes. But it faces critics and obstacles. Chapter 5 is dedicated to consideration of these, some of which unite odd bedfellows. Higher minimum wages may fail to address poverty, or launch broader reforms for the labour market, or they may eventually encounter major resistance if unemployment rises. This chapter focuses on a necessarily speculative set of longer-term problems that involve employer strategies and 'competition' from alternative policies. Employers may well outmanoeuvre the living wages movement through some combination of work intensification, automation, non-compliance, and outsourcing work through global mechanisms. One pivotal question is whether higher minimum wages will only result in greater automation, especially for routine low-paid jobs. Future assessments vary dramatically. But if history is a guide, capitalist labour markets will continue to produce new forms of work from which business owners profit – in the words of Levitz (2019): 'Human beings are very good at inventing new uses for each other.'

While the neoclassical right and corporate-dominated politics point to the futility of a living wage movement, elements of the progressive left have abandoned an emphasis on paid work on the assumption that technological forces will eliminate millions of the jobs that are the focus of living wage campaigns. The project of worker-led democracy and mobilisation is imperilled by the threats of automation and artificial intelligence and also what critics see as the limited prospects for improving low-wage jobs (like cleaning, basic care, and gardening) compared to a radical programme built around a universal basic income. Chapter 5 considers the prospects of a universal minimum income as more limited than its protagonists would hope. That is in part because of a mix of electoral opposition, implementation hurdles, and fiscal consequences. But those prospects are more limited in part because a basic income does not have a large organised constituency like the one the living wages movement has been able to build. Still, the chapter offers concrete suggestions for the welfare model implied by a living wage welfare state, a subject reflected on further in the Conclusion.

1

Minimum wage workers and the low-wage labour market

The first two chapters focus on the social experience of low-wage employment in the liberal countries. In this chapter, the investigation is set out in three parts. The first shows empirically that the liberal countries have smaller middle classes and more low-income households than other clusters of rich democratic nations. Discontinuous and weak wage-earner institutions are not the only cause of small middle classes and large, growing shares of poor people. Tax and welfare institutions are, of course, central. But if the further development of conventional tax and spend measures is 'blocked' by liberal, conservative, and increasingly populist right politics, then wage-earner institutions become more critical to distributional struggles in the liberal world. The second part develops a clearer sense of who minimum wage workers are, where they work, and the social and economic pressures they experience. The focus is extended to a wider group of workers – the lowest third of the income distribution – to draw on reliable samples from survey data for four of the six countries. As we shall see, in the 2010s, low-wage earners were under financial pressure, buffeted by less stable working and financial lives. Job insecurity for many was not the overwhelming issue that it will be in the post-COVID-19 recovery of the 2020s. The third part accounts for minimum wage institutions across the six countries. Institutionally dormant in many cases, minimum wage-setting has become subject to activist politics and policy development. The rest of the book seeks to explain why – and to draw out the implications of these developments for the liberal world in the rocky realities of the 2020s.

This chapter deals with income distribution and minimum wage-setting trends. But this is only half the story. Chapter 2 follows up with an exploration of the broader context of low-wage work: threats to the living standards of low-wage workers. Three causes are identified: housing costs, indebtedness, and aggressive welfare reform. Both chapters keep to the path set out in the Introduction – to draw selectively on empirical evidence from across the six countries to develop central arguments and perspectives.

Poor people in rich (liberal) worlds

To provide an overall perspective on the low-wage problem, a stronger sense of the particular distributional problems facing the rich liberal world is needed. The bulk of this analysis comes in Chapter 4, where I outline the structural and social forces driving wage protests and institutional reform, which dominated the 2010s and will shape the post-COVID 2020s. But first a broad sweep is necessary, showing that the liberal world has significant distributional problems.

Income distributions are shaped by powerful generative mechanisms in the capitalist economy and welfare systems that cushion these. *Predistributive* controls on that distribution include, for example, farmers' cooperatives that set milk or grain prices, or guaranteed employment for workers during 'downtimes', or strong wage-earner institutions that distribute the fruits of production more fairly between wage-earners and shareowners. *Redistributive* controls centrally involve the state, with the most direct and visible mechanisms being taxation of factor incomes. Proceeds from taxes are returned to the community in welfare or transfer payments or public goods. When both contribute – for example through unionised collective bargaining at work and progressive taxation from government – nations devote institutional power to the quest for greater class equality. By contrast, when weak predistributive institutions such as ultra-liberalised labour markets combine with equally weak redistributive mechanisms like regressive tax regimes, they entrench inequality and stratification.

Chapter 4 takes up 'regime' comparisons in more detail. For now, it is useful to explore the distribution of income by 'classes' in comparative terms to address a central question. Are the liberal countries producing a larger share of low-income households than comparable high-income European or Asian countries? The answer is yes. Recent OECD data produced for the *Under Pressure: The Squeezed Middle Class* (OECD 2019a) report is primarily focused on the disappearing middle class. But the report in effect highlights the other problem: large numbers of low-income households. Table 1.1 confirms that the liberal countries do indeed produce a greater share of low-income households. OECD data has been reclassified into a four-way comparison of regimes to establish the facts. These regimes are: the five liberal countries (New Zealand is not included) and the four Nordic countries, five Continental European states (Austria, Belgium, France, Germany, and the Netherlands), four Southern European states (Greece, Italy, Portugal, and Spain), and two very high-income East Asian countries, South Korea and Japan.

Table 1.1: Smaller middle classes in five liberal countries, %

	Lower income	Middle income	Higher income
Australia	32	58	10
Canada	32	58	10
Ireland	31	60	9
UK	30	58	11
US	35	51	14
Liberal English-speaking	**32**	**57**	**11**
Greece	32	57	11
Italy	33	59	9
Portugal	29	60	11
Spain	33	55	12
Southern Europe	**32**	**58**	**11**
Austria	26	67	7
Belgium	29	66	5
France	25	68	6
Germany	28	64	8
Netherlands	25	69	6
Continental	**27**	**67**	**6**
Denmark	27	69	4
Finland	27	68	5
Norway	25	71	4
Sweden	30	65	5
Nordic countries	**27**	**68**	**5**
Japan	27	65	8
South Korea	31	61	8

Note: Middle-income households are defined as the share of households recording equivalised incomes between 75% and 200% of the median.

Source: OECD (2019a) *Under Pressure: The Squeezed Middle Class*: www.oecd.org/social/under-pressure-the-squeezed-middle-class-689afed1-en.htm

When equivalised household incomes are compared by regime, the Continental and Nordic countries and Japan produce relatively small low-income populations (27%) and smaller high-income groups (defined as above 200% of equivalised median household incomes). This means they produce large middle classes ranging from 61% to 67% of the population. By contrast, the middle-income share of the liberal average is just 57% – 11 percentage points below the Nordic average. The average is influenced by the unequal US, which has the smallest middle class – on this measure at 51% of the population. Taken together, the liberal countries do no better than Southern Europe, which has been disrupted by a decade-long Eurozone crisis. The US has over one-third of households (35%) in lower-income locations.

Under Pressure accounts for long-term trends producing greater inequalities. The share of households earning between 75% and 200% of equivalised median household income fell from 64% in mid-1980s to 61% in mid-2010s (OECD 2019a, p 13). This change does not look like a particularly large shift. But it is consistent with predictions of critics of deregulated labour markets and smaller governments. The OECD (2019b, p 16) captures the underlying forces as follows:

> Many middle-income households face a considerable *risk of sliding down* into the lower-income class: one-in-seven households in the middle 60% of the income distribution and one-in-five of those living in the second-lowest income quintile slide into the bottom 20% over a four-year period. These risks have increased over the past two decades.

In accounting for 'risks' building up for the middle class, *Under Pressure* has a twin focus on labour markets and the costs of living. The latter pressures related to the cost of living are centrally relevant to claims for a living wage and they are analysed in Chapter 2. On the incomes side, the report identifies the *predistributive* forces acting on unequal labour markets, making it clear they are central to the inequality problem (OECD 2019a, p 135). One important insight is that the widely acknowledged polarisation of jobs by skill – on its own – is making only a small contribution to income polarisation that shows up as a shrinking middle and more poor households (OECD 2019a, p 76). A complex reshuffling is under way. Across the OECD, greater numbers of higher skilled workers are not making it into high-income positions. Instead, they occupy a new and smaller middle class. This trend involves a further displacement: fewer two-earner households where neither worker has high skill levels are making it into the middle class (OECD 2019a, p 77). To put it bluntly: access to middle-income security is becoming less and less normal for working-class households. These problems are also cast intergenerationally. The polarising class structure for millennials suggests that these trends have forward momentum. Middle-class income positions are shrinking and becoming harder to obtain, especially for younger individuals and households without access to high levels of education (OECD 2019a, p 55).

Fiscal institutions – large-scale progressive taxation and transfer payments – help ensure that middle-class positions are available for a diverse set of households whose opportunities are shaped by access to education, economic geography, and class networks. Damaged or unresponsive wage-earner institutions add to poor fiscal foundations to block mobility and limit redistribution. Once strongly pro-deregulation, the OECD identifies the lack of collective bargaining rights as central, advocating their extension to 'non-standard workers' as critical to equalising labour earnings (2019a, p 137). This extension is politically feasible in OECD countries with strong collective bargaining systems that potentially stretch existing policies to cope with employment dualisation and/or fragmentation. However, collective bargaining has been significantly weakened in most liberal countries, with trends less evident in Canada and Ireland. These problems are discussed further in Chapter 4. The point here is this: ultra-liberalised labour markets lack the institutional tools and the political consensus to address widening earnings inequality.

Liberal problems: institutions of low wages and low mobility

The literature treats liberal welfare states as the main bloc of countries occupying the liberal market economies described by Hall and Soskice (2001). The weak and discontinuous features of their labour market institutions are central to that depiction, confirmed in other leading accounts (Freeman et al 2007). Over the past 20 years, institutional and political developments in the liberal welfare states have worsened the situation for wage-earners. Key developments relevant to our account can be summarised as follows:

- Liberal states are principally responsive to powerful employers and/or industries. One can point to Wall Street, big tech, private health, and large retail in the US, and to powerful mining companies and banks in Australia. In the UK, London finance is dominant. States preoccupied with powerful corporate interests risk losing system-wide technical and developmental capacities. The loss of manufacturing in the liberal market economies illustrates this problem and so does uneven regional development (northern England and the Rust Belt of the US, for example).
- There is now widespread recognition of the rising power of employers and weakening power of workers and their collective institutions (Manning 2020; Stansbury and Summers 2020). Profit shares have soared but productivity performance has stalled – both trends are consistent with class-based strategies to redistribute income and wealth from labour to capital.
- Managerialism in larger organisations promotes top-down control of the workforce. A winner-takes-all economic system (Hacker

and Pierson 2011) has, in turn, favoured huge salary increases for top managers (Alvaredo et al 2013; Piketty 2013; Stansbury and Summers 2020, p 50). These shifts are now a central feature of widening dispersion of earnings, particularly in the US (Stansbury and Summers 2020, p 50).

- Profit-seeking managerialism incentivises top managers to extend use of temporary labour, contracting, outsourcing, and deunionisation or union avoidance. The consequences include smaller core workforces and the expansion of temporary labour markets and gig employment.
- 'Winner-takes-all' public policy has promoted governments responsive to the interests of industry as well as tax cuts for the wealthy (Hacker and Pierson 2011; see also Piketty 2013). At the same time, the social system becomes more tightly organised around opportunity hoarding processes by the upper-middle class.
- Expansion of highly skilled and low-skilled employment coincides with a hollowing out of medium-skilled jobs and middle-class social locations. One implication, reinforced by OECD findings, is that a growing number of workers are poorly paid for their skills and contributions to productivity. Improvements in 'job quality' over time using sophisticated new measures devised for the UK (Williams et al 2020) are being offset by overwork and control. The authors conclude: 'work [in the UK] for all occupational categories is becoming more routine, more controlled and more intense' (Williams et al 2020, p 123).
- Weakened wage-earner institutions become unresponsive to the inequalities of new industrial organisation, entrenching new forms of work and class stratification.

As will become clear, the evolution of organisational and employment structures has major implications for understanding the political opportunity structure for minimum wage activism and politics. No doubt the trends highlighted above mostly characterise the socially unsettling conditions prevailing in the US, which is a democratic outlier. But other liberal countries face similar scenarios. Writing of the contemporary UK, Major and Machin (2018) give a sense of where deeper stratification along these lines leads: 'Britain's emerging industrial model is that companies directly employ elite graduates as core workers, and contract out lower-level work to temping agencies and other contractors.' Where industrial organisation creates impermeable boundaries, it also damages class mobility, as it relates to an ability to improve one's job or even occupation over time. If the jobs structure becomes more polarised and there is greater competition for fewer good jobs, then mobility into middle-class job locations becomes less likely.

New and greater forms of social stratification produced by the reorganisation of employment undermine one of the strongest defences of liberal market inequalities. That defence points to the dynamics of markets and its opportunity structure as promoting reward and mobility. As Bosch (2009, p 341) puts it: 'From a social policy perspective, short periods in low-wage employment are less problematic than a situation where low-wage jobs are concentrated among certain groups and those concerned have no prospect of moving into more highly paid employment.'

Liberal countries, according to OECD evidence, do not have high-income mobility on the measures they use. The Nordic social democracies do. But, taken as a group, liberal welfare states are not the worst either – they do reasonably well on several measures related to earnings and occupations (OECD 2018a, p 16). In fact, most do better than the more equal but conservatively stratified countries of France and Germany. The latter countries, however, do a better job at keeping the share of low wage-earners smaller (see Table 1.1) because their institutions keep more of the working class in the middle of the income distribution. To illustrate: a French worker on the national minimum wage may well pass on low mobility prospects to their children. But this does not mean that those children will have particularly harsh working lives.

Low-income mobility over a working life, and across generations, becomes a more serious problem when it entrenches a large and poor working class because of inequalities in opportunity, organisational, and fiscal structures. This combination of low mobility and a large share of poorer households is already apparent in the US – an outlier in inequality terms for the rich democracies. Like Germany, the US has a 'sticky floors' problem, locking in low mobility out of poor earnings and income positions (OECD 2018a, p 37; see also Pickert 2019). But this problem is more sociologically concerning in the US than in a country like Germany because the share of low-income households is already significantly larger and, in relative terms, poorer. The OECD (2018a, p 74) remarks that: 'When measured over a longer time period, the United States has the largest share of low-income people stuck at the bottom.' Similar stickiness problems apply at the top end of the US income distribution (OECD 2014, pp 3–4). Moreover, new evidence confirms long-term declining earnings and occupational mobility across generations in the US (Schultz 2019; Song et al 2020; see also Beckfield 2020).

The American story applies, to some extent, to the contemporary UK but less to the other liberal countries where fiscal and wage-earner institutions are slightly more intact. Still, the trends have wider implications for the liberal world where deregulated labour markets almost guarantee widening earnings inequality. Declining mobility into middle-class positions built into work organisation and wage-earner and fiscal institutions adds to the risk of a sustained low-income sector, which then worsens intergenerationally. My argument is that higher minimum wage floors are being recruited to deal with the living standard losses of this cohort of workers and their households. The OECD (2019a, p 137) recognises this: 'In countries or sectors with no collective agreements or low coverage, statutory minimum wages can help ensure fair pay and raise wages higher up the distribution.' This advice reverses course. One long-standing objection to high minimum wages is that they are a blunt instrument to deal with working poverty and therefore an ineffective distributional tool (for Australia, Cranston 2019). The OECD (2019a, p 137) states: 'There is a relatively broad consensus that minimum wages are not very effective at reducing poverty, because poor households frequently have no-one in work, while many minimum-wage earners live in non-poor households.'

However, this problem turns out to be advantageous in the search for tools in the liberal countries that can improve the distribution of earnings. As the OECD (2019a, p 137) explains:

> middle-income households, particularly those on lower middle-incomes, directly benefit from minimum-wage increases. In some countries, moreover, the minimum wage has been shown to have a so-called 'ripple' or 'knock-on' effect, with companies raising wages further up in the distribution to maintain wage differences between lower- and higher-paid workers.

One path for higher minimums to achieve a broader predistributive impact occurs through dual-income households, particularly where formal skill levels are mixed between the household's wage-earner members. Levin-Waldman and Whalen (2007, p 66) explain in the US context:

> if [minimum wage workers] are not the primary earners, they are at least essential secondary earners (defined as those earning as much as half their family's total income). Those

who are earning slightly less than half of the total family income could be considered essential secondary earners because their income is essential to the maintenance of their families.

Better-paid secondary earners keep working families in the middle of the income distribution, just as higher minimum wage floors reduce poverty and social stress on the households of poor workers.

Minimum wage workers

The rest of this chapter looks at the social and occupational profile of minimum and low-wage workers, ending with a survey of current minimum wage-setting arrangements across the six countries. Public perceptions of minimum wage workers are captured by stereotypes: a younger worker in a temporary job who is combining work with other life goals, particularly study; a recently arrived migrant who – with some difficulty – is imagined to progress through the narrow opportunity structures of wage labour and home ownership; and a 'drifter', following some mix of precarity and dreams across geographic locations, jobs, and welfare.

Often, commentators in public debates write about minimum wage workers when they really mean a larger group of poorly paid workers or even the working class more generally. This cultural extrapolation is actually useful for two reasons. First, minimum wage workers often migrate into better-paid jobs that are still reasonably low paid, and second, minimum wage policies have 'spillover' impacts on the pay and job prospects of many more low-paid workers. For these reasons, this chapter not only focuses on the profiles and experiences of minimum wage workers, but also low-income workers generally. A broader focus on the bottom third of workers also helps with obtaining a sociological profile, given the limited sample sizes available in high-quality cross-national survey data. The ISSP's most recent Work Orientation module offers insights into four of our target countries in the decade before COVID-19, where low wages – not job insecurity – emerged as the dominant pressure faced by workers.

Let's begin with minimum wage employment in the strict sense. In the UK, 1.6 million minimum wage workers are concentrated in three main industries – retail, cleaning, and hospitality – with around half of all minimum wage jobs found in these sectors (Low Pay Commission 2018, p 46). Over 60% of minimum wage job holders are women and over half of these jobs are part time. The rising UK national minimum wage has been particularly important where living standards have been undercut by underemployment or the lack of time availability of carers. All three industries were already prone to severe industry-wide disruption prior to the further dislocations of COVID-19. For example, retail has been changing rapidly with the demise of traditional 'high street' and department store shopping. Restaurant and food industries continue to be transformed by home delivery services. Digital technologies, advanced further with distancing problems during the pandemic, are playing a transformative but highly disruptive role for employment patterns and work organisation.

In the US, Bureau of Labor Statistics (2018, p 1) show that the number of US workers employed *at or below* the federal minimum wage – currently $7.25 – has plummeted since 1979. Only 2% of American workers earn the federal minimum or less, compared with 13% in 1979. This decline tells us a lot about the declining relevance of the US federal minimum to most low–wage workers. That wage has not been increased since 2009 due to Republican control or blocking power in Congress. Given entrenched hostility to the working class in Washington, states where Democrats and unions have greater influence have moved ahead of the federal minimum. Once minimum wage workers on state or city level are included, the numbers change. The total number of minimum wage workers in the US was around 7 million (Tedeschi 2019) or approximately 4–5% of the employed population. This number would rise sharply with a universal $15 minimum wage.

Federal minimum wage workers in the US have a similar profile to UK minimum wage workers. Workers are commonly employed in the service occupations, that is, in food preparation and serving, personal and healthcare support jobs, protective services, and cleaning jobs (Bureau of Labor Statistics 2018, p 10). Food preparation and food server jobs attract the largest share of *below* minimum wage workers, earning some of their weekly wages in tips. The social profile of federal minimum workers reflects general social inequalities. Women, workers from minority backgrounds, young people, and workers in some southern US states are all strongly represented (Bureau of Labor Statistics 2018, pp 1–2).

Canada's rising minimum wages demonstrate how rising minimum wage floors change the profile of workers earning these wages. Like the US, Canada has maintained relatively low minimum wages, as measured by Kaitz scores. However, as I discuss in Chapter 4, that situation is changing with major wage gains in Alberta, British Columbia, and Ontario. A much larger share of Canada's workers now earn minimum wages (over 10%), with Ontario's minimum wage workers reaching 14% of its workforce (Dionne-Simard and Miller 2019, p 5). Researchers reinforce a key message. Minimum wage workers no longer fit the stereotype of young people living with their parents who have upward mobility to look forward to. More workers are older, work in larger firms, and live in cities, with retail workers now making up the largest group of minimum wage workers (Dionne-Simard and Miller 2019, pp 5–9).

For decades, Australia and New Zealand stood apart from the other English-speaking welfare states when it came to wage-setting for ordinary wage-earners. Both countries developed an independently determined award wages system over the 20th century. However, NZ abruptly abandoned that system during a 'big bang' neoliberal reform period in the early 1990s (O'Neill 1993, p 16). By the late 1990s, NZ began to place greater importance on minimum wages. Once a moribund industrial tool, the NZ minimum wage has risen dramatically in relative terms. Consistent with changes underway in Canadian provinces like Ontario, NZ minimum wage workers now make up a larger and larger share of the workforce. The minimum wage is currently paid to around 4% of workers, with a high representation of low-skill service sector industries (that is, retail and hospitality jobs) and some presence of jobs in administrative services and arts and recreation industries (Ministry of Business, Innovation & Employment 2018, p 38).

However, the number of minimum wage workers is likely to increase sharply. The Labour-led government of Prime Minister Ardern (2017–) brought the minimum wage up to NZ$20 on 1 April 2021. Government estimates suggested that a higher minimum would directly benefit around 350,000 workers or approximately 13% of the workforce on my calculations (Ministry of Business, Innovation & Employment 2019, p 7). The result will be that NZ's rising minimum wage moves closer in overall coverage to Australia's award wage-earners.

Unlike NZ, Australia preserved its complex award wages system determined by commissioners through the Fair Work Commission. Perhaps the best comparison for understanding this system is to see it as a formal, universally anchored 'wages board' system. Its legacy has been high minimum wages in relative terms. Moreover, its pervasive 'welfare function' led Castles (1985) to characterise Australia as a wage-earners' welfare state. On purchasing power measures, the Australian minimum wage – determined by the lowest pay rungs in particular industry awards – is the highest in the world (Charlton 2018). Temporary or casual workers get an additional loading of 25%

or more, which means that minimum wage workers employed under those arrangements can earn around A$25 per hour. Even though industrial awards now play a smaller regulatory role over wages, they remain important to the Australian system of minimum wage floors and central to determining the incomes of many workers. Just under a quarter of Australia's employees were paid directly via industrial awards in 2018 (Australian Bureau of Statistics 2019).

Few workers in Australia *literally* earn the national minimum wage because it is the wage floor in award wages in low-paid sectors like hospitality and horticulture. A study in 2006 attempted to create a profile of minimum and near-minimum wage workers in Australia. At that time, the relevant hourly rate was A$12.50. The minimum wage workforce by this measure totalled around 12% of employees, noting that some of these workers were employed in family enterprises, and so on (Healy and Richardson 2006, Table 1, p 7). Similar to patterns already identified, minimum wage and near-minimum wage workers in 2006 tended to be younger and/or less educated, and were more likely to be women. They were concentrated in occupational areas such as routine service jobs (business services, hospitality, personal retail, and agriculture industries) or labouring jobs (Healy and Richardson 2006, Table 2B, p 13).

To summarise key findings: there are consistent worker demographic patterns across the five jurisdictions discussed above. Minimum wage workers are more likely to be women, younger, to work part time, and to work in industries such as hospitality and retail, or in routine service jobs like cleaning and care work. Recent statistics on the social and occupational composition of the minimum wage workforce make it clear that rising minimum wage floors will broaden the demographic and industry profile of this workforce.

Minimum wage and low-wage workforces

Further perspective on the minimum wage is gained by expanding our focus to the wider low-wage workforce. First, as we have just seen, rising wage floors mean that minimum and low-wage workforces will overlap further. Second, even with wider coverage, the spillover effects of better minimums will benefit workers on above-minimum wages. UK data suggests that minimum wage adjustments benefit workers up to the 30th percentile of the distribution (Low Pay Commission 2019, p 17). US analysis concludes similarly, with estimates that a national $15 minimum wage would benefit around 27% of workers (Economic Policy Institute 2019). Third, even when minimum wage workers make progress to better paid jobs and occupations, many remain in the low-wage workforce (see Schultz 2019 for the US). A final reason for looking at more than minimum wage workers is pragmatic. High-quality sociological data allows us to consider the demography and work attitudes of workers. But decent sample sizes are needed to draw conclusions, so it makes even more sense to make comparisons for the lower third of wage-earners by income.

US data provides insights into the occupational base of low-wage employment by ranking job categories where more than 50% of workers earn less than two-thirds of the full-time median income (Schultz 2019, p 181). These jobs include many occupied by minimum wage workers in cleaning and care work, cashier work, and waiting tables. But the list also includes cooks and chefs, expanding out to include manual jobs held by sewing machine operators and agricultural workers as well as clerical work and teaching assistant positions (Schultz 2019, p 181). Detailed data is available for the large US state of California with a population around 40 million. Table 1.2 provides occupational data for low-wage workers who earned hourly wages below \$14.35 in 2017. This threshold is consistent with the two-thirds of median full-time earnings used extensively in the literature. Just under 5 million workers, or 32% of Californian workers, fell into this category in that year.

Table 1.2: Occupation categories of low-wage workers in California, 2017, %

	%
Retail sales workers	9.9
Personal care aides, childcare workers, and other personal care and service workers	5.7
Cooks and food preparation workers	5.7
Material moving workers	5.4
Customer service representatives and other information and record clerks	5.1
Waiters, waitresses, bartenders, and other food and beverage serving workers	4.1
Janitors, maids, and pest control workers	4.1
Material recording, scheduling, dispatching, and distributing workers	3.8
Agricultural workers	3.8
Construction trades workers	3.6

Note: Low-wage workers are defined as earning below \$14.35 per hour in 2017. The data represents the shares of the low-wage workforce in California that belong to the top 10 occupational categories, and the total does not tally to 100.

Source: University of California Berkeley Labor Center (n.d.) *Low Wage Work in California*: http://laborcenter.berkeley.edu/low-wage-work-in-california/#industries-and-occupations

California's patterns closely follow what Schultz identifies for the wider US. Just over 50% of the total low-wage workforce are employed across 10 occupational groups that mostly belong to the service industry. California's retail, care, and hospitality workers top the list. But there is some representation of traditional blue-collar employment as well, with material moving workers, agricultural workers, and construction workers making up a total of over 10% of the low-paid workforce. When even larger occupational groupings are compared, the category of 'office and administrative support occupations' emerges as the largest, ahead of sales and food-related jobs (University of California Berkeley Labor Center n.d.).

Consistent with federal patterns, low-wage workers in California are more likely to be women. Some 37% of women are low paid compared to 32% of workers overall who are classified as low wage. Many workers have lower levels of formal education: some 43% of those with high-school-level education are low paid. Racial diversity is a feature: 40% and 45% of Black and Latinx workers, respectively, are low-paid workers. The study also finds that while low-wage workers are younger (average age is 36), they are only slightly younger than the average Californian worker, who is aged 40 (University of California Berkeley Labor Center n.d.).

Retail workers, waiters, hairdressers, gardeners, material movers, farm workers, and data entry staff are among the occupations earning low wages. I have focused here on the US, but similar groups of workers make up the low-wage workforces of all six liberal countries and, of course, other rich countries. Several industries dominate the low-wage workforce: hospitality, retail, administration, and care industries along with some parts of manufacturing and agriculture.

Low-wage workforces are made up of many workers who perform what industrial sociologists and economists call 'routine jobs'. Over the years, skill classifications have been challenged by feminists and other social scientists who identify processes of social devaluation involved in those classifications (see Tilly 1999; Rose 2004). And the pandemic has only made the arbitrariness involved in these valuations obvious. Complex forms of societal dependence on low-wage workers has been made visible by the many essential functions these workers have performed during a global health crisis. Social devaluation of often difficult work goes hand in hand with the social patterns of inequality and discrimination. The data shows that women, people with lower levels of formal education, immigrants, and younger workers are all more likely to perform low-wage work. However, higher minimum wages that cover more of the workforce might slightly broaden the social profile of this workforce over the next decade or so.

Surveying low-wage workers

The multicountry International Social Survey Programme (ISSP) Work Orientations IV (ISSP Research Group 2017) dataset provides valuable survey data on the work experiences of respondents in four liberal countries. There is no data for Canada or Ireland. The data was collected in the mid-2010s. ISSP data adds to labour force surveys and opinion polling because it uncovers the broader social experience of work. Tables 1.3 and 1.4 provide the sample characteristics and work attitudes for respondents in paid employment and in the lowest third of self-reported incomes. Some caveats apply. Respondents included in the low-income sample were selected by personal, not household income. Moreover, reported incomes could include contributions from sources other than paid work. Although the data presented here is weighted by the ISSP for population characteristics, these weights do not adjust for labour force parameters. As a result, sample estimates differ somewhat from population parameters on key workforce characteristics. For example, the weighted ISSP sample still overrepresents the share of women in paid employment, including in the low-income cohort where women are already overrepresented.

Does the ISSP data confirm the profile of low-wage workers that we are already building? The answer is a reassuring yes. Table 1.3 compares sample characteristics for low-income and higher-income worker cohorts (n = 816 and n = 1,712 respectively). It separately reports the results for the low-income sample in all four countries, noting that headline figures for the individual country samples are subject to large errors. Overall, 44% of the low-income sample are aged under 40 and a majority are women (65%). Gender differences are substantial, reflecting inequalities entrenched by occupational and industry segregation as well as disproportionate childrearing commitments. Low-income earners are less likely to hold post-secondary qualifications (43% versus 66%), reflecting class disadvantage and the impact of a younger cohort still acquiring skills. Low-income workers work fewer hours on average. A majority (52%) work full time, defined as working more than 30 hours per week, but this share is much lower than the 93% full-time employment reported for the comparison group of higher-income earners. There was wide variation between the Australian and US samples on this count; the

Table 1.3: Characteristics of low-income workers in four liberal countries, 2015–16

	Australia*	New Zealand	United Kingdom	United States	4-country average (low income)	4-country average (average and high income)
Social characteristics						
Women	73	65	61	60	65	40
Aged under 40 years	50	38	49	43	44	37
Full-time (>30h p/w)	40	44	61	63	52	93
Post-secondary education	32	48	75	74	43	66
Occupation ISCO Major Group						
Managers	9	11	7	7	9	17
Professionals	23	23	9	9	16	31
Associate professionals	16	17	8	9	13	17
Admin workers	14	5	14	7	10	8
Service workers	24	23	34	37	30	7
Agricultural workers	1	4	2	0	2	1
Manual workers	4	2	4	7	4	9
Machine operators	4	2	7	8	5	6
Unskilled manual workers	6	13	15	16	12	4
Unweighted N	*143*	*142*	*311*	*220*	*816*	*1,712*

Notes: Samples includes only those currently in paid work (includes self-employed), on two separate measures, and reporting an income. Low-wage sample includes lowest 'third' of wage-earners determined for each country by taking personal income response category closest to 33rd percentile (that is, monthly: AU $3,600, NZ $2917, GB £1,100, US $1,875). US/UK zero reported income excluded. Occupational categories are International Standard Classification of Occupations (1 digit, main groups). *Individual country samples have large sampling errors. Fieldwork conducted in 2015 and 2015–16 in Australia and 2016 in the US.

Source: ISSP Research Group (2017), weighted by ISSP weighting variable

US low-income sample has 63% working full time. That compares to data suggesting 57% of low-wage workers in the US work full time (Ross and Bateman 2019).

Consistent with earlier data, the survey results confirm that low-income wage-earners are concentrated in particular occupational groupings graded by the International Standard Classification of Occupations (ISCO) scale. When compared to higher-income wage-earners, the low-income cohort is strongly overrepresented among service workers (ISCO Major Group 5) and unskilled manual workers (ISCO Group 9). A large share of Australian and NZ low-income earners work as professionals and associate professionals (ISCO Groups 2 and 3). This fact suggests sampling biases or a high concentration of part-time employees in these occupational groups. It is worth noting that, despite these high shares, professionals and associate professionals are both under-represented in the low-income cohort.

Evidence on the social experience of low-wage employment is presented in Table 1.4. Not surprisingly, low-income workers reported many worse employment experiences than better-off workers. The top half of Table 1.4 shows data on respondent perceptions of various dimensions of job quality, while the bottom half includes useful data on work disruptions (over five years) as recalled by respondents in Australia and NZ only. Country-level sample sizes are reasonably small, so the main comparisons are drawn from aggregate responses reported in the last two columns.

In the mid-2010s, low-income workers reported slightly lower job security than the rest of the sample (64% versus 72%) and, correspondingly, slightly higher job loss worries (25% versus 21%). By contrast, low-income workers reported significantly worse prospects for advancement (23% versus 35%) – consistent with objective indicators of poor mobility discussed earlier in the chapter. The COVID-19 jobs recession in several of the liberal countries has affected key sectors of the low-wage workforce (hospitality and tourism in particular), while bolstering employment in others (transport, supermarkets, cleaning work). In the 2020s, the 'low-pay' story reported above for the 2010s is likely to generalise into widespread social stress about the combination of low wages and insufficient employment.

Job satisfaction reported in the 2010s followed expected patterns. More low-income workers would have preferred to change their jobs (46% versus 36%). Fewer found their jobs interesting (69% versus 78%). Still, around seven in ten low-income workers found their jobs interesting. Consistent with a higher share of physical work among

Table 1.4: Attitudes and experiences of low-income workers in four liberal countries, 2015–16

	Australia*	New Zealand	United Kingdom	United States	4-country average (low income)	4-country sample (rest)
Current work experience and attitudes (agree and strongly agree)						
My job is secure	56	57	64	77	64	72
Worry (a great deal or to some extent) about losing job	27	30	27	17	25	21
Disagree with the statement: My pay is high	75	75	64	67	70	31
Opportunities for advancement are high	13	16	27	37	23	35
I would change type of work	47	43	42	50	46	36
Work is (often and mostly) stressful	33	29	29	30	30	41
Work is interesting	66	72	66	73	69	78
Work is (often or always) hard physical work	32	34	41	52	40	30
Workers need strong unions to protect their interests	54	61	59	50	56	43
Current union membership	14	9	23	4	13	22
Work discrimination in past 5 years	25	27	46	24	31	17
Prefer to work longer and earn more money	23	42	35	49	37	25
Work experiences over past 5 years						
Finances 'worse off'	29	29			29	15
Took additional job	31	30			31	11
Unemployed longer than three months	26	39			33	20
Changed occupation	36	46			41	27
Changed employer	45	56			51	41
Unweighted N	143	142	311	220	816	1,712

Notes: Samples includes only those currently in paid work (includes self-employed), on two separate measures, and reporting an income. Low-wage sample includes lowest 'third' of wage-earners determined for each country by taking personal income response category closest to 33rd percentile (that is, monthly: AU $3,600, NZ $2917, GB £1,100, US $1,875). US/UK zero reported income excluded. Occupational categories are International Standard Classification of Occupations (1 digit, main groups). *Individual country samples have large sampling errors.

Source: ISSP Research Group (2017), weighted by ISSP weighting variable

low-income workers, a higher share reported that their jobs often or always involve 'hard physical work' (40% versus 30%). Hard physical work is not only more commonly reported by respondents in the ISCO major groups covering manual labour; the largest group of low-wage service workers (ISCO Major Group 6) are also more likely to report physical stress. By contrast, low-income workers are less likely to report that their jobs are often or mostly 'stressful' (30% versus 41%), an indication that stress is more commonly interpreted by respondents as mental or emotional pressure.

In the 2010s, the major difference in responses was pay adequacy. Some 70% of low-income workers disagreed that their pay is high; this compared to 31% of better-off workers. Pay inadequacy was also projected into the future: only 23% of low-income workers reported 'high' opportunities for advancement compared to 35% for other workers. These findings are mostly consistent with the problems identified with 'blocked mobility'. However, it should be acknowledged that the highest perceptions of mobility came from the admittedly small (n = 220) sample of low-wage workers from the US, the liberal country with the worst mobility. Low-wage earners were also significantly more likely to prefer longer working hours (37% versus 25%), reflecting the respective impacts of low pay and shorter hours.

Additional Work Orientations data available for Australia and NZ provides insights into five-year work experience reports from low- and higher-wage respondents alike. This data gives important insights into disruptions in working life that low-income workers are more likely to endure. The share of low-wage workers who reported that their finances were worse off was almost double that for the rest of the sample (29% versus 15%). Low-income workers were three times more likely to have taken on an 'additional job' (31% versus 11%) in the previous five years and significantly more likely to have changed occupations (41% versus 27%). Just as significantly, low-wage workers were more likely to have experienced unemployment for more than three months (33% versus 20%). The COVID-19 jobs crisis will add to the long-term unemployment experiences of low-wage workers and involve even greater contact with welfare systems than that suggested by these 2015–16 findings.

Two of these findings warrant further comment. First, survey results pointing to additional job-taking among low-income workers indicate 'earnings stress' resulting from a varying combination of low hourly pay and inadequate hours. Additional job-seeking can be an entry point to gig employment and contracting arrangements that bring certain payoffs but significant risks for workers. Second, low-income workers had more commonly experienced long-term unemployment – pointing to higher levels of contact with welfare agencies and, speculatively, workfare policies. In Chapter 2, the relationship between workfare and low-wage employment is addressed in more detail, largely because of the risks of 'scarring' for workers subjected to tough benefit systems.

ISSP results also highlight patterns in workplace discrimination. Low-income workers are more likely to experience discrimination at work than higher-income counterparts (31% versus 17%). This difference in part reflects the social diversity of low-income workers reported earlier; and it accords with media reports about discrimination (see Semeuls and Burnley 2019). A closer inspection of responses reveals a wide spread of personal assessments of the reasons for this discrimination, which identify age, disability, nationality, as well as gender. Activist worker movements like Fight for $15 in the US have mobilised workers over a wide range of social justice and discrimination issues experienced by their constituency as well as over core claims for living wages.

In the mid-2010s, low-wage workers in these four liberal countries reported, not surprisingly, greater problems with pay adequacy, and, in limited data from Australia and New Zealand, had more disrupted working and financial lives than better-off workers. Longer periods of unemployment and frequent job changes hint at problems addressed in Chapter 2 – the threats to low-wage workers' living standards posed by expensive housing, mounting debt, and harsh welfare policies. And given clear evidence of their social diversity, low-income workers confirmed greater reports of discrimination at work.

Still, the findings confirm a broad attachment to work – over two-thirds of low-income workers found their jobs interesting. The impression from the mid-2010s data does not confirm either key elements of Graeber's (2018) thesis about pointless work or Standing's (2011) idea of a radical precariousness of institutionally detached workers. The picture is probably closer to Wright's (2015) characterisation of the insecurity experienced by a broadly defined working class. Of course, the post-COVID 2020s may undermine persistent attachments to work if the economic recovery in the liberal world promotes even greater emphasis on gig or temporary jobs or 'make-work' schemes that confirm predictions of radical critiques. In the mid-2010s, however, low-income workers held onto pro-work outlooks – and in one critical respect. They held significantly more positive views of unions: 56% agreed that 'workers need strong unions to protect their interests' compared to 43% of the rest. This result contrasts with actual density. Union membership was 13% compared to 22% for the rest. The gap between union support and membership is a crisis of interest representation that higher minimum wages indirectly attempt to address.

Evolving minimum wage-setting institutions

Minimum and low-wage workers are concentrated in service and manual jobs in key industries. Postindustrialisation paths via low-wage service-oriented labour markets, often centred on open and large metropolises, have made minimum wage floors central to the living standards of more workers. The profile of this constituency resembles a broader slice of a multicultural working class with continuing overrepresentation of women and younger people. Social survey data from four liberal countries shows that, in the mid-2010s, low wages, limited opportunities for advancement, and experience of discrimination were the dominant job pressures facing workers.

If minimum wages are destined to assume a larger role – and the evidence in this book suggests that they already are – then we need to know how they perform now and how they differ across jurisdictions. Table 1.5 provides an overview. The scope of this final section is synoptic, with the politics and social forces producing institutional change addressed in Chapter 4. Over the rest of this book, it becomes clear that minimum wages are now a very active area of reform in jurisdictions where they have remained dormant, often for decades, and that reforms are edging towards local or national living wages when measured in hourly rates. What is also clear is that minimum wage determination is becoming more political: legislatures are deeply involved in wage determination. At the same time, minimum wage settings are not well integrated into broader wage-earning institutions – a legacy of institutional discontinuities built into the liberal model, themselves the result of power struggles and resistance to encompassing protections.

Australia and NZ minimum wages

Let's start with Australia and NZ. Castles (1985) identified Australia and NZ as wage-earners' welfare states for the central role that minimum or 'basic' wages played in their early, progressive experiments in state-building. Awards served an important dual 'welfare' function designed to cover family living costs, initially of male breadwinners, and to

Table 1.5: Current minimum wage determination in the liberal countries

	National and subnational	Main determination mechanisms	Living wage criteria
Australia	Federal system with the national minimum wages determined by national awards. Some awards specify concessional rates (e.g. for junior staff or apprentices). Most states set some awards	National: Fair Work Act 2009. Annual wage review by an independent statutory authority, the Fair Work Commission. Most states maintain awards with minimums	No direct provisions. Federal legislation requires consideration of relative living standards of low paid
Canada	Narrow coverage federal minimum wage with provincial minimum wages acting as minimums	Levels, exclusions and coverage vary by province. Seven provinces or territories have automatic yearly adjustments based on either CPI or another formula. Periodic legislative adjustments elsewhere. British Columbia has advisory Fair Wages Commission	No direct provisions, except for British Columbia's Fair Wages Commission has 'living wages' advisory role. Ad hoc legislative responses to cost of living pressures
Ireland	National with concessional rates for workers aged under 20	Low Pay Commission (since 2015) makes recommendations to the Minister for Employment Affairs and Social Protection who in turn makes an annual National Minimum Wage Order. Minimum wages in some sectors higher and set by Joint Labour Committees	Minimum wages should be 'fair and sustainable' and adjusted 'incrementally' but without 'adverse consequences for employment or competitiveness'
New Zealand	National minimum wage with sub-minimum wages for trainees and younger workers	Minimum Wage Act 1983. Minister of Labour recommendation to NZ governor general Advice from Ministry of Business, Innovation and Employment	No direct provisions. Coalition agreement between governing parties (Labour and NZ First) committed to NZ$20 minimum wage by 2021

(continued)

Table 1.5: Current minimum wage determination in the liberal countries (continued)

	National and subnational	Main determination mechanisms	Living wage criteria
UK	National Living Wage set by UK Secretary of State 5 minimum wage rates	National Minimum Wage Act 1998 Low Pay Commission – statutory body for monitoring and advisory functions but now subject to government-set targets	2016 Regulation, though the hourly rate of the National Living Wage is considered below estimates of London and UK living wages
US	Overlapping federal, state and city minimums	Federal legislation dating back to Roosevelt's New Deal (Fair Labor Standards Act 1938). Highly ad hoc and partisan increases determined by Congress States vary in determining their rates, concessional rates, exclusions, and coverage Cities have minimum wage ordinances or living wage policies for staff and contractors	Some city-level policies assess living wage needs for minimum wage workers States pay below a living wage, although some states are closer to recognised living wage rates Federal policy has no regular adjustment or wage adequacy advisory commission

Sources: Australia: Fair Work Act 2009: www.legislation.gov.au/Details/C2017C00323. Canada: see provincial government webpages for policy details or https://en.wikipedia.org/wiki/Minimum_wage_in_Canada for an up-to-date and comprehensive overview of province and territory minimums. Ireland: see www.irishstatutebook.ie/eli/2000/act/5/enacted/en/html and www.citizensinformation.ie/en/employment/employment_rights_and_conditions/pay_and_employment/pay_inc_min_wage.html. NZ: Minimum Wage Act 1983: http://legislation.govt.nz/act/public/1983/0115/latest/DLM74093.html and www.govt.nz/browse/work/workers-rights/minimum-wage/. UK: www.gov.uk/government/organisations/low-pay-commission and www.gov.uk/national-minimum-wage-rates. US: see 'State Minimum Wage Laws', www.dol.gov/whd/minwage/america.htm#stateDetails; or here: www.epi.org/minimum-wage-tracker/#/min_wage/

ensure independent household living. These state-regulated minimums were more ambitious and encompassing than the wages boards of the UK and Ireland or minimum wage laws in Canada and the US, where the focus was very low-paid women in the sweating industries. Australia and NZ minimum wage-setting diverged after the 1990s, with NZ abandoning award determination altogether. Australia's minimum wages continue to be minimum rungs on the award wage system, which is overseen by the Fair Work Commission – a statutory institution with its roots in Australia's early arbitration courts that settled disputes and undertook basic wage-setting functions. Award wage minimums are directly influenced by the Annual Wage Review by the Commission. What remains distinctive about the Australian approach is the independence of the Commission's wage decisions and their direct impact on the significant share of the workforce (exceeding 20% of employees). These independently administered award wages delivered relatively high minimum wages – in 2000, the Kaitz index score sat at 58%, which was then the highest in the OECD (see Table 4.5).

Conservative governments tolerated Australia's extensive Commission-led wage determination when the alternatives were unpredictable strikes and industrial contention. By the early 2000s, the conservative Coalition government of PM John Howard (1996–2007) finally gained legislative approval to undertake major reform called WorkChoices. It stripped the main Commission of award pay-setting functions and empowered a short-lived Australian Fair Pay Commission to accommodate business interests on wage levels (Buchanan and Oliver 2014, p 106). Just as significantly, the government introduced individual contracts that would weaken wages and conditions delivered by the two-tier system of collective enterprise bargaining that sat above industrial awards (Buchanan and Oliver 2014, pp 105–6). Howard's government, already long in power, overreached, with the union movement and Labor Party opposing the reforms. Howard fought and lost the 2007 election on this issue (Bean and McAllister 2009; Wilson and Spies-Butcher 2011).

After the election of the Rudd Labor government in 2007, the Fair Work Act 2009 rebuilt some traditional features of the Australian model on the legal foundations of WorkChoices, ending the former government's individual contracts. But Labor 'modernised' awards, restricting their scope and function (Buchanan and Oliver 2014, pp 106–7).

The Act's minimum wage-setting powers establish four main objectives for the Fair Work Commission's annual wage review. The first two relate to considerations of the 'competitiveness' of the economy and promoting 'social inclusion' through 'workforce participation' (Fair Work Act 2009, s 284), although the latter could be construed as a 'living wage' consideration in that social inclusion at work might arguably be construed as a living wage job. However, this provision is an orthodox policy construction, implying that wage levels should maximise employment because work is inherently a social good. The third consideration relates to 'relative living standards and the needs of the low paid', which hints at 'living wage' principles without explicit commitments. Although these guidelines formally guide the Fair Work Commission's reviews, the Commission's decisions have been cautious, never restoring the relative minimum wages that prevailed prior to big bang reform. For this reason, the federal Australian Labor Party proposed to move towards a 'living wage' as part of its unsuccessful 2019 election campaign (Karp 2019). Labor's proposal recognised that Australia's minimum wages have gradually departed from the living wage foundations set in the Harvester decision in the early 20th century (see Chapter 2). By contrast, the current Coalition is closer to the US Republicans, assuming a consistently hostile position on higher minimums in its submissions to the Commission.

New Zealand's system of industrial award wages was never as institutionally central as Australia's. However, when that system was abandoned in the 1990s under a conservative National government (O'Neill 1993, p 16), the country was left, like the UK, with few mechanisms to either alter the wage distribution or prevent the expansion of the working poor. Although the Labour government of Helen Clark returned to a limited system of collective bargaining, the new government gave previously marginalised minimum wage legislation a greater emphasis. These reforms were similar to those pursued by the UK's Blair government from the same period. The minimum wage was to act as the functional equivalent of the country's abandoned award wages system.

The determination of the minimum wage involves a yearly review by the Minister of Labour, which is then prescribed by the NZ governor general (Minimum Wages Act 1983, s 5). The Ministry of Business, Innovation & Employment (MBIE) advises on increases based on a range of tests, some determined by the legislation and the ILO Minimum Wage-Fixing Machinery Convention that NZ has signed. But the decision about the minimum wage level is ultimately a *political* one determined by the government. For example, the Labour-led government of PM Ardern continued the Clark government's higher minimum wage floor, promoting the living wages agenda as part of its governing arrangements with the NZ Greens and a small nationalist party, NZ First. Living wage politics has also been influenced by strong community campaigns for living wages alongside other welfare initiatives. The MBIE's assessment of living wage costs, for example, suggested that New Zealand's 2018 minimum wage – assessed on 2016 living costs – was below a living wage for an Auckland family with two children but not radically so (Ministry of Business, Innovation & Employment 2018, p 26). By 2020, NZ had the highest Kaitz index of any rich OECD nation, embarking on a wages experiment that gets closest to a living wage in a liberal country.

Canada and the US

Historically, Canada and the US never developed comprehensive wages boards or independent minimum wage commissions like Australia and NZ or even as the UK and Ireland did. The initial focus of minimum wages was on the pay and conditions of very low-paid and marginalised women. But the minimum wage became central to Roosevelt's New Deal employment policies (Stabile 2016) and long-standing provincial institutions in Canada. Again, starting points and early failures or successes determine paths. Subnational institutions have remained important in North America; and, in Chapter 4, we will see how much more so, given recent reforms. Weak institutional legacies have meant, however, that North American Kaitz scores have remained at the lower end of the OECD. Living wage agendas have been resisted politically and by the powerful 'North American' economics consensus.

Canada's federal system maintains a central place for provincial governments in labour law and minimum wage determination, although there are federation-wide protections for union recognition and collective bargaining. Unions remains strong in the public sector and parts of Canada's industrial economy. After 1996, the federal minimum wage set for workers in the federal sphere reflected the corresponding provincial minimum wage (Employment and Social Development Canada 2019, p 2). As expected, the provinces and territories set these minimums differently – 'in legislation or regulations; by the government-of-the-day or an independent board' – and they are adjusted 'based on inflation, average wage rates or other economic factors' (Employment and Social Development Canada 2019, p 2). Rates also vary by age and employee status (reflecting apprenticeship status), often reduced for 'liquor servers' or drinks waiters.[1] Where adjustment takes place, automatic formulas depend on the Consumer Price Index (CPI) – a measure that, in Canada and elsewhere, is prone to fall gradually behind productivity growth and wages.

Minimum wage activism at the provincial level has become important to programmatic reform in three large provinces – Alberta, British Columbia, and Ontario. Alberta's one-term New Democratic Party (NDP) government of Premier Rachel Notley passed legislation increasing Alberta's minimum wage to C$15 in 2018, a remarkable achievement in that conservative-leaning jurisdiction (Employment and Social Development Canada 2019, p 3). However, the Conservative government of Premier Jason Kenney reduced rates for teenagers after taking office and it appointed a panel to review wage rates. The legislature holds responsibility for adjusting minimums, which means an uncertain, partisan-based adjustment process and therefore relative deterioration under Conservative governments.

In British Columbia, another NDP administration took action on the provincial minimum, introducing the Fair Wages Commission in late 2017. Like the UK commission, its role is advisory. But its third mandate is 'to advise the government on ways to begin to address the discrepancy between the minimum wage and a living wage in our province' (Government of British Columbia n.d.). Here, there is a direct acknowledgement of the living wage objective in the current government's and in the Commission's objectives. However, this objective does not amount to a statutory power to determine the minimum wage with reference to a living wages formula or panel-based deliberation. In Ontario, the Liberal government of Premier Kathleen Wynne used a significant package of labour reforms to increase the minimum wage to C$15 in 2017. The incoming Conservative government of Premier Doug Ford, however, limited the proposed increase to C$14. Ontario's minimum is adjusted yearly with reference to changes in Canada's CPI.

Canadian reforms have a partisan character, with the NDP most active in pursuing higher provincial minimums, although the Liberal Party is moving similarly towards living wages policies. Recent Conservative governments in Alberta and Ontario have either halted, reversed or reviewed reforms. With more activist policies on the political left on this issue in Canada, minimums are likely to rise because Conservative governments are wary of the political impact of cutting minimum wages. Massive COVID-19-related unemployment may provide renewed political opportunities for opponents.

Like Canada, US minimum wage institutions reflect its federal structure. National legislation was the result of legislative struggles over

Roosevelt's New Deal reforms, which culminated in the Fair Labor Standards Act 1938 (Stabile 2016). Consistent with weak national institutions (Weir 1992), Congress determines the minimum national rate politically. There is no formal advisory commission or automatic adjustment for inflation or productivity or economy-wide earnings growth. Still, over the decades Congress regularly acted. Federal laws assumed such policy dominance that Waltman and Pittman (2002, p 53) remarked: 'State minimum wage laws have long been overshadowed by the federal minimum wage. Nonetheless, state laws represent an important aspect of American labor market policy.'

How things changed over the first two decades of the 2000s. Long periods of Republican control in Congress have meant that Roosevelt's legislation has become, in the words of journalist Eric Morath (2019), 'an irrelevant labor policy'. Despite signs that President Trump initially prevaricated over policy, Republicans have continued their decades-long hostility to a higher federal minimum.

Long periods of Republican intransigence have spurred city- and state-level activism. US state minimums, and how they are determined, vary enormously. They are prohibitively exhaustive to summarise here, but regularly updated information is available at: www.epi.org/minimum-wage-tracker/#/min_wage/. The partisan divide is clear: Republican-dominated states, particularly in the country's south, act as bulwarks, tending to rely on the federal minimum (or conservative state-wide settings). State-based conservatives have even pre-empted progressive city-wide ordinances in those 'red' states from exceeding state policies (Huizar and Lathrop 2019).

Elsewhere, Democratic-controlled administrations have been more responsive. Most Democratic states now produced significant improvements to state minimums, often staggered over years, either through legislation or ballot measure or constitutional change. In 2020, at least six states and Washington DC made legislated changes to reach $15. The best policies in California and New Jersey include automatic adjustments via indexation. These make the preservation of the real value of $15 more likely, even if cost of living adjustments do not account for broader wage and productivity growth.

Chapter 4 looks closely at grassroots union and community organising, notably Fight for $15, as well as city-level living wages that have become springboards for state and national action. As it turns out, the $15 minimum, which has symbolised the living wages struggle, emerged from New York fast-food workers who picked a wage rate that they could live on (Greenhouse 2019, p 235). Worker judgements can be combined with sophisticated measures that now track local, state, and national living wages levels in the US. These technically advanced efforts undermine claims that setting living wage minimums is too complex and depends on too many local and family factors.

Consider the Massachusetts Institute of Technology's (MIT) living wage calculator produced by Amy Glasmeier. According to their website, living wage estimates are determined conservatively, assembled around the bare basics without including savings (that is, for home ownership) or restaurant meals (Glasmeier/MIT 2020). The authors note:

> The living wage is the minimum income standard that …
> draws a very fine line between the financial independence
> of the working poor and the need to seek out public
> assistance or suffer consistent and severe housing and food
> insecurity. … the living wage is … a minimum subsistence
> wage for persons living in the United States. (Glasmeier/
> MIT 2020)

Readers are able to consider a wide array of estimates made for states and even counties that also compare living wage calculations adjusted for household size and type with both poverty wages and actual wages.

These calculations are clear. Raising a family on a living wage in America still requires two adults to be working. This realisation does not reject the living wage principle or efforts to develop better calculations. It reminds us that buttressing labour market institutions that guarantee decent work are needed, along with targeted social protection for single-income families. Both subjects are addressed in Chapter 5.

Ireland and the UK

Finally, to minimum wages in the UK and Ireland. The UK case is considered first because reforms in Ireland followed later, sharing common features. Like NZ Labour in the late 1990s, the Blair government dealt with an institutional void. Thatcherism had weakened unions and the Major government abolished the remaining wages councils in 1993. Low-income workers had few institutional protections. New Labour established the Low Pay Commission through the National Minimum Wage Act 1998. The Commission has had an important advisory and oversight role (Brown 2017) but has none of the statutory power to make wage determinations like Australia's Fair Work Commission. UK national minimums are adjusted yearly and there are currently five rates dealing with adults (25 years and over), juniors, and apprentices. The responsible secretary of state makes determinations about the National Minimum Wage along with these concessional rates on the recommendation of the Commission (National Minimum Wage Act 1998).

Cautious incremental improvements to the Kaitz index marked the initial phase of the National Minimum Wage. The situation changed in the mid-2010s with the Conservative government unexpectedly setting a living wage target. Conservative Chancellor George Osborne added Regulations to the 1998 Act to introduce the 'National Living Wage' in 2016, set initially at £7.20 with staged increases planned over coming years. Although the Conservatives were signalling to the wider electorate that they supported the principle, at least, of living wages, the current rate remains below what the Living Wage Commission considers a living wage for both high-cost London (the rate was around 25% below) and the UK more generally (around 13% below) (www.livingwage.org.uk). The Conservatives' living wage commitment was criticised by the Labour Party, which campaigned for an immediate increase to a living wage of £10 in the December 2019 election, which would have been close to estimates of a London living wage (Mayor of London/London Assembly 2020).

The UK shift in rhetoric and policy is one of the most fascinating. Starting out as a cautious Labour reform, prompted by concessions to UK's labour movement, it has resulted over time in more ambitious targets. The Conservative Party's shift is a conversion of sorts, given their former hostility to minimum wages. The reasons for this are partly strategic and electoral, as discussed in Chapter 4.

Irish wage-setting involves a multilayered institutional process and history. There have been experiments in social partnership between trade unions and Fianna Fáil governments, a stable system of collective bargaining, and continuity in wages boards (abandoned in the UK) for low-wage industries. These trades/wages boards are called the Joint Labour Committees. Still, Ireland introduced a national minimum wage in 2000. Ireland followed the UK with new legislation that placed greater emphasis on a national minimum wage as a stronger wage floor. Later, the Fine Gael/Labour coalition government followed the UK by establishing a Low Pay Commission. That Commission makes 'recommendations to the Minister of Employment Affairs and Social Protection designed to set a minimum wage that is fair and sustainable' and seeks to 'assist as many low-paid workers as possible without harming overall employment or competitiveness' (Low Pay

Commission [of Ireland] 2020). The Irish government announces increases in the annual Irish budget.

The 2019 increase in the national minimum wage to just over €10 remained below an assessment of a living wage from Ireland's Living Wage Technical Group, which assessed that wage at over €12. The difference between the national minimum wage and the assessed living wage is around 20%, similar to the gap estimated for the UK. Ireland's rapid but unsteady economic growth path has combined with multilayered wage-earner institutions to improve overall living standards. But inequality has worsened and, for this reason, a politically restive Ireland may look to greater minimum wage progress through the 2020s.

The story so far

This chapter lays the groundwork for our investigation of evolving minimum wage policies. The results are summarised below:

1. The liberal countries have smaller middle classes and large and growing shares of low-income households. Limited redistributive budgets are a major feature of the institutions maintained by the power resources of business. Chapter 4 develops a more complete picture of the contribution of weak wage-earner institutions to the structures and inequalities of Anglo-American labour markets. Not surprisingly, the OECD recognises a larger role for statutory minimums, given the weakness of collective and industry bargaining derived from the power resources of corporations.
2. Earnings mobility is poor in the US, but the other liberal countries tend to group in the middle of the OECD pack. Weak mobility emerges as a serious problem where it is difficult to escape a high probability of low-paid work or living for extended periods in poor households. Such a combination contributes to a large working poor – the target of the Fight for $15 mobilisations under way in the US.
3. Minimum wage workers are more likely to be women, young workers, and people with few formal qualifications working in low-wage service industries that have grown over the past few decades. However, as minimum wage floors rise, the profile of minimum wage workers would trend closer to the profile of the broader workforce.
4. In survey research about the experiences and attitudes of low-wage workers in the mid-2010s, the central issues that distinguished

low-income workers from the rest were low pay and perceptions of limited low mobility – and more common experiences of discrimination. Survey results from Australia and NZ confirm that low-wage workers experience greater labour market disruptions that implicate the central problem of low pay. Low-income wage-earners had very low union membership but express stronger support for unions. The gap in representation is no doubt a factor in greater state intervention across the liberal world.

5. Minimum wage institutions vary considerably across the liberal countries – a result of starting points, path dependence, the success of recent policy interventions, and processes of cross-country policy learning. Chapter 4 presents evidence of rapidly rising Kaitz scores across the liberal world over the past decade or so. These successes point to the role of both contentious politics and political bargaining in minimum wage transformations.

6. Minimum wage-setting outside Australia involves partisan legislative interventions with clear incentives for centre-left governments to lift minimums. Conservative and pro-business parties divide over higher minimum floors. As we shall see, there is continuing strong Republican resistance to improvements in the US, but greater accommodation in Ireland, NZ, and the UK. Boeri (2012) observed that, historically, legislatures produced lower minimum wages. Recent politics and policy suggest that the pattern is now changing.

7. No statutory minimum wages meet an objectively determined living wage standard. Some jurisdictions are now closer than others, with living wage criteria either guiding advisory commissions (British Columbia) or party political positions, that is, policy stances of Australian Labor, NZ Labour, and both the UK Labour and Conservative parties.

The pressure for higher money wages has wider foundations than struggles against relative pay injustice. Material insecurities, as we shall see, are built into the social architecture of living standards in the liberal countries. Living is expensive in privatised worlds. Chapter 2 explores three pressures on living standards: debt accumulation, unresponsive welfare systems, and emerging exploitative employment practices.

Low-wage workers and threats to working-class living standards

We now have clearer perspective of who earns minimum wages and how minimum wage institutions across the liberal countries affect the low-wage workforce. Pressure on these institutions to respond to the needs of low-wage workers emerges from three types of evidence. First, the liberal countries, particularly the US, produce more low-income households than comparable welfare states. Later, Chapter 4 provides further evidence on how weak labour market institutions contribute to this problem. Second, low-income workers report greater insecurities relating to both pay levels and opportunities for advancement as well as more frequent disruptions to working life. COVID-19 adds to these problems by wiping out the employment growth over the past decade. Third, deficits in wage-earner institutions of the liberal regime mean that minimum wage institutions are an obvious target for activists and policymakers in addressing pressures on low-wage workers.

The reports of poor pay, limited mobility, and disrupted working lives that emerge from the ISSP data capture only part of the pressures on low-wage workers and their households. This chapter looks at three particular stresses on the social architecture of working-class lives – debt, workfare, and threats to future jobs. Household debt is a central indicator of the poor health of households. Debt reflects poor wages, a troubling relationship to money and finance, and, critically, high housing costs. At the same time, welfare now adds to social stresses on low-wage households rather than cushioning them. Harsh reforms in at least three liberal countries – Australia, the UK, and the US – are indicative of the long-term attack on social protection for unemployed wage-earners. The result is an 'engineered dependence' on low-paid jobs or deepening poverty outside paid employment. Finally, future jobs are threatened by more than technology. The organisational forces described in Chapter 1 are driving the growth of insecure, low-paid jobs. Gig employment and the systematic underpayment of workers are part of that problem, consolidating low wages and unstable working lives.

The focus on threats to the social architecture of low-wage working life is not intended to be comprehensive. Nor does it suggest that the liberal countries are the only affluent countries that are adding to the burdens of working-class households. However, trends in market economies – the privatisation of public goods, unresponsive wage-earner institutions, and hostility to social protection – are particularly discernible features of the politics and policy of the English-speaking countries. The final section of this chapter returns to the historical mobilisation for the living wage. Exploring the historical social forces that pushed living wages to the fore provides an important context for understanding contemporary pressures on workers. The weakness of organised labour to influence low-wage sectors is a reminder of past pressures for intervention and reform.

Expensive housing and indebted workers

Pressure for higher money wages has a major cause: high living costs in a privatised economy and society. Central to household financial stress is the high cost of housing emerging from higher mortgage costs and expensive rents. Table 2.1 uses recent data from the OECD's *Better Life Index* to make an assessment of housing expenditures, which are then organised and presented by regime type. The liberal countries have the second highest average expenditure on housing at 22.3% of household income. Average expenditures in Southern European countries are slightly higher at 22.5%, noting that income growth

Table 2.1: Household housing expenditures and household debt by welfare state, as % of household income

	Average expenditure	Range in expenditures	Average rank (highest = 40)	Household debt ratio
Liberal countries (n = 6)	22.3	19–26	27/40	155
Nordic countries (n = 4)	20.5	17–23	21/40	211
Continental countries (n = 6)	20.7	19–22	21/40	145
Southern European countries (n = 4)	22.5	22–23	31/40	107
East Asian countries (n = 2)	18.8	15–22	14/40	147
Eastern Europe/Russia (n = 7)	21.0	18–23	21/40	69

Notes: Continental countries are: Austria, Belgium, France, the Netherlands, and Germany. Southern European countries are: Greece, Italy, Portugal, and Spain. East Asian countries are Japan and South Korea.

Source: OECD (2019c) *Better Life Index*: www.oecdbetterlifeindex.org/topics/housing/; OECD household debt statistics: https://data.oecd.org/hha/household-debt.htm

has been poor across the regime since the Eurozone crisis. Still, two liberal countries earn the top two positions on the list of 40 nations. NZ and the UK have the highest housing costs as a share of household income at 26% each. Canada's housing expenditures are also above the OECD's 40-country average (22% versus 20%). However, Australia, the US, and Ireland are closer to the OECD average expenditures on housing.

However, when the focus turns to lower-income households, the US joins NZ and the UK among those OECD countries with expensive housing. Bottom quintile measures available from the OECD do not perfectly capture the relative income position of low-wage working households, but the class gradient evident in housing costs is still illuminating. Sometimes, low-income *renters* are paying very high housing costs. Other times, housing stress shows up among low-income *mortgage holders*. NZ features in the top 3 countries (out of 35) for the share of disposable income absorbed by rents in households in the bottom quintile – and the US is ranked fifth (OECD 2019d, Figure HC1.2.2, Panel A). The US also ranks highly for *mortgage costs* as a share of disposable income in the bottom quintile and is joined by Canada as highly ranked on this measure (OECD 2019d, Figure HC1.2.2, Panel B).

Another OECD measure compares countries by the overall share of low-income households who are 'overburdened' by housing costs – that is, paying more than 40% of disposable income in housing expenditures. Of the 32 countries analysed, NZ, the US, and the UK all emerge at the top or near the top on combined measures (OECD 2019d, Figure HC.1.2.3). When average housing expenditures are compared, the US is not an outlier nation. But poorer households face unusually high burdens. One report suggests that low-income households in large US cities face severe housing stress because of investment in high-end real estate and the lack of investment in affordable housing (Stein 2018). Similar patterns are found in large Australian cities. A clear contrast example is provided by France, which deploys its large social housing sector to limit poor and working-class housing stress (OECD 2019d). Not surprisingly, city-wide ordinances in the US that substantially raise minimum wages cite dangerous levels of housing unaffordability in their claim-making. Similar claims are advanced by voluntary organisations such as the Living Wage Foundation to encourage business commitment to pay a higher London-wide living wage (Cominetti 2019).

As discussed in Chapter 1, more frequent work disruptions add to the financial instability faced by working-class households. One US report has investigated the role of 'negative income shocks' on the financial capacity and wealth of American households. The report notes that income shocks actually continued to rise after the global financial crisis (GFC). The author observes: 'The share of families who have seen a negative income shock – meaning their income was less than usual in the previous year – grew from less than 18 percent before the Great Recession to 22.3 percent since then' (Weller 2018, p 2). The report relates this trend to the rising job instability built into the employment system – even when labour markets improve. The extent of disruption was picked up in the ISSP results for Australia and NZ reported in Chapter 1.

Low-income households do not hold most debt: higher household debt is strongly related to the capacity to pay of higher-income households. In the US, for example, Mason (2018) convincingly shows that the US debt build-up has been concentrated among richer households pursuing opportunities and assets relative to their capacity to pay. Poorer households, over time, have absorbed rising inequality in the US by constraining their living standards (Mason 2018). However, other evidence suggests that debt problems related to the GFC hit the poorest households hardest (Kim et al 2017). Even prior to the subprime mortgage crisis, scholars were already observing the class character of risky US debt accumulation (Foster 2006; see also Mason 2018). Since then, one cohort in particular has continued to experience the risk of debt-related hardship produced by downward mobility risks. Households experiencing 'negative income shocks' had a higher chance of unsustainable debt burdens and a greater risk of falling behind on repayments (Weller 2018, pp 8–9). These risks make housing acquisition – the main form of working-class wealth – less likely. Moreover, high debt burdens leave households with poor borrowing records even when circumstances improve.

A similar scenario has developed in the UK after the GFC. The Trades Union Congress (TUC), the main union body, has implicated poor labour market conditions in rising household debt problems, particularly in unsecured debts (Collinson 2019). As reported in *The Guardian*:

> Public spending cuts and years of wage stagnation are key reasons for the increase in unsecured debt, the TUC said, adding that working families are on average worse off today than before the financial crisis. The rise of the gig economy and zero-hours contracts are also thought to be a significant contributing factor. (Bignall 2019)

Scholars at the Bank of Italy investigating national comparisons of household debt identify a multitude of contributing causes, including a central role for housing finance (Coletta et al 2019, p 1204). Comparisons put the liberal countries towards the top of the list of indebted households. Curiously, they are not at the very top. The Nordic countries have the most indebted households. This is the result of high house prices in countries such as Denmark and also the liberalisation of credit supply in Nordic countries (Reiakvam and Solheim 2013, p 17). Coletta et al (2019) implicate welfare state arrangements in their explanation for high debts in the liberal and Nordic countries. They state that welfare policies:

> in turn may have contributed to the rise in households' mortgages. The issue is interesting as household debt is high both in countries with a social democratic system, such as Denmark, the Netherlands and Sweden, and in nations with a liberal welfare state, such as Australia, Canada, Ireland and the UK. (Coletta et al 2019, p 1191)

However, high indebtedness in the Nordic and liberal countries differs for an important reason. Coletta et al (2019, p 1191) explain: 'households decide the desired level of long-term debt, such as mortgages, taking into consideration long-term assets provided by welfare systems... [and that]... deficiencies in the welfare state can prompt households to seek private substitutes such as home ownership'. In the Nordic countries, as Reiakvam and Solheim argue, higher debts are related to *trust* in the welfare state: 'Strong welfare schemes to cover the loss of income due to illness or unemployment also limit the need for private savings' (Reiakvam and Solheim 2013, p 12, see also p 16).

By contrast, rising Anglo-American household debt is driven by the opposite problem: the need for households to counteract weak welfare states. Even for non-poor households with stable jobs, household debt in rich countries points to deeper problems with a social contract under threat from unresponsive governments, social competition, and the declining provision of public goods. Here, I am referring to opportunity hoarding in the 'markets' set up for housing and education (Andriotis et al 2019; OECD 2019a). Better-off households build up private assets in the absence of encompassing public institutions as a form of savings for future income shocks. Poorer households or households facing 'negative income shocks', by contrast, use debt to stabilise their incomes through choppy periods in the labour market. Adding to this problem intergenerationally are high and rising student debts, particularly in the US. Young workers are entering unequal labour markets, more sharply defined by class-based opportunity structures. Poor jobs prospects, rising student debt, and high housing costs (rather than ideological shifts) are more plausible explanations for the sharp generational patterns in support for ultimately unsuccessful though influential challengers on the left in the UK and the US, Jeremy Corbyn and Bernie Sanders.

A final remark about debt and living wages. The accumulation of household debt complicates effective living wage rates for cities and wider jurisdictions. This complication is illustrated by turning to living standard measures used in social policy to measure benefit adequacy or poverty thresholds. *Normative* budget standards determine the income needs of households to avoid poverty. In theory, they are set so that low-income households can cover daily or weekly contingencies. However, these can differ from the real *behavioural* income needs of low-income households, given the dynamics of real-world situations (Saunders and Bedford 2017, p 10).[1] Rising debt burdens, or steep area-specific housing costs, are examples of problems for determining anti-poverty thresholds. Studying consumer debt burdens, Pressman and Scott (2010, p 9) conclude that: 'High interest payments mean that living standards for U.S. households are lower than median household income would suggest, and that more people in the United States have disposable income below the poverty line than is indicated by current poverty measures.'

The same conundrum must apply to determining living wage rates. Unclear numbers of low-income households have accumulated debts related to poor pay, expensive housing, and work disruptions. High money wages embedded in living wage claims are an obvious response to these often-hidden pressures and the absence of state investment in basic living infrastructures.

Welfare paternalism and the churn of work and welfare

As the survey research presented in Chapter 1 shows, low-wage workers are more likely to report disrupted working lives. These disruptions showed up as more five-year reports of unemployment, changes of occupation, and changes of employer. The Work Orientations IV module, on which the responses are based, does not ask about welfare experiences. However, the findings – especially the higher incidence of long-term unemployment – provide clues about the disproportionate contact of low-wage workers with welfare systems (for Australia, see Buddelmeyer et al 2010; for the US, see Boushey 2002). I am not referring to access to benefits for childcare or wage subsidies, but rather income support payments for unemployed workers, single parents, and people living with disabilities. Many minimum and low-wage workers have limited or even negligible contact with welfare. And, even when they do have contact, some workers successfully move on to better jobs as opportunities become available. But, as we shall see, positive experiences are far from universal. Too many workers get caught between overly policed, harsh welfare systems and low-paid jobs.

One source of compensation for choppy and unstable labour markets is a responsive social security system, guaranteeing minimum incomes. This protection could be achieved through a mix of in-work payments and unemployment benefits. Or more ambitiously, it could be achieved through a basic income, one likely to involve potentially significant policy compromises, given the power resources built into the liberal regime. However, welfare reforms have travelled in quite the opposite direction in at least three of the liberal countries covered here.

Workfare policies continue to entrench low-wage labour markets as the sole source of income support. Williams (1997, p 542) remarks that: 'The development of welfare laws has always been connected to low-wage labor markets.' A centuries-old antagonism continues to pit the power resources of business and politics to maximise dependence on paid work against worker and community resistance to harsh reforms. Indeed, pursuit of punitive dependency on labour markets has its origins in the reform of the English Poor Law in 1834, famously described in Polanyi's *The Great Transformation* ([1944] 2001, p 86). However, during the late 19th and 20th centuries, workers and communities fought back. Capitalist labour markets proved unstable and damaging to many, stimulating the countervailing power resources of unions and social democracy. As state administrations gained revenue and budgets, a broader 'struggle for recognition' (to use philosopher Axel Honneth's phrase) compelled government to recognise entitlements for other disadvantaged groups with limited access to paid work, particularly single women with small children and people living with major disabilities. Even so, entitlements for unemployment remained barely adequate whether delivered through time-limited North American insurance schemes or low replacement, flat rate payments in Australia, NZ, and the UK (which also has a National Insurance benefit).

The 1990s was a turning point for liberal welfare states. A neoconservative current flowed through Anglo-American policy debates. Decades of conservative attack on small but important social programmes broke through politically, informing policy not only in America but increasingly elsewhere across the liberal world. Before this success, the US had not been a source of social policy inspiration, even for the liberal countries. The country had a poor record on employment and poverty through the 1960s when other affluent democracies were near full employment and narrowing inequalities. Well-known political blocks on comprehensive reform had limited the progress of policy seen elsewhere (see Weir 1992, for example). Democratic administrations have only garnered sufficient political capital to act in periods of crisis such as the 1930s and 1960s. Obama's limited programme illustrates that declining political capital despite his charisma and popularity as leader. The programme was restricted to GFC-era improvements to food stamps and temporary unemployment insurance measures. Longer-term improvements to healthcare fell well short of universal public insurance.

Strong employment growth towards the end of the 1990s, a technological revolution, and apparently bold efforts in finally dealing with 'dead-ends' of US social policy held greater sway. The 1990s welfare reform agenda had lasting paradigmatic impact on social policy across the liberal world. Australia, the UK, and the US are our focus here because they have pursued neoconservative welfare reforms furthest. By extension, they provide the most striking illustration of the impact of welfare reforms in 'engineering dependence' on low-wage labour markets. This dependence has had a critical background influence on labour market developments that have led to bolder minimum wage claims.

The 1990s agenda has its origins in reactions to the social unrest of the 1960s, even though one of its principal targets was a Roosevelt-era programme, Aid to Families with Dependent Children (AFDC), which supported single parents. Public discussion of welfare in the 1960s focused on African American families and their poverty and unemployment. This focus has been continuous in welfare policy debates for decades, from the Moynihan Report of 1964 (Geary 2015) through to Charles Murray's provocative *Losing Ground*, published in 1980. These debates also shaped the more cautiously argued but ultimately more influential book, *The New Paternalism*, which Lawrence Mead published in 1997. The content of these debates was not confined to the seminar room. They had political currency as well. An often racially charged politics of welfare has proved a powerful wedge issue for Republicans marching to the right and looking to win over disaffected and angry voters to their widening electoral coalition.

Welfare became a political headache for all but the most hard-headed Democrats. President Clinton, whose pragmatism had helped him survive the conservative sweep of Congress in 1994, ceded major ground. The defining moment was his signing of Republican legislation, the Personal Responsibility and Work Reconciliation Act in 1997. This legislation ended the AFDC, time-limited public assistance to dependent families, and devolved the replacement programme, Temporary Assistance to Needy Families (TANF), to state governments (Weaver 2000). TANF has since become a 'zombie' policy in some states, unresponsive to the needs of struggling families (Weissmann 2016). In the 1990s, some states like Wisconsin emerged as temporarily emblematic of a national reform effort to end welfare dependence through limited benefits and 'tough love' for non-working Americans.

Optimism was high. Early successes of welfare reform in America gave centre-right and centre-left politicians elsewhere an opportunity to make major reforms to benefit systems. But reforms came as a 'package' of sorts: deregulated labour markets and loose monetary policy would provide jobs to sustain aggressive reforms designed to engineer departures from welfare reliance. This three-part prescription imploded a few years later and America's labour market has never recovered.

Welfare reform's political success in part depended on its rhetorical energy – and powerful backers for that rhetoric. But it held broad appeal to disparate interests building its chances of success. Centrally, it appealed to low-wage employers looking to take advantage of an unexpected services economy boom in the late 1990s. It appealed to policymakers looking to limit the growth of welfare budgets. It appealed to neoconservatives hostile to the social remit of advancing welfare and the swing electorates it could conscript. And it appealed to centre-left politicians looking to survive the anti-welfarist mood of the 1990s by promoting a new path to full employment involving the free markets and popular, tougher social policy – not big government.

The ultimate success of these reforms hinges on two things. The first is widespread electoral appeal of claims that forceful social policy compelling job search could end welfare dependence.[2] The second is clear evidence of declining US 'welfare rolls' after reforms began. Interviewing Lawrence Mead for *The Guardian* a decade later, in 2010, Ramesh noted: 'There's little doubt that Mead's thinking is becoming increasingly influential in the UK.' Welfare reform had begun with New Labour's signature hybrid policy combinations. Labour had also spent significantly more to promote fair employment (such as tax credits for working families) but sought tougher penalties for noncompliance with benefit conditions (Deeming 2015). When the Conservatives finally returned to power in 2010, they used the frame of budget repair to tighten austerity. The new Coalition was hostile to tax credits for workers, making major cuts to the benefit system after 2010 (MacLeavy 2011). Those efforts eventually combined welfare payments into a flawed, tightly policed, and widely loathed universal credit scheme (Beatty and Fothergill 2018).

In Australia, Mead's paradigm became the central force for the conservative Howard government's 'mutual obligation' reforms (Abbott 2000). Since then, Australian governments have actively expanded their own tools for pushing social policy in a neoconservative workfare direction. Two decades later, income support programmes have become highly conditional, subject to close and haphazard digital scrutiny for overpayment. Like the US, access to cash payments is increasingly limited by expanding cashless welfare policies. Highly disadvantaged jobseekers are further distracted with onerous job search requirements and a poorly designed system of obligations and penalties. The unemployment benefit, JobSeeker, is not time limited, but its replacement rate is very low by comparative standards (Henriques-Gomes 2020; Morris and Wilson 2014; Wilson 2020).

Consequences of workfare

Media discussion and public commentary about welfare dependence has declined over the past few decades. A recovery in employment in the 2010s, falling welfare rolls, and widespread support for tougher benefits policies are credited with creating effective solutions to a policy problem. But does this mean that workfare policies have succeeded – at least on the terms that advocates set out for measuring reform? Let's consider three goals promoted by the reform agenda: greater work participation, reduced benefit dependence, and a long-term reduction in poverty.

Workfare policies are supposed to increase employment in several possible ways, direct and indirect. By creating deterrents to long-term benefit dependence, they promote finding work and keeping it. Or they may encourage dropping out of the labour force entirely. Supporters of workfare argue that where these policies are assisted by ultra-liberal labour markets, then both employers and unemployed workers have incentives to create and keep employment. Looking at the big picture, the two workfare decades from 2000 to 2020 coincided with marked improvements in overall employment rates in Australia and the UK (see Table 4.1). However, in the US, where the benefit regime has become either restrictive or nonexistent, employment rates have trended *down* since the late 1990s. In Canada, NZ, and Ireland, where workfare reforms have been less dramatic, employment rates have risen as well. Admittedly, these three other English-speaking countries share at least one common feature with the toughest regimes: low replacement rate unemployment benefits that reinforce reliance on low-wage work. Still, on these broad comparisons, it is difficult to identify clear and unambiguous improvements for countries with the toughest benefits systems. If workfare has encouraged employment, these effects are not clear-cut trends in the aggregate employment data.

Looking more closely at welfare cohorts, US studies causally attribute higher employment to workfare (Moffitt and Garlow 2018). Reviewing the evidence, Moffitt and Garlow (2018, p 19) suggest that the impact of initial US welfare reforms on reduced welfare dependency may have even been *underestimated*. They are, however, cautious: strong counterfactuals have influenced trends in work participation. In the US context, Moffitt and Garlow (2018, p 18) point to ongoing uncertainty about whether welfare reform made the difference or whether it was the 'pro-job' Earned Income Tax Credit that 'incentivises' low-paid work. Equally, secular improvements in employment growth might be credited. All three influences may have made significant independent contributions. My interpretation of these findings is this: a combination of expansionary policies and work subsidies may well have achieved similar improvements without the hardships imposed by tough policy. In any case, very poor US employment performance since 2000 makes it difficult to accept that workfare regimes outperform other employment and social protection systems, with limited benefits mostly detected at the micro-level or for specific cohorts.

Elsewhere, the evidence supporting the employment benefits of workfare is not at all convincing. Analysis of the UK's Tory-led welfare reform between 2010 and 2016 is clear about one thing: reforms reduced the incomes of the poorest communities (Beatty and Fothergill 2017, p 175). UK researchers Beatty and Fothergill (2018, p 950) state that 'evidence from a pilot study in Scotland suggests that the reforms have had little impact on levels of worklessness', concluding that 'there is little evidence that the welfare reforms have delivered lower numbers on benefit and higher numbers in employment'. And in Australia, analysis and data indicate that workfare has little or no benefit. One early study even suggested that Australia's work for the dole scheme harmed employment outcomes, stigmatising beneficiaries (Borland

and Tseng 2004) and distracting participants from job search (Borland and Tseng 2011). Later on, the federal government's own departmental data supplied to a Senate inquiry into Newstart in 2013 provided a grim assessment of the employment outcomes of jobseekers (Morris et al 2015, pp 51–2).

Evidence about the aggregate employment impact of workfare is very limited. However, there is evidence to support the second goal of workfare: reductions in welfare dependency. What is less clear is workfare's role in causal explanation. Moffitt and Garlow (2018, p 18) note that the number of beneficiaries in the US following major reforms dropped 'by 40 percent over the next three years, coincident with the transition from AFDC to TANF. By 2000, half as many people were receiving welfare.' They further observe that 'even the Great Recession in 2007–2009 caused only a small increase in caseloads. By 2013, about 4.1 million people collected welfare, about the same number as in 1964' (Moffitt and Garlow 2018, p 18). Given that some workers are ineligible for unemployment insurance, which is in any case time-limited assistance, the combined evidence suggests that the US welfare system has not resolved hardship related to joblessness. Rather, it has become unresponsive to the problem.

Australia also saw declines in welfare dependency between 2001 and 2016 (Wilkins and Lass 2018, p 40). The largest decline in welfare reliance occurred among single parents with young children (Wilkins and Lass 2018, p 41). Benefits for single parents have been gradually reformed, lowering benefits when dependent children are older and adding work tests. Again, what is less clear is the contribution made by welfare reform to reduce dependence levels and that made by employment growth. Similar uncertainty pervades interpretations of the UK experience. Evidence from Scotland suggests that falling Jobseeker's Allowance (JSA) claims *appear* to be associated with improved local employment. But Beatty and Fothergill (2018, p 963) note that: 'the biggest percentage point reduction in JSA unemployment during the recent upturn, which were also the places hit hardest by welfare reform, are the same places that experienced the biggest reduction in claimant unemployment during previous upturns'. On this basis, Beatty and Fothergill (2018, p 963) conclude that 'reductions in JSA unemployment cannot be attributed to welfare reform'.

Published data on welfare dependency is clear from all three countries: it fell considerably before the severe employment impact of COVID-19 in 2020. What is sketchier is evidence that workfare reforms *themselves* contributed to greater employment participation. That impact may be strongest for traditionally welfare-reliant cohorts, such as single parents with young children. However, general growth in low-wage employment remains the key counterfactual in explaining falling dependency. In the US, falling dependency coincided with worse, not better, overall employment outcomes. This anomalous result points to the pernicious impacts of workfare: it has a powerful deterrence impact that leaves too many potential claimants without support. This confounding outcome may be the outcome of overlapping responses to limit eligibility and impose Poor Law-like regulation of welfare. Potential claimants might instead stay in bad jobs, rely on welfare fleetingly to manage transitions, live off credit and/or savings, or withdraw from the workforce and social security system altogether. These deterrent effects are an important problem for social scientists to study in the 2020s.

The final claim is that, by promoting work first, workfare outperforms liberal alternatives as an anti-poverty policy. For tough benefit systems to make inroads on poverty, they rely on the availability of secure living wage jobs for ex-claimants. Certainly, examples of individual successes can be highlighted. But welfare-to-work transitions depend on supportive policies that create opportunities for often highly disadvantaged jobseekers. Failure to achieve these interlocking improvements in practice illustrates why US 'caseload' reductions have not reduced poverty rates, which remain high. Declines in aged poverty were the main reasons for US improvements before COVID-19. By contrast, there are few signs that poverty in the 18–64 years (working-age) cohort fell in the era of welfare reform (Semega et al 2019, p 16, Figure 11). Similar failures to reduce poverty rates have occurred in Australia and the UK. In the latter, poverty rates fell during the Labour government. But they rose again during the GFC and under the Conservative-led governments since (OECD 2020b). Poverty in Australia declined slightly under the Rudd and Gillard Labor governments (due to pension benefit reform), but the trend since 2000 shows no overall improvement. This stasis comes after two decades of employment growth and falling welfare reliance (Davidson et al 2018, p 32).

A pattern of falling dependency and persistent poverty points to the reality of post-welfare transitions and, speculatively, the impact of benefit toughness on deterrence. Moffitt and Garlow (2018) confirm difficult transitions out of welfare in the US. They write:

> Many women took low-wage jobs, and the increase in their earnings was often cancelled out by their loss of welfare benefits, leaving their overall income relatively unchanged.

And welfare reform seems to have made matters worse for a significant number of single mothers ... About 40 percent of former welfare recipients are not working, and Rebecca Blank estimated that 20–25 percent of all low-income single mothers were neither working nor on welfare in 2007. (Moffitt and Garlow 2018, p 19)

These findings are supported by other researchers. Mallon and Stevens (2011, p 113) noted that:

less well publicized is the economic fate of these 'welfare leavers.' Extensive evidence shows that, despite the fact that as many as 60% exit with a full-time job, within a year or two approximately one half of all welfare leavers – and their children – fall into poverty.

Writing in *The Atlantic* in 2016, Semuels observes:

A study of Maryland welfare recipients exiting TANF, for example, found that just 22 percent found stable employment five years after leaving welfare, and for many more the only work available was either temporary or paid poverty wages. There is little hope of moving up.

Finally, Shaefer and Edin's analysis of the Current Population Survey suggests that the welfare reform era coincided in dramatic rises in severe poverty. The authors measure this as access to $2 per day or less in cash. They state:

the count of annual extreme poverty among children in single-mother families peaked in 2011 at nearly 895,000, and in the last year in our series it stood at 704,000 (3.5%) in 2012. These figures reflect a 748 percent increase in the number of children (660% increase in the percentage) of single-mother families experiencing annual $2-a-day poverty between 1995 and 2012. (Shaefer and Edin 2018, p 24)

A parallel problem of extreme exclusion has been flagged for some American men. Blanchflower (2019, p 26) also notes:

There is a major concern about what prime-age men in the United States in particular who are neither employed nor unemployed are actually doing with their time ... It appears that these men have simply given up because there are no decent jobs available. It is by no means obvious what they are doing.

What roles are being played by institutional gaps in social policy, severe localised unemployment, discrimination, or welfare deterrence caused by overly punitive benefit systems require urgent further study.

Tough workfare policies have contributed to reductions in welfare reliance, especially for some well-studied cohorts such as single parents in the US. Assessing the scale of this impact and the actual mechanisms involved is more difficult. The real impact may not be successful transitions in quality employment, but rather engineered dependence on unstable low-paying work or the consequences of dropping out of work and welfare altogether. When aggregate data on employment and poverty is considered, there is little sign that reduced welfare dependency has improved overall poverty levels. It is also unclear whether much of the improved employment performance after 2000 – where it actually happened – could be attributed to workfare. Two conclusions can be drawn. First, the neoliberal and neoconservative alliance that produced workfare has created much greater reliance on low-paid work for welfare claimants and other vulnerable working-age groups. Second, this reliance is contributing to greater and more successful claims for justice – not through social security but through the struggle for living wages in low-wage workplaces. In the post-COVID-19 world, living wage claims must necessarily expand to encompass the availability of decent jobs through sustained pro-worker government intervention in the labour market.

Normalising underpaying workers

This chapter has addressed the particular impact of housing costs and workfare reforms on the living standards of low-wage workers. There are clear signs that the liberal world has performed badly on both fronts. Severe housing costs problems emerge in NZ, the UK, and the US. And Australia, the UK, and the US have all imposed harsh rationalisations of benefit systems available to unemployed workers that have engineered dependence on low-wage labour markets. Both trends, in their own ways, add pressure to living wage claims: cities are too expensive to live in and social security systems have become unresponsive to the needs of poorer working populations. A further set of problems growing in labour markets needs brief discussion. These relate to a combination of, first, technology-dependent reorganisation of work in the gig economy and, second, the pervasive underpayment of workers.

Liberal countries pride themselves on pro-employer labour markets. Rhetorically, these markets are sold as a win–win. Workers get easy access to jobs that best the social welfare system in providing opportunities and escaping from poverty. Entrepreneurs can experiment with innovation at low cost delivered by a flexible labour force. Evidence confirms some benefit of gig employment markets: they appear to prevent even greater falls in worker pay (Adams-Prassi 2020). But both features have unquestionable downsides: they provide near-perfect conditions for the fragmentation of jobs produced by the gig reorganisation of employment and the deepening exploitation of workers.

In theory, labour market deregulation creates incentives for employers to innovate through a greater capacity for flexible reorganisation of workforces. In practice, weak rules mean employers can use 'innovation' to push the costs of adjustment onto workers who, at worst, are treated as expendable. The results are indeed a growing stream of profits. But these profits are built on a community of insecure workers and indebted households, combined with surprisingly anaemic economy-wide productivity gains or real innovation. Australia's low-wage regime, for instance, is built on a high level of casual employment – insecure employment paid by the hour with no guarantees of work. The UK has institutionalised zero-hours contracts that entrench insecurity. But insecure work is not solely a feature of the liberal regime. As scholars of European welfare states recognise, 'dualised' labour market conditions mean that reliance on temporary jobs for 'outsiders' is a much wider problem for the rich world. However, at least in those instances, the architecture of wage-earner protections is available for extension and renovation and does not need to be built from scratch.

The fragmentation of employment generated by the gig economy presents normative as well as organisational challenges. The utopian version is one of skilled workers choosing between interesting jobs, blending employment with their own entrepreneurship, and managing carefree lives that combine periods of intense work, rest, and travel. For those who have won the opportunity-hoarding race, such a utopia of networks and short-term highly paid gigs might be within reach. But, for most, gig work maximises benefit to employers who exploit labour laws to define temporary workers as contractors – to be paid strictly for hours worked. Insurance and job-related expenses, such as often expensive equipment, are covered by workers.

The number of workers now involved in the gig economy explains the rapid growth in scholarly attention to this area (Kaine and Josserand 2019). One UK report indicated that around 10% of the UK workforce has had 'gig' work experience (Partington 2019). The entry point to gig employment frequently involves efforts by workers to supplement poor earnings from their main jobs or to meet high living costs. Gig online 'platform' work activities vary greatly. The most exploitative situations emerge in low-wage industries that employ delivery drivers, ride-sharing services, accommodation 'hosts', and 'crowd-sellers'. In capturing some of its unifying features, Stewart and Stanford (2017, p 421) state:

> Gig workers typically face irregular work schedules, driven by fluctuations in demand for their services. In most positions, the worker provides some or all of the capital equipment used directly in their work – from a bicycle for food delivery, to more complex and expensive transportation or computing equipment in other jobs. Many gig workers also provide their own place of work: at home, in their car or elsewhere. Most jobs are compensated on a piecework basis, with payment defined according to specific tasks rather than per unit of time worked. Finally, gig jobs are usually understood to be organised around some form of digital mediation, like a web-based platform.

At worst, cutting-edge 'innovation' is actually gloss for organisational control over workers, strategies reliant on legal advantage-taking and technology. Stewart and Stanford (2017) consider five different strategies to address the damaging effects on workers. These focus on expanding legal definitions of 'work' and 'workers' as well as redefining the status of the employer. Given the threats to living standards, as well as to safety and wellbeing, activism in the gig economy has centred on poverty wages, unsafe work situations, severe stress, and migrant vulnerability.

Under pressure, lawmakers have begun to act. One focus has been sub-minimum wage employment. Stewart and Stanford (2017, p 424) note that

> two Uber drivers were indeed found to be 'workers' [by a UK Employment Tribunal in October 2016] and hence entitled to minimum wages, holiday pay and other benefits ... The tribunal delivered a scathing assessment

of Uber's use of 'fictions' and 'twisted language' in characterising its operations.

California legislated in 2019 to ensure ride-sharing and other gig workers are legally defined as employees and entitled to minimum wage protections of the state (Conger and Scheiber 2019). These reforms have been the subject of a successful state-wide ballot in November 2020, effectively overturning the laws, and then further legal challenges to the ballot in 2021. Elsewhere in 2019, New Jersey, which has improved its minimum wage laws, fined Uber Corporation $649 million for 'unpaid employment taxes' associated with efforts to define workers as 'independent contactors' (Haag and McGeehan 2019). These examples are a reminder that techno-pessimism is not justified: activism can push legal and policy institutions to deal with the exploitation of workers.

One further problem is deliberate employer evasion of the correct pay entitlements and other employment standards – a potential problem for higher wage floors, especially with high joblessness and desperate workers. The situation in Australia, where minimum wages are comparatively high, involves now weekly scandals mostly in low-wage industries like the restaurant trade but also in public sector organisations including Australian universities. This problem is far from confined to ultra-competitive industries like food services where profit margins are often low. Large oligopolistic employers, such as supermarket chains, have been subject to union and media scrutiny for systematic underpayment (Powell and Patty 2020).

Severe cases of underpayment of wages have involved Australia's large temporary migrant workforce. These workers face multiple disadvantages where visa conditions are attached to exploitative situations or fear of deportation (Wilson 2018). Similar problems have emerged for migrant workers elsewhere where visa rules contribute to the problem. As a Canadian lawyer wrote in the *Globe and Mail* of her country's rules: 'Canada's system largely excludes working-class individuals and families from permanent immigration. Workers are needed to fill jobs in Canada at all levels of the economy, but working-class migrants must come to Canada with precarious temporary status, without their families' (Faraday 2019).

The wages evasion problem in high minimum wage countries like Australia provides grounds for some to doubt the ability of the living wage movement to outwit employers. These problems are addressed in Chapter 5. My argument is that these are formidable obstacles in achieving wage justice but they are not insurmountable. They are one of the major challenges for unions and policymakers attempting to humanise a 21st-century liberal model.

Past and present: 21st-century living wages

This chapter has focused on three serious problems for the living standards of minimum and low-wage workers. Housing costs at the lower end of the income distribution in several liberal countries are among the most elevated in the OECD. Moreover, typically cautious working-class households are relying on debt to manage disrupted working lives. Workfare has added to these deficiencies by undermining social protections for workers in at least three states. Moreover, low replacement rate benefits across the liberal countries reinforce a reliance on low-paid work.[3] The next wave of workforce reorganisation is having an impact. Gig employment adds to temporary and insecure workforces and this employment may accelerate if business dominates the COVID-19 recovery. Reliance on overextended, poorly regulated labour markets for low-wage workers creates the structural basis for conflict over minimum wages and, more broadly, the welfare compact for wage-earners. The rest of this book explores how the policy consensus in favour of low minimum wages has been disrupted by new evidence and living wage campaigners alike. But before addressing these themes, it is useful to recall the claims and context for living wages that predated modern welfare states and the era of big industry, unions, and collective bargaining after World War Two.

The last part of this chapter considers that history, highlighting four themes. The first is that, a century ago, progressive liberals had realised that deficiencies in utilitarian market liberalism meant that it had no solution to poverty wages. Minimum, and even living, wages would emerge as necessary compromises if an unequal and even cruel division of paid labour was ever to be humanised. Second, advocacy started to rely on emerging *sociological* inquiry into the actual living conditions of poor workers. Third, cross-country differences in institution-building reflected divergent political opportunities, ideological casts, and gender politics. Finally, union weakness in low-wage sectors of the early 20th-century economy drove the need for state intervention. Chapter 3 focuses on the post-1970s low minimum wage 'policy monopoly' and how it has come under significant intellectual and social challenge. And, in key respects, history has repeated itself. Doubts about the social misery caused by unconstrained 19th-century 'liberalism' and its ideological support extended beyond trade unionism and socialist causes. Similar doubts are now apparent with respect to contemporary neoliberalism and the policy architecture it has committed national states to.

New liberals and progressives on both sides of the Atlantic, but also in the emergent postcolonial Antipodes, realised that liberal doctrine needed major modification. The scale of hardship opened up a massive problem for social institutions. But part of the motivation of the liberal class was pre-emptive, to resist growing intellectual commitments to socialist and public ownership. The challenge recognised that some forms of intervention were needed for markets to deliver '*positive* freedoms' in the forms of basic fairness and justice (Fawcett 2014, pp 186–97; Waltman 2008, p 41). Other shifts in thinking were important, given associational alliance common for the times. Progressive currents, especially in North America, could be traced to the 'social gospel' (Waltman 2008, p 51; see also McCallum 1986, p 39 on Canada) as well as Catholic social teaching that influenced Australia's change-making judge, Henry B. Higgins (Rickard 1984, p 173).

Pressures for minimum wages were not purely moral responses. Writing of the progressive era economists, Prasch (1999, p 224) notes that enlightened US economists had 'reasoned that improved "rules" would bring out the full potential of the marketplace by ensuring that competition did not take socially destructive channels – such as a perverse "race to the bottom" featuring demoralized workers, indolent managers, outmoded technology, and a vice-ridden society'. Waltman (2008, p 52) makes a similar point: 'When it came to justifying the minimum wage, Progressives turned to the same arguments as their British counterparts: ending extreme poverty, driving out parasitic industries, efficiency, and the like.'

Minimum wage movements could rely on a new form of intellectual support that went beyond principles and moral reasoning. Reformists and activists both encouraged and were responsive to empirical *sociological* enquiry into the living conditions of poor workers and their households. Waltman (2008, p 43) noted these influences, including:

> Charles Booth's investigations of London and Seebohm Rowntree's studies of York. Rowntree, for example, found that 15% of the working class population lived in dire poverty. In over half these cases, this was directly attributable to low wages. Another 22% of the working class, he demonstrated, earned wages totally inadequate for a larger family.

Statistical reports on living costs also assisted Canadian reformers in the same time period (McCallum 1986, pp 32–3). Henry B. Higgins, Australian reformist judge and central actor in the Australian wage-earner model, also promoted a sociological over a narrower economic perspective on wages. Higgins went about investigating the empirical living conditions of workers (Lake 2019, p 126). Forgotten to history, the Piddington Royal Commission of 1920 in Australia was similarly dependent on empirical studies in its investigation of wages and living costs.

Major differences did emerge, however, over the minimum wage reform paths taken by liberal countries. Antipodean progressivism benefited from the power resources of a nascent trade union and labour movement, with liberal reformers and pro-labour politicians agreeing to build institutions that were delayed, resisted, or more limited elsewhere (Castles 1985). NZ minimum wages were the world's first. However, the Australian living or 'basic' wage for male breadwinners, which became associated with Higgins' Harvester Judgment of 1907, was the most significant reform. Influences on Higgins' determination of the Harvester wage were evidently wide. These included the papal encyclical, *Rerum Novarum*, of 1891; Higgins' reference to providing for 'the wage-earner in reasonable and frugal comfort' was first made in this foundational Catholic statement (Rickard 1984, p 173). Higgins (1915, p 25) also recognised structural inequalities as grounds for intervention: 'The strategic position of the employer in a contest as to wages is much stronger than that of the individual employee.' The judge's explanation is the same as that provided by Marxist sociologist Erik Olin Wright in explaining exploitation to students in his *Class Counts* (2000). Citing a judgment, Higgins (1915, p 25) notes: 'The power of the employer to withhold bread is a much more effective weapon than the power of the employee to refuse to labour.'

This multidimensional framework for living wages had far-reaching influence, as a recent history about the reach of Australian ideas in America by Lake (2019) points out. She notes that:

> Higgins's historic definition of that wage as sufficient to meet the needs of workers, defined as human beings, living in a civilized society, would prove influential not only across Australia, as M.B. Hammond told American readers, but also, as historian Lawrence Glickman has noted, in the United States. (Lake 2019, pp 126–7)

However, the focus of Canadian, US, and UK minimum wage reforms was the development of *minimum* wage in a narrower sense. Outside the Antipodes, reform encountered greater resistance. US minimum wages were hampered by major court challenges in the 1910s and 1920s and legislative resistance continued all the way through to Roosevelt's efforts to pass national minimum wage legislation as part of his New Deal (Waltman 2008, pp 49–61). And the UK made only limited progress towards a national minimum at the time via the Trade Boards Act of 1909. These limits were the product of severe political compromises and, eventually, shifting priorities on the part of reformists. The boards covered just four industries, with efforts to expand them failing. As Waltman (2008, p 65) notes: 'the original four had barely had time to begin operating before they were eclipsed by the war. As for the second batch of five, none of them had even issued a wage order when war came.' Institutional gaps were never fully corrected, later compounded by the postwar emphasis on collective bargaining. Wages boards were eventually abolished by the Conservative government in 1993, making way for a durable institution in the National Minimum Wage later that decade.

Differences in approach pursued in the Antipodes[4] and other liberal countries had implications for the development of gendered wage institutions. The focus was not on male breadwinners but poor women in sweating industries. Concern was focused on 'sweating industries' employing women as secondary earners in industries and jobs not paying 'living wages' (Seager 1913, pp 3–4; see also Waltman 2008). In Great Britain, a narrow 1907 legislative focus on wages boards resulted, covering the four sweating industries employing women. This focus resulted from resistance from Board of Trade officials and tactics by the Anti-Sweating League aiming to guarantee parliamentary support for legislative reform (Waltman 2008, pp 48–9).

The preoccupation on minimum wages for women was multifaceted, some of which related to the spread of policy responses across national boundaries. Other factors also mattered. In the US, constitutional obstacles for an encompassing minimum wage – a problem resolved in the New Deal era – had an impact. McCallum (1986, p 30) notes: 'individual [US] states specifically restricted their minimum wage laws to women and minors in order to circumvent the protection of freedom of contract in the Fourteenth Amendment of the federal constitution'.

Canada followed American states in erecting minimum wages boards across the provinces but these applied, with some exceptions, to women's work (Derry and Douglas 1922, pp 185–6; McCallum 1986). Derry and Douglas (1922, p 186) pointed out at the time: 'Canada shows a reluctance to follow England and Australia in extending the protection of the minimum wage to men, and rather copies the

American commonwealths in restricting its application to women and to female minors.' McCallum's (1986) history explains why the development of provincial minimum wages boards focused on women. These reasons included the role of women's advocacy organisations (p 33), union support for equal pay rates to protect male breadwinners (p 37), and a business preference for minimum wages boards over more far-reaching legislation (p 39).

One further remark on history. State intervention became 'inevitable' in low-wage work because of glaring exploitation and limited union capacity to organise these industries. At the same time, unions occasionally had varying, sometimes ambivalent, commitments to statutory minimum wages. In Australia and NZ, the system of award wages brought under a court-like form of arbitration won support from unions because strike-related claims could be settled through this process. Australia's 'living wage' was one that unions would own and defend, and even enhance over decades of semi-institutionalised struggle.

However, union resistance to minimum wage laws elsewhere was noteworthy. Waltman (2008, p 53) notes: 'The major craft unions had formed the American Federation of Labor, and its president, Samuel Gompers, was a lifelong opponent of minimum wage laws, fearing they would undermine collective bargaining. However, he could not control state branches, and sometimes they were somewhat more sympathetic to the cause' (see also Derry and Douglas 1922, p 155). Canadian unions, by contrast, were sympathetic to minimum wage laws (Derry and Douglas 1922, p 155) for reasons that included the elimination of competition for jobs from low-paid women (McCallum 1986, p 37). Additionally, unions had reasons to support legal intervention in low-wage industries where workers were more difficult to organise (Waltman 2008, p 44).

Old problems in new forms

In the postwar era, the strength of organised labour reached its peak. Unions used the capacity to strike to lift their control over capitalist surplus and to change the rules of the industrial game. Collective bargaining, along with progressive taxes on capital, produced not only a more equal distribution of income but combined to lift labour's share of economic surplus.[5] In the UK, Waltman (2008) observes that minimum wages were never central to workers' wages until the late 1990s. And even in the US, Waltman (2008, p 61) notes that 'for nearly three decades the minimum wage was a central feature of federal policy ... it too lost out in time to social insurance and public assistance as major poverty fighting tools'. Modern welfare states developed other means to partially protect vulnerable populations from low-wage work and low incomes with redistributive social programmes acting as 'functional rivals' to living wages.

A renewed focus on higher minimum and living wages – as well as low-wage labour markets – bears similarities to the debates and struggles of over a century ago. The costs of proscriptively severe and overconfident economic liberalism are once more under question, even among quite orthodox economists. Equally, the social sciences are actively analysing the consequences of low wages, highlighting their social and psychological costs, and finding evidence of improvements in wellbeing and social outcomes from higher pay. The weakness of unions is another striking parallel with earlier times. Union weakness is only marginally the consequence of individualism (Peetz 2010). Instead, it is the product of complex changes in work and society – and a particular consequence of state aggression towards unions in at least three of the liberal countries. This weakness once more provides the context for a return of state intervention in low-wage labour markets. Still, as we shall see, labour movements remain major actors in this story.

There are also important differences a century ago and now. The world is much more affluent and technologically advanced. When poverty and inequality are a focus of political pressure, policymakers have a wider toolset to respond with – well beyond the levers of wage rates. At the same time, political and electoral constraints on further tax-and-spend redistribution are also clearer. This problem will apply to the post-COVID-19 social environment in the 2020s if austerity policies return with some degree of electoral support. Changing realities suggest that the predistributive institutions of the economy, including the regulation of low-wage employment, will be central to addressing inequality. Critics of the living wage movement, on the back foot for a decade, will likely find new audiences willing to listen to attacks on minimum wages as a distributive tool. Left and right will variously point out that:

- wages ultimately depend on the state of the labour market;
- single living wage floors have trouble with the needs of different households, which means-testing and taxation rates cope with better;
- monetised gains in the forms of higher wages will not overcome low living standards without investment in public goods;

- living wages are 'blunt' tools in the fight against poverty and do not build workers' power.

My argument is that these objections do not constitute obstacles to the greater use of minimum wage floors to improve living standards in low-wage labour markets, especially when combined with relevant and robust social policies. These problems are taken up in more detail in Chapter 5. Before then, it is necessary to address how a low minimum wage consensus emerged in the first place and how and why this consensus has been challenged since. These are the tasks of Chapters 3 and 4.

3

The crumbling orthodoxy: arguments for low minimum wages

> The rise in the legal minimum-wage rate is a monument to the power of superficial thinking. (Milton Friedman, September 1966)

> On June 16, 2019, we surpassed the record for the longest period of time without an increase to the federal minimum wage. (www.epi.org)

Improved minimum wage floors and living wage campaigns are addressing the problems of low-wage work. These efforts are a reminder of the power of institutional change: minimum wage reforms have been so significant they have produced higher pay growth at the *bottom* end of the US and UK labour markets for the first time in decades. These gains, as I have stressed, are relative: the weakening of collective bargaining means that gains for low-wage workers through state intervention look better because of failures higher up the earnings distribution.

Low wages at the tail of the distribution are, however, our immediate subject. The goal of this chapter is to briefly chronicle the circumstances and forces behind arguments in favour of keeping minimum wages low. Our argument is that a policy monopoly (Meyer 2003) emerged that promoted this socially risky approach – particularly in North America. In turn, sympathetic economists and policymakers anticipated problems, proposing compensatory fiscal measures to staunch inequalities from such an approach. Our argument is that this monopoly has been disrupted over the past decade by two forces: improved evidence and analysis about the impact of higher wages and energetic policy experiments, some in response to worker mobilisation over poverty wages. This chapter deals with the first disruption: a challenge from the economics profession itself to the arguments against minimum wages as a tool of social policy. This area of economic policy-making, however, remains subject to intense disagreement. Higher unemployment in the 2020s will bring new attention to potential employment disincentives from overly ambitious wage floors. Fittingly, the final section is devoted to a consideration of economists' arguments against the use of higher minimum wages as social policy.

Constructing a market for workers

As noted at the beginning of this book, it is no surprise that the liberal countries have been particularly influenced by neoliberal orthodoxies. These core policy and political beliefs reactivated older and bitter ideological resistances to encroaching workers' power and the reach of government. Gradually, however, the neoliberal framework supplied the arguments and tools to establish policy monopolies in central areas of policy. The problems that led to this ascendancy have been rehearsed in the academic literature and public commentary for decades, so only the briefest recount of themes is necessary here:

- Widespread stagflation in the 1970s was followed by high unemployment caused by worldwide recession in the early 1980s. Hardline market reformers finally got the upper hand in policy debates. Reformers took power in the UK, the US, and NZ, with harsh reforms in Canada, Australia, and Ireland either delayed or moderated by domestic political institutions.
- Class conflict intensified across the liberal world. Employers, along with their state allies, used legal and industrial weapons to reduce union organising and collective institutions (Greenhouse 2019; Moody 1997). Union repression was severe in the US and the UK under Reagan and Thatcher respectively. Australia elected anti-union governments for lengthy periods after the mid-1990s. Equally, NZ unions reeled from late 1980s and early 1990s shock therapy. Anti-union activity in Canada was more limited, confined mostly to the actions of various provincial governments.
- Collective bargaining coverage has fallen across the liberal world. Australia's high 60% coverage is boosted by its award wages system, which counts as collective wage determination. Elsewhere in the other five English-speaking countries, collective bargaining is declining (OECD 2020c). Coverage ranges from around 12% in the US to above 30% in Canada and Ireland, noting that the Irish statistics are from 2014. Mishel (2012) illustrates through the experiences of once-unionised Michigan, a state that saw blue-collar collective bargaining coverage fall from 54% in 1983 to 26% in 2011. The broader impact is instructive: 'A more general mechanism through which collective bargaining has affected pay

and compensation practices beyond the workers directly affected is the institution of norms and established practises that become more generalised throughout the economy' (Mishel 2012, p 11). Mishel (2012, p 11) further notes that 'these norms and practices have particularly benefited the 70 percent of workers who are not college educated'.

- By contrast, collective bargaining rates outside the liberal world generally remained higher or more stable. They are high to very high in the Nordic and most Continental European countries, but not a deconstructed Greece (OECD 2020c). Eastern European rates are trending downwards, starting to resemble the English-speaking nations. Japan and South Korea have similarly low collective bargaining coverage (also Cazes et al 2017).

- The minimum wage situation from the early 1980s to the late 1990s added to the problems with collective bargaining. Minimums were either left dormant, abandoned altogether, or recalibrated in the direction of wage deflation. In the US, the federal minimum wage was left to deteriorate in real terms under Presidents Reagan and Bush (Waltman 2008, p 131). Contradicting Roosevelt's famous efforts to promote a living wage, President Reagan said in 1980 that the minimum wage had 'caused more misery and unemployment than anything since the Great Depression' (Waltman 2008, p 131). And, as already discussed, minimum wage institutions were dismantled in NZ and the UK, with Australia diminishing its commitment to centralised wage determination over decades but without abandoning awards.

The neoliberal ascendancy has been deep and multifaceted – and subject to extensive discussion inside and outside the seminar room. The overriding promise of liberalisation and wage deflation has been simple: to re-establish a flexible, dynamic, and buoyant private sector for jobs. Let's turn to how this argument gained ascendancy in the minimum wage policy debate.

Low minimum wage orthodoxies

The low minimum wage orthodoxy is in key respects a product of American thinking and policy-making. Here, the post-1970s views of the minimum wage are situated within a powerful policy monopoly. It has been dominated intellectually by the US economics profession, which, as I noted in the Introduction, broadly opposed higher minimum wages or their use as a predistributive tool. The low minimum orthodoxy began to monopolise policy-making in other liberal countries over the same time period. Perhaps French President Mitterrand's reflationary experiment – criticised at the time – was the final effort at democratic socialist policies of that era. The socialist government presided over large real increases in the minimum wage, the SMIC (Sachs and Wyplosz 1986). This is telling because, as a result of this reform – one against the current – France's Kaitz score has remained high, at around 60% of median wages (OECD 2020a).

The French experiment proved the exception. A US-style orthodoxy gradually became a widely appealed to source of policy advice. Most emblematically, the OECD began to promote this orthodoxy in its *Jobs Study* series in the 1990s (Visser 2016). We need to consider the successful defence mounted by economists, as well as allies in politics and policy, for low minimum wages before considering the factors leading to the disruption to this consensus. This coverage does not aim at a complete history of ideas, but rather to establish the key features of the policy monopoly in question.

The economic crisis of the 1970s and 1980s provided ultra-free-market economists a political opportunity to influence policy-making across the US government. Keynesian policies, only ever partially adopted and often focused on the financing of industry or war, were losing influence in the political economy of ideas. Business was seeking a far more robust intervention of a different kind from government to restore and build profitability.

Although the timing of this challenge is rightly dated to the 1970s, the US economics profession had been fomenting opposition to living wage ideas for decades before. President Roosevelt's eventual success with the Fair Labor Standards Act of 1938 had prompted condemnation from senior representatives of the economics profession. Nobel economist George Stigler's (1946) paper 'The economics of minimum wage legislation' crystallised this opposition and many of his arguments have proved durable critiques of living wages. Other economists, notably Lester (1947, p 142), stunningly attacked the Stigler and marginalist analysis of the impact of minimum wages, describing it as 'unreal' and lacking in a detailed understanding of historical policy and actual wage-setting, which Lester characterised as far more local, idiosyncratic, and sales driven.

Stigler had strongly refuted the Roosevelt reforms, predictably highlighting job losses from retaliating employers as minimum wages were increased. His refutation contained early arguments against the impracticality and inefficiencies of uniform wages as an instrument to curtail poverty. These arguments rehearsed 19th-century refutations about the disincentives, inefficiencies, and self-defeating consequences of principled government intervention (Leonard 2000, pp 123–4). Stigler did not sidestep the claims of indifference to poverty levelled at cold-hearted economists. His preference, however, advanced the case for the 'thinnest' of policy mechanisms – the negative income tax. This framework was to have a lasting influence on policy responses, such as the US's Earned Income Tax Credit (EITC) later on. It also consolidated policy alternatives to predistributive 'interference' with wage levels.

After Stigler's intervention, it was Milton Friedman's influence on minimum wages protections that became a general point of reference. Friedman become a global adviser of sorts to governments, pushing monetarist and severe neoliberal 'doctrines', most notoriously to Chile's military junta (Klein 2007). Friedman is sometimes thought of as a marginal figure on public policy, too fundamentalist in his commitment to free-market dogmas to influence policymakers. However, Friedman was 'immensely influential' (Ip and Whitehouse 2006) in policy domains. Indeed, the outlines of Friedman's and Stigler's critique of the US wages and social policy has had a lasting impact on US policy.

Social scientists Myles and Pierson highlight that influence in their provocatively titled account, 'Friedman's revenge', published in 1997. Friedman was determinedly opposed to minimum wages, which he characterised as a mistaken interference in the welfare-maximising function of free markets. He did, however, rightly identify minimum wage policies as part of the architecture of welfare states. Friedman (1966, p 8) noted that 'the welfare iceberg includes also measures that impose restrictions on private transactions, and do not require direct government expenditures, except for enforcement. The most obvious is minimum wage rate legislation.' The incursion of welfare-minded interference in the labour market crossed an important boundary that the economic orthodoxy continues to defend.

Friedman's criticisms of minimum wage legislation build on Stigler's. The first points to inevitable welfare losses to unemployed workers (and the economy as a whole) when minimum wage floors 'price' workers out of work. The second points to a 'weakening of incentives' (Friedman 1966, p 6) that comes from the consequences of unemployment – that is, paying unemployed people benefits to subsist outside paid work. The third and fourth elements are closely related. Friedman objects to the tax burden posed by the welfare state (maintaining the unemployed) and the growth of welfare-related bureaucracy. The last element is particularly important because it again relates to social equity and opportunity. In an obvious reference to US racial tensions, Friedman (1966, p 8) argues that high minimum wages create unemployment among minorities whose prior skill disadvantages already weaken their risk of joblessness.

President Reagan's 1980s administration provided the vital test for the new labour market orthodoxy. Reagan's dislike of minimum wages was well known. And his administration achieved a decline in the federal minimum wage through the 1980s and 1990s. The Bush administration in the 2000s followed a similar path until it lost control of Congress in 2006. Republicans had an effective 'veto' over improvements in the federal minimum wage in the decade following their 2010 Congressional victory. They then kept control of the Senate until 2021, blocking the necessary double-majority for higher minimums. Reagan-era wage austerity, combined with heavy military spending, was hailed by both neoliberals and neoconservatives as the major force in a sharp improvement in US unemployment. These achievements signalled to the world that a tougher, pro-business, and market-driven economy had ended the stasis that was the 1970s.

The reality on the ground looked very different. Unions were being sidelined by tougher, even ruthless, management tactics, and key parts of US manufacturing went into serious decline, faced with global competition and the nonexistence of a coordinated industry policy in the US outside the military. Critics quickly saw the consequences of Reagan's intransigence: this approach ensured a worsening of structural problems over time. Economists Bluestone and Harrison (1988) acknowledged that Reagan's America was creating jobs, but they were already finding a worsening polarisation marked by increases in low-wage employment, especially in areas that had lost their manufacturing base. Causes of polarisation are made clear: 'this [trend] has to do with such factors as the decline in unionization, the erosion in the real value of the minimum wage, the widespread existence of wage concession bargaining, and the institution of two-tier wage structures in a number of large industries' (Bluestone and Harrison 1988, p 128).

Other economists began to attribute rising wages inequality in the 1980s to deliberate policies of low minimum wages. In a cautious paper, Lee (1999, p 1016) noted that, when it came to the *observed* wages distribution, there was strong evidence that declining minimum wages had contributed to wages inequality: 'cross-state variation in the "effective" minimum wage imply that a great majority of the observed growth in inequality in the lower tail of the distribution is attributable to the erosion of the real value of the federal minimum wage rate during the 1980s'.

Later, critical economists on the left began to highlight the consequences of the tough, deregulated and unequal 'US model' (Mishel and Schmitt 1995). They warned other democratic nations against this approach because of its mounting social and economic costs. But, as is well documented, similar hardline policies were to shape Thatcher's UK in particular. The Conservative government confronted the unions and promoted Friedman-style deregulation that caused high unemployment, devastating regional Britain. At the time, the UK had already moved its focus away from minimum wages but those institutions were in the government's sights. Waltman (2008) recalls the mood at the time, noting that Thatcher's administration considered the wage-setting functions of the remaining wages councils as nothing more than market interference. Two notable legislative attacks occurred via the Wages Act 1986, which 'removed those under 21 from coverage ... [and] ... restricted the councils' actions to setting a single minimum wage' (Waltman 2008, p 74). Later, the Trade Union Reform and Employment Rights Act 1993 ended wages councils altogether. Wages and employment in the most affected industries, contrary to confident claims, then fell (Waltman 2008, p 74). Labour PM Blair made the restoration of the minimum wage a central claim prior to his landslide 1997 election victory.

In Australia and New Zealand, austerity wages policies also had some bearing on liberalising reforms. In the 1980s, Australia's Labor governments used a series of generally progressive Accord agreements with unions to negotiate a reduction in real wages, something later criticised by some unions and the left. The process of moderation was, at least, coordinated and offset by social expenditures, and not comparable to Reagan and Thatcher's approach. By contrast, New Zealand undertook sweeping neoliberal reforms, first under a Labour government influenced by a radical free-market finance minister, and then conservative National governments that followed with employment deregulation. As stated, NZ departed from the award system that had protected basic wages, installing individual contracts and decentralised firm-level bargaining. Not surprisingly, NZ's experiment did not achieve the promised outcomes; it suffered from poor economic growth and widening inequality (Kelsey 1995).

The zenith for policy confidence in radically liberalising labour market policies came with the OECD's publication in 1994 of *The OECD Jobs Study* (OECD 1994; Visser 2016). This report is now over a quarter of a century old. Of course, a radically pro-business agenda was already dominating the power and policy networks of the Anglo-American democracies. Still, OECD support for deregulation to deal with unemployment sent a signal. The study promoted the deregulation of labour markets (and the restructuring of wage-earner entitlements and training) on the basis of US and UK employment performance. Schmitt and Wadsworth recall:

> As part of the effort to sell the flexibility prescription, the OECD has ... held up the United States and, to a lesser degree, its closest European counterpart, the United Kingdom as models of labor-market flexibility. Indeed, through most of the second half of the 1990s, both countries enjoyed low unemployment and high employment rates relative to most of the rest of the OECD. (Schmitt and Wadsworth 2002, p 1)

The OECD Jobs Study encompassed more than minimum wage recommendations. However, recommendations in that domain were severe. It called for member countries to:

> Reassess the role of statutory minimum wages as an instrument to achieve redistributive goals, and switch to more direct instruments. If it is judged desirable to maintain a legal minimum wage as part of an anti-poverty strategy ... [then policymakers should consider] ... indexing it to prices, rather than average earnings [and] ensuring sufficient differentiation in wage rates by age and region to prevent the minimum wage from harming employment prospects for young people or low-productivity regions. (OECD 1994, Policy Recommendation 5)

The study's recommendations followed the Stigler and Friedman doctrine: the minimum wage was not a desirable anti-poverty tool, and that its uniform application imposed the greatest welfare losses on workers in vulnerable labour market positions, that is, young workers or low-skilled workers in economically depressed regions.

Two points encapsulate national responses to the study. First, the greatest 'compliance' with its recommendations came from the liberal countries. An analysis of 21 OECD nations showed that *all six* of the English-speaking states appeared among the eight most *compliant* countries, with the UK, the US, and Australia occupying the top three positions (McBride and Williams 2001, p 291). Switzerland and Denmark also appeared in the list of eight. The researchers note that the 'compliance scores are revealing. The OECD had very little to tell the United States and the United Kingdom. Their policies were close to the "ideal" neoliberal thrust of the Jobs Strategy' (McBride and Williams 2001, p 291).

It is notable, however, that liberalisation was also pursued in the two least compliant states. The 'purple coalition' government of Labour Prime Minister Wim Kok of the Netherlands undertook pro-market labour and social security reforms, and the Hartz IV reforms of Social Democratic Chancellor Gerhard Schröder were similarly disruptive to the industry-focused German model. But many countries resisted reforms or followed different directions – the OECD-endorsed approach was beginning to encounter resistance in liberal countries. Although moderate in scope and ambition, both the NZ and UK Labour governments of the late 1990s began to inch away from the damaging and extreme deregulation settings established in the early 1990s, which had left both countries without effective wage-earner institutions. And, as noted earlier, an emboldened labour movement convinced Australian voters to eject the conservative Coalition in 2007 after it attempted further labour market deregulation. Outside the Anglo-American world, a French leftwing coalition led by Prime Minister Lionel Jospin also ignored OECD directives, managing to slightly reduce unemployment through greater regulation of maximum working hours.

National reluctance, and mounting signs of the costs, likely factored in the OECD retreating from proscriptive neoliberalism. Visser (2016, p 29) notes: 'Ten or fifteen years ago the OECD's advice had no takers ... [and] ... in 2004 the organization admitted that the evidence had probably not been as straightforward and convincing as had been presented in the 1994 study.' Visser (2016, p 29) adds that the OECD 'conceded that the general trends of rising wage inequality and persistence of low pay had made governments wary of instituting reforms that tend to make such trends worse'.

A major redirection, however, was not on the cards in several liberal nations. Stronger employment growth in the UK and the US in the 1990s secured the orthodox consensus, even as UK Labour installed a national minimum wage and extended union bargaining. The US model was supercharged in the 1990s by rising confidence, low interest rates, and a pro-Wall Street administration under President Clinton. As noted in Chapter 2, the combination of more jobs in a deregulated labour market and tough welfare reform to boost work participation and cut spending became attractive policy for rightwing governments in Australia and the UK. Centre-left parties partly humanised, but still accepted, the direction of reform.

Employment triumphs were nowhere as strongly associated with deregulation as the orthodoxy asserted. Schmitt and Wadsworth (2002, pp 25–6) conclude that macroeconomic strength, not extreme forms of 'flexibility' at work, drove success. They note:

> despite the high praise of the OECD for the flexible US and British economies, younger workers and less-educated workers had no better employment or unemployment outcomes in absolute or relative terms in those economies at the end of the 1990s than did similar workers in other far less flexible economies. (Schmitt and Wadsworth 2002, p 24)

Schmitt and Wadsworth (2002, p 24) also remark that, 'in relative terms, the prospects facing these marginal groups were often substantially worse in the United States and especially the United Kingdom'. Far less policy attention was paid to the US model after the 2001 recession. The country began a long period of poor labour market performance with heightened signs of social distress, compounded by the global financial crisis.

Social liberal compromises

Pro-business reforms reshaping labour markets across the liberal world between 1980 and 2000 affected the capacity of labour movements to respond. Support for trade unions among centre-left politicians began to wane. Calls for pro-worker interventions in unequal labour markets were dismissed as misguided challenges to the proven superiority of the market. The new policy consensus carved out territory for centre-left parties to promote as part of their third way transformation. Third way politics reversed Esping-Andersen's (1985) characterisation of social democracy as 'politics *against* markets'. The benefits of markets could overcome the 'old' politics without sacrificing the social democratic goals of higher employment and reduced poverty. The third way movement accepted the consensus about a free market for labour as superior to full employment policies engineered by expanded government. It endorsed the orthodox insistence that social objectives would be better met through non–distorting fiscal tools rather than through deficits, the public sector, and collectivism. Centre-left parties adopted elements of Stigler and Friedman's approach. Social protection would involve fiscal benefits to low-paid working families who would be kept in work by freer employment markets.

In the 1990s and the early 2000s, the liberal countries expanded their fiscal support to low-income working families. These programmes vary but the common emphasis addressed labour market insecurities through social expenditure. Kenworthy (2015, p 24) notes that the largest 'cash transfers' or 'tax credits' are available to workers in Ireland, NZ, the UK, and the US. In the UK, Labour's Chancellor Gordon Brown built a generous but administratively fraught system of tax credits for working families. Similarly, Helen Clark's Labour government in New Zealand pursued tax credits, ones that excluded non-working families from direct assistance (Wilson et al 2013). Australia's efforts under the Hawke Labor government earlier in the 1990s followed a similar logic of compensating low-income families for instability in labour markets. Later, the Gillard Labor government introduced a higher 'tax free threshold' so that low-income workers kept more of their earnings (Wilson et al 2013). Canada's family tax benefits, also introduced in the 1990s, similarly apply to working and non-working families alike (Myles and Pierson 1997, p 448).

The Earned Income Tax Credit (EITC) in the US is the most instructive of these reforms because it has been well studied, achieving bipartisan support for its 'pro-work' and 'pro-family' design. This programme is tiny in terms of GDP (around 0.3%), providing a tax credit to low-income workers. The 'phase in' generosity encourages work and a tapered 'phase out' promotes self-reliance at higher earnings. The programme is designed to be more generous to workers with children. In fact, it is of marginal benefit to poor single workers. The same low coverage of singles also reduces the anti-poverty scope of UK tax credits (Hick and Lanau 2019).

The EITC's growth since its inception in the 1970s is emblematic of Friedman-inspired social policy. The policy was designed to sustain a low-wage employment recovery in a post-industrialising America, satisfying both pro-business and anti-welfare Republicans, who had little reason to oppose it, and ultimately Democrats, who were on the back foot politically and hardly likely to reject Congressional spending on poor families. Myles and Pierson (1997, p 451) make it clear that the EITC was supported by a 'powerful political coalition', because the policy suited times of budgetary austerity, it was consistent with 'increasing labor market flexibility', and involved 'gradually phased-out benefits ... widely considered to be more effective than traditional means-tested programs in sustaining work incentives'.

The EITC survived successive administrations, and has grown to around $70 billion, which is still a very small share of the $20 trillion US economy. The EITC has a modest anti-poverty impact. Around

6 million Americans are lifted above the official poverty line with the programme's assistance and around half of those benefiting are children. The programme also reduced the 'severity of poverty' for an even larger number of Americans (Center on Budget and Policy Priorities 2019). There is no doubt that the EITC is an effective programme with a high level of support among policy scientists and politicians. Given its small budget commitment, the EITC benefits a remarkably large share of the US working population, estimated at one in four Americans (Kenworthy 2015, p 7). Its success as a policy is, however, closely related to the growth in the problem the EITC was designed to alleviate, namely: 'stagnant wage levels for Americans on the lower rungs of the wage ladder' (Kenworthy 2015, p 7).

Apart from its very limited redistributive impact, the EITC has problems relevant to this discussion. Kenworthy's analysis, for example, affirms many of the EITC's successes. He highlights the benefits to poorly educated women with children, a target of welfare reform (Kenworthy 2015, p 11). But he notes that evidence about the EITC (and the UK's tax credits) promoting superior labour market performance is limited. He concludes:

> Overall, the evidence suggests that an employment-conditional earnings subsidy tends to boost employment in US- and UK-type economies, but the labour market institutions of those two countries, including their earnings subsidies, don't appear to yield superior employment performance compared to the institutions of many other rich nations. (Kenworthy 2015, p 16)

However, Kenworthy (2015, p 16) adds that an EITC-style approach may outperform comparable countries in assisting employment for 'low-skilled immigrants'.

The tax credit fiscal approach may indeed yield modest employment and poverty benefits. The policy does, however, subsidise profitable employers who could lift pay for low-wage workers. Political perceptions of this subsidy problem have begun to change. Senator Bernie Sanders (2020) highlights the multi-billion dollar subsidies in tax credits and Medicaid that the US government spends to effectively subsidise the poverty wages paid by highly profitable corporations. Do programmes like the EITC subsidise employers and keep in place a low-wage economy? Kenworthy reviews the UK and US evidence, which suggests that these policies *do* reduce wages. He concludes: 'overall, the evidence suggests that a US- or UK-style employment-conditional earnings subsidy may reduce wages somewhat but we need more research on this question' (2015, p 18; see also Rothstein and Zipperer 2020).

Kenworthy (2015, p 18) agrees that the low wages problem can be effectively addressed by higher wage floors. Economists and researchers who promote higher minimum wages, however, still defend the EITC and similar policies. And they do so for a good reason. A much higher wages floor, once established, would mean that the *same* expenditures on tax credit resources would realise greater redistributive impact (Rothstein and Zipperer 2020). Some US states have pursued higher EITC payments and higher minimum wages. Congressional efforts to extend the EITC, along with its $15 an hour legislation, need to overcome obstacles presented by the US Senate.

Income tax credits boost the post-tax incomes of low-income working families. They were a pro-market response at the height of the orthodoxy's influence over policy. Critics, however, are right to identify their modest impact and the public subsidies they provide to rent-seeking employers. This approach made sense to centre-left labour parties and to the US Democrats looking to preserve pro-worker fiscal institutions, given the prevailing low-wage orthodoxy. Although the 1990s represented peak confidence in these pro-market visions, that decade was a starting point for major intellectual disruption to the low minimum wage consensus. Before long, politics and activism would leap ahead, seeking a transformation of poverty wages.

Disruption in the 1990s

Not all US minimum wage policies followed Reagan's austerity for workers. In the early 1990s, economists David Card and Alan Krueger began publishing their research on the effect of New Jersey's increase to the minimum wage on the incomes, jobs, and hours of fast-food workers. The reform affected parts of the state differently, with the maximum impact of the wage rise being 19% or 0.80¢ per hour. Card and Krueger (1993) compared New Jersey's response with its neighbouring state Pennsylvania, in a 'natural experiment' investigating how minimum wages affected workers in reality. The study then appeared in book-length form in 1995. Entitled *Myth and Measurement: The New Economics of the Minimum Wage*, it disavowed testing 'that or that theory' in favour of a natural experiment in real-world policy effects (Card and Krueger [1995] 2015; see also Leonard 2000, p 132).

Their research started a revolution. Card and Krueger (1993, p 34) challenged the consensus on labour markets: 'Contrary to the central prediction of a text book model of the minimum wage, but consistent with a growing number of studies ... we find no evidence that the rise in New Jersey's minimum wage reduced employment at fast-food restaurants in the state.' The study's significance was greater because orthodox predictions forecast that young workers' jobs would be harmed. Krugman (2019) captures the study's impact:

> before Card and Krueger, most economists just assumed that raising the minimum wage leads to lower employment. ... What Card, Krueger and the research that follows tell us is that labor markets are a lot more complicated than we thought, that market power matters a lot and that there may be much more room for public policy to raise wages in general than Econ 101 would have it.

Card and Krueger's contrarianism far from ended the battle. This area of economics remains territory for fierce contests over models, data, and methods. Card and Krueger ([1995] 2015) made a further provocative contribution, suggesting that the type of analysis of minimum wage effects was 'biasing' the conclusions drawn from the published literature. In effect, they argued that the methods themselves promoted the idea that higher minimum wages reduced employment. Although a later meta-analysis criticised these pioneering authors' methods, it confirmed Card and Krueger's findings, that is, publication biases contributed to the findings that higher minimum wages produced 'negative elasticities' for employment (Doucouliagos and Stanley 2009). In fact, in their corrections for these biases, these researchers found a very small *positive* elasticity, that is, that employment goes *up* with rising minimums.

Doucouliagos and Stanley (2009) offer two explanations for why the policy conclusion from 'Econ 101' (as Krugman calls it) might be faulty. The first is an idea we have already encountered. Monopsony power among leading firms meant that they had an untapped capacity to absorb higher wages. The second is the impact of efficiency wages – Doucouliagos and Stanleys' preferred explanation, given their findings (2009, p 422). This idea of efficiency wages has relevance to the major themes of this book. In fact, the 'efficiencies' of living wages far exceed conventional economic accounts of the stabilising impact of better wages on productivity. In a sociological sense, these efficiencies include a much larger and poorly catalogued social dividend, including lower suicide rates and higher levels of worker wellbeing.

Another battle for Seattle

It is 25 years since *Myth and Measurement* shook the influential but intellectually complacent monopoly on ideas about minimum wages. Has subsequent evidence confirmed Card and Krueger's findings? The answer is mostly yes, but not conclusively so. Prior to COVID-19, the evidence pointing to minimal employment disruption from higher minimum wages was strengthening. Arindrajit Dube's review for the UK government of the international evidence on the impacts of minimum wages concludes:

> Overall, the most up to date body of research from US, UK and other developed countries points to a very muted effect of minimum wages on employment, while significantly increasing the earnings of low paid workers. Importantly, this was found to be the case for the most recent ambitious policies. (Dube 2019a, p 2)

It is striking that one of the liberal market countries – Australia – has maintained high Kaitz index award wages over decades. Moreover, it had done so without significant departure from OECD employment rates. This reality has had zero impact on the policy monopoly that has kept insisting on the welfare losses, inefficiencies, and damage to incentives caused by higher wage floors. Similarly, the fact that much higher Nordic wage floors, especially combined with activist labour market policies, had produced *low* unemployment appears to have had no influence on the central debates over minimum wages.

One intense intellectual battle over minimum wages centred on the Democratic-leaning city of Seattle, which has led the US with its local minimum wage experiment. That minimum reached $16.39 (about €15 or £12.50) for large employers in January 2020 (Lathrop 2019). It is now above the Australian minimum wage (approximately US$14.50). Two groups of economists, one from University of California, Berkeley and the other from the University of Washington, conducted investigations into the impact of these increases. They initially produced findings at dramatic variance. The Berkeley team found no negative employment impact, while the University of Washington found substantial negative impact.

Why? Dube's account of these discordant findings emphasises a few things. Initially, the University of Washington study did not account for the possibility that the observed loss of low-wage jobs could have resulted from 'spillover effects' leading to more, better-paid jobs because 'many people ... [were]... getting raises' (Dube 2019a, p 36). Later, those researchers used a different methodology that focused on what happened to low-wage workers (rather than low-wage jobs). They found a 'negligible impact on headcount employment' (Dube 2019a, p 37).

By contrast, the Berkeley study used 'a synthetic control based on other US areas' to study the Seattle impact and, on that basis, found 'no discernible job loss' (Dube 2019a, p 37). Dube reports on one further study that compared six cities (led by Nadler), which reached similar conclusions. Although Dube (2019a, p 37) stresses caution 'in interpreting the findings causally', the implication from Seattle is that real wages for low-wage workers could be increased without significant job losses. This finding is consistent with the meta-analysis cited earlier.

What about evidence from elsewhere in the liberal world? The UK experience has provided an important national 'experiment' in a higher minimum wage floor, a result of sustained adjustment. The Low Pay Commission (2019) published its findings after 20 years of the National Minimum Wage (NMW). It notes that minimums now cover more workers, especially men and younger workers, redistributing some £60 billion to workers (Low Pay Commission 2019, p 17). The NMW has also led to pay compression, improving absolute and relative pay for the bottom 30% of wage-earners (Low Pay Commission 2019, pp 16–18). In turn, the UK's Kaitz index has risen dramatically. Although the Low Pay Commission (2019, pp 22–3) notes that employers in some industries or cases have reported reduced profits, with others passing on price rises (especially at the beginning), there is little evidence of job losses. The report also notes record levels of employment over the time that minimum wages have increased (Low Pay Commission 2019, p 23), as well as equity gains for women as well as younger and older workers, three cohorts more likely to benefit from higher minimums (Low Pay Commission 2019, p 21). The UK pays workers under 25 as well as apprentices a minimum wage below the National Living Wage. The Commission reports that, for a range of reasons related to higher minimums, greater age coverage, industry change, and work patterns, more young workers now earn minimum wages (2019, pp 9, 19).

Improvements are, however, qualified by adverse developments highlighted by the Commission. It found more employer interest in work intensification and more non-standard jobs as well as cutbacks to 'non-wage labour costs', while, significantly, there was a trend towards 'fewer tiers of pay' in the presence of a higher minimum (Low Pay

Commission 2019, p 24). One implication of this is the greater use of the higher wage floor to cover more jobs.

The Low Pay Commission notes that the largest improvements in the Kaitz index, however, have taken place in New Zealand, where the minimum wage increased to NZ$20 per hour in 2021, with a Kaitz index close to 70% of median hourly wages. Further context is relevant here. NZ per capita earnings are lower than the other five liberal countries. But this bold experiment lifts the purchasing power of minimum earnings (that directly benefit over 10% of NZ workers) closer to the average for the liberal countries. It will also ensure a further stimulus to the NZ economy as it recovers from its successful COVID-19 response in 2020.

What about job losses? Prior to COVID-19, New Zealand had very low unemployment – around 4% in early 2020. Government forecasts of slightly slower jobs growth, attributed to Kaitz index increases, need to be considered in that context. In a detailed report, the NZ Ministry of Business, Innovation and Employment (Hikina Whakatutuki) projected a small negative jobs impact in 2020 (2019, pp 5–6) that has been since complicated by COVID-19. However, better minimum wages combined with tax credits were keeping full-time workers – with and without children – above the poverty line (Ministry of Business, Innovation & Employment 2019, p 27). The report also noted that 2019 wage rises occurred with labour underutilisation at near-historic lows (Ministry of Business, Innovation & Employment 2019, p 6). Large improvements in minimum wages have helped working-class living standards in a country with high housing costs (see Chapter 2), which is still recovering from shock therapy a generation ago.

As the rest of this book establishes, disruptions to the policy consensus have left its defenders on the back foot. Up until COVID-19, wage reforms were proceeding apace. Heterodox evidence and ideas from economists and social scientists were gaining credibility and intellectual energy. Still, defenders of the orthodox consensus have continued to raise objections to the interventionist use of high wage floors as a form of social policy. These objections range from professional caution about overreach and ambiguities in the evidence to fierce ideological rejection of living wages. The rest of this chapter addresses the most compelling objections. Two further objections related to living wage policies – that high wages hasten the technological demise of low-wage jobs and that employers will evade wage obligations to pay higher wages – are taken up in Chapter 5.

Like 'water running uphill'

Libertarian James Buchanan captured the economics discipline's scepticism about increasing minimum wages. He stated: 'Just as no physicist would claim that "water runs uphill," no self-respecting economist would claim that increases in the minimum wage increase employment' (Buchanan 1996, cited in Leonard 2000, p 137). Although careful empirical studies lend support to Buchanan's 'iron law', recent broad-ranging studies by Dube (2019a) and Doucouliagos and Stanley (2009) refute his position. They find no clear negative impact on jobs from raising minimum wages. And as noted, the latter study – which was a meta-analysis – even found weak evidence for a *positive* impact on jobs. Still, there are scenarios where caution about large increases haunt the policy debates and literature. These include: the impact of *larger* minimum wage increases; the impact of higher floors on 'youth' labour markets; and the effect of higher wages on the jobs of those with few formal skills. These questions are addressed over the next two sections.

Internationally, large shifts in minimum wages have not been common experiences, given the prevailing climate of low inflation and pro-business politics. As a result, these are rarely studied. However, highly industrialised South Korea has made a series of bold increases, making it the rising star of the predistributive use of minimum wages as social policy. Centre-left President Moon dramatically increased minimum wages – by 16% and 11% in 2018 and 2019 respectively (Yon 2020). As noted in the Introduction, these decisions have had the largest impact on any OECD Kaitz index since 2000. In 2020, mixed reports have emerged of the consequences. However, business and opposition predictions of mass unemployment did not eventuate over 2019. In fact, the South Korean unemployment rate remained below 4% in the second half of 2019.

The Korea Labor Institute analysis relied on Statistics Korea census data in a 2020 study. It identified very large increases in *hourly* wages for the lowest deciles of workers between 2017 and 2019 – consistent with the planned redistributive effects of reform (Yon 2020). However, the same study found overall take-home earnings for the lowest two deciles of wage-earners actually fell in response. This is because employers shortened work hours to offset labour costs. They managed to accomplish this by exploiting a loophole available under South Korea's Labor Standards Act (Yon 2020). Still, Moon's bold wages experiment does not appear to have added to South Korea's unemployment, which remains very low. And these moves have dramatically reduced wages inequality when it comes to *hourly* earnings. However, offsetting reductions in work hours at the bottom appear to have limited worker gains, leaving more workers on low wages (Yon 2020). A broader policy response is needed. The report called for changes to South Korea's labour law to prevent exploitation of short-hours arrangements (Yon 2020).

Dube (2019a) notes the 'limited' evidence base about larger minimum wage increases in drawing together analysis from the US, the UK, and Hungary. He notes, however, that the employment effects of bigger adjustments are 'not very different from the broader evidence base' (2019a, p 52). The reason that these real-world adjustments differ from orthodox predictions relates to the wider menu of adaptations available to firms. Many of these avoid sacking workers. As Dube (2019a, pp 50–2) notes, rising prices, falling profits, improved productivity, and the monopsony power of firms can all 'absorb' the impact of higher minimum wages. The South Korean case will no doubt add to the evidence across the 2020s.

What about the negative impacts of raising minimum wages on the jobs of young workers? As Chapter 1 reports, concessional wages are frequently in place for teenagers and young adults. These are maintained in part because of policymaker and business insistence on the risks posed by unrealistic wages to the hiring of young workers who are acquiring skills and experience. For instance, those claims have been central to Alberta's Conservative government's response to the former New Democratic Party administration's decision to raise that province's minimum wage to C$15 in 2019. Economists argue that youth hourly wages are justified on two grounds: the lower productivity of employees acquiring skills and experience, and the importance of finding work in preventing long-term unemployment when younger workers most need opportunities (Low Pay Commission 2019, p 19).

David Neumark, a major contributor to the minimum wage debate and careful critic of high minimum wage policies, summarises the evidence for young workers in the following terms. He states: 'Neumark and Wascher (2004) found little clear evidence of youth disemployment effects in countries with restrictive labor standards and generous employment protections, but elasticities in the −0.2 to −0.4 range in countries with the least regulated labor markets' (Neumark 2018a, p 5). However, Neumark further notes that 'a later paper by Sturn (2018) disputes these conclusions and suggests that the findings of negative effects are fragile' (2018a, p 5). Neumark's recent co-authored research on this topic has indeed confirmed a negative impact of minimum wage rises of teenage employment. But Neumark and Shupe's research also makes a particularly novel finding. While asserting that the 'role of minimum wages has been largely ignored in explaining the trend decline in teen employment' (Neumark and Shupe 2019, p 51), they find that the disincentives attached to *higher* minimums may have *positively* affected school retention and therefore the acquisition of human capital (Neumark and Shupe 2019, p 64).

A further point should be made. Even when small job losses can be accurately attributed empirically to higher minimum wages, these losses may not be sufficient to justify policy stasis. Commenting on findings of small employment disincentives of minimum wage changes relating to pre- and post-GFC periods, Neumark (2015) remarks: 'This is a small drop in aggregate employment that should be weighed against increased earnings for still-employed workers because of higher minimum wages.' Maximising employment alone misses the broader benefit of higher wages to low-wage workers. Other employment and social policies are arguably better placed to maintain employment levels.

Injustices of wage ambitions

Spanning back to Stigler, orthodox economists point to the social injustices that arise from job losses or reduced hours produced by living wage campaigns. The first highlights economic losses to less-skilled workers or jobseekers who are 'priced out' of competitive labour markets. The second relates to the social discrimination that higher minimums allegedly worsens. The claims carry significant rhetorical force in the liberal countries where jobs are expected to provide all of a worker's economic welfare. These claims are literally *made* true by the deteriorating safety net in some liberal states. It is correct that, without a generous social safety net, any job loss can become associated with deep poverty. Where low wages are attached to other socially patterned forms of discrimination, job losses from wage ambitions can be seen as harming broader equality. Friedman (1966), for example, emphasised the unintended consequences of ambitious wage agendas at the height of racial conflicts in 1960s America. He sees workers who are already in vulnerable labour market positions because of discrimination as most likely to suffer from job losses. This argument can be – and indeed is – applied to the situation facing *any* disadvantaged group – women, people with disabilities, workers with few formal skills, or migrants who still acquiring language skills and social capital.

Recent US research underlines some of these impacts. Neumark (2018b, p 7) points to recent research suggesting worse outcomes for some 'less-skilled minority men' in states where both EITC allowances and minimum wages are higher. But other multicountry findings can be suggested as interpreting otherwise. Sturn's (2018) analysis covers 19 OECD countries between 1997 and 2013. He concludes that cross-national minimum wage patterns 'provide little evidence of substantial disemployment effects for low-skilled, female low-skilled, or young workers. The estimated employment elasticities are small and statistically indistinguishable from zero' (Sturn 2018, p 647). This finding does not mean there is no patterned discrimination in labour markets. But it does provide cross-country evidence that more generous minimum wages are not a clear cause of job losses for socially disadvantaged workers.

Living wages don't help poverty

Social justice arguments against high minimum wages go further than highlighting the potential losers from ambitious reforms. They raise doubts about who *benefits* from this kind of redistribution. Economists as far back as Stigler (1946) have driven a wedge between legitimate policy ambitions of reducing poverty and the actual consequences of raising minimum wages. Stigler's initial illustration of the problem attends to now-familiar complications. Of course, workers must be *earning*, and not unemployed, to benefit from higher hourly pay. But then, workers might *combine* their more generous minimum pay to generate more-than-adequate family incomes. Conversely, larger families would require even higher wage rates if genuine equality in poverty reduction was the goal (Stigler 1946, pp 362–5). These anomalies lead Stigler to argue for a fiscal, and not a wage, response to aid poor workers. His solution is remarkably similar to a later policy, the EITC.

Similar arguments – along with supportive evidence – are rehearsed today. First, economists emphasise that very poor households have low labour force participation – they miss out on a justice project focused on higher minimums. Second, low-income workers also live in *non-poor* households – typically young workers living with their parents or women who are secondary earners in male breadwinner families. For these reasons, the anti-poverty impact of higher minimums is either poorly understood by advocates or, ultimately, is rather limited. Neumark's (2015, p 1) research recognises that a 'higher minimum wage reduces the inequality of wages earned by workers'. But the author points out that the overall anti-poverty effect of higher minimums is not well studied and he is not convinced that higher wages likely improve on the efficiency of EITC-type arrangements.

Neumark's reasoning is similar to Stigler's: anti-poverty benefits made available through taxes and transfers are determined by actual earnings and can therefore be tailored to need. Still, it should be noted here that recent work by Dube (2019b) has found consistent anti-poverty effects from higher US minimum wages, suggesting that the evidence base is gradually widening.

Finally, technical problems in setting a single living wage level overlap with questions about the capacity of a living wage to produce justice. Sympathetic economists such as A.B. Atkinson (2015) puzzle over how a single 'living wage' rate could be determined if indeed the goal is to eliminate poverty in all its manifestations across diverse households. Indeed, scholars determining effective living wage levels acknowledged these difficulties (Anker 2006; Johnson et al 2019, p 322).

There are several responses to claims that living wages are blunt, ineffective anti-poverty tools. The first response acknowledges the reasoning behind these criticisms. Transfer payments are indeed better suited to addressing poverty in very poor households where joblessness is the obvious problem. Even if job guarantees or extended social Keynesian measures could be put in place to produce more living wage jobs, there is a clear need for fiscal support to poor households that cannot be dealt with by living wages. The second response rejects a juxtaposition of policy responses, recognising that low-wage households need living wage initiatives to be combined with progressively targeted tax and transfer benefits. Given that employers 'capture' some of the benefit of progressive tax credits like the EITC, the presence of higher wage floors improves the progressive impact of benefits. As Rothstein and Zipperer (2020, p 1) put it: 'a sufficiently high minimum wage can prevent this dilution, ensuring that low-wage workers receive the full benefit of the EITC'.

A third response seeks a shift in the minimum wage discussion. The US policy debate tends to see poverty alleviation as the main, and even *only*, distributional question in designing pro-worker social policies. Broader distributional issues are just as important – and always have been. Widening earning inequalities account for a stressed and shrinking middle class. Broader worker frustrations about pay and job security are creating restive publics, successfully targeted by rightwing populists and business interests in politics attempting to weaken any redistributive electoral coalition. High wage floors contribute to a fairer distribution of earnings. Australia and NZ, with higher Kaitz index scores, have kept their share of low-wage full-time wage-earners below the other four countries (see Table 4.2). As we shall see in Chapter 4, NZ has recorded a dramatic decline in low-paid workers to just 8.5% of full-time wage-earners. Other countries with concerted policies to raise minimum wages are reporting progress on this measure, too. The UK's Office for National Statistics (ONS) reports that the share of low-wage workers – defined as earning low *hourly* wages below two-thirds median full-time wages – has fallen from 22% of wage-earners in 1997 to 16% of wage-earners in 2018 (ONS 2019). This result represents the lowest share since the ONS began reporting this data. The *weekly* low-pay trends were not as pronounced, dropping from 28% to 27% (ONS 2019).

More than a cold calculus

The orthodox consensus insists on a rather cold calculus. Higher minimum wages mean fewer jobs, with most welfare losses going to already disadvantaged communities. Moreover, high wage floors are a poor and inefficient form of poverty alleviation. Evidence for the first two claims turns out to be weaker than economists have insisted. Claims about the ineffective impact of minimum wages on poverty tend to be meaningful only when poverty thresholds are low (and exclude most workers) or where broader distributional issues – such as the number of workers just above poverty thresholds – are not considered.

Moreover, a narrow focus on small, even marginal impacts of higher minimums on hours, pay, or job losses constrains the field of vision. It excludes new contributions from social scientists about the benefits of better minimum pay for worker wellbeing, job quality, and productivity. Such insights provide valuable context for policymakers. And they also identify the policy terrain of the sociology of low-wage labour markets in the coming decade. Sociologist Matthew Desmond's (2019) essay in *The New York Times* makes this point. He remarks:

> For years, when American policymakers have debated the minimum wage, they have debated its effect on the labor market. Economists have gone around and around, rehashing the same questions about how wage bumps for the poorest workers could reduce employment, raise prices or curtail hours. What most didn't ask was: When low-wage workers receive a pay increase, how does that affect their lives?

Desmond's essay mentions the experience of one minimum wage worker, now earning at least US$15 in his two jobs. He reports actually cutting back his work hours – consistent with evidence that low-wage workers use higher hourly pay to devote time to non-work activities. Desmond (2019) also surveys the mounting evidence of the prosocial impact of higher minimums – fewer reports of 'child neglect', fewer 'low-birth-weight babies', fewer premature deaths. Desmond's list can be extended; higher minimum wages improve worker wellbeing on a wide range of social indicators (APHA 2016) and they contribute to fewer suicides among the high-school-educated population in the US (Kaufman et al 2020). The suicide study finds that minimum wage effects were strongest at times of higher unemployment (speculatively, because high unemployment also reduces feelings of isolation among jobless people), while making it clear that other redistributive policies can also reduce suicide rates (Kaufman et al 2020, pp 221–3).

Another study led by Dow et al (2019) illustrates the impact of redistributive policies on non-drug suicide. They find that 'a 10 percent increase in the minimum wage reduces non-drug suicides among adults with high school or less by 3.6 percent; a 10 percent increase in the EITC reduces suicides among this group by 5.5 percent' (Dow et al 2019, p 26). Moreover, a 10% increase in the value of both policies would reduce suicides by 1,230 in the US annually (Dow et al 2019, p 26). Gertner et al (2019), who also find that higher US state-level minimum wages reduce suicides, provide further insight. They argue that: 'minimum wage laws in the U.S. may be particularly important for providing financial security given the fewer labor protections and higher volatility U.S. workers experience compared with workers in other high-income countries' (Gertner et al 2019, p 653). This important observation reinforces a broader claim. Greater societal reliance on low-wage employment only adds to the case for living wages. As Desmond (2019) says: 'A higher minimum wage is powerful medicine.'

A crumbling orthodoxy

The orthodox consensus sees the quest for living wages as a well-intended but muddled and ultimately costly instrument for achieving justice. For these economic rationalists, one could read their 'realism' as adhering to an oddly Marxist calculus. It is a world where employers always have the upper hand. Any move by workers, unions or activists will be trumped by superior options available to rational, profit-seeking employers. Efforts to intervene too greatly with the functioning of labour markets in turn produce the greatest harm to those most vulnerable to job loss in an era of rapid change, welfare austerity, and global industry and trade.

The consensus built a powerful policy monopoly that promoted labour market deregulation across the liberal countries, particularly from the 1980s to 2000, narrowing the range of redistributive measures to relatively modest, non-distorting tax credits. It took some cracks in the orthodoxy, ones opened up by economists skilled in regression analysis and big datasets, to force a re-examination of the orthodox consensus. Card and Krueger's ([1995] 2015) book was critical in this respect. Krugman (2015) noted that 'our understanding of wage determination has been transformed by an intellectual revolution – that's not too strong a word – brought on by a series of remarkable studies of what happens when governments change the minimum wage'.

That disruption to the policy monopoly indeed came from within the US economic profession. But that challenge crucially depended on the 'natural experiments' of substantial minimum wage rises across the liberal countries and elsewhere. The forces that gave rise to these policy experiments are addressed in Chapter 4.

Enter the new politics of the living wage

What Card, Krueger and the research that follows tell us is that labor markets are a lot more complicated than we thought, that market power matters a lot and that there may be much more room for public policy to raise wages in general than Econ 101 would have it. (Paul Krugman, *The New York Times*, 19 March 2019)

'I think $15 may be enough to have a life and have the necessities.' It was as simple as that. It wasn't an MIT calculation. (Fight for $15 organiser, Kendall Fells, on the determination of the $15 minimum wage goal, in Greenhouse 2019, p 235)

Rising inequalities, weakened power resources

The liberal states never fully developed social democratic institutions like some European and all the Nordic countries did. This was not because there was a universal commitment to the institutionalisation of a market-driven liberal ethos. Unions and progressive parties sought to build social democracies. But resistance from the right was tougher, electoral arrangements favoured the political right, and industry would not tolerate state coordination of markets. Across employment and welfare policy, the US made the least progress, failing to develop the national institutions after World War Two. This left the country with, as Weir (1992, p 4) puts it, a 'truncated repertoire of policies to deal with employment issues'. The same can be said about social welfare.

Of course, the antipodean states, the UK, and Canada all went further, building employment and welfare state institutions that reflected the power resources of labour and the political left. Still, the 'truncated repertoire' remains an enduring problem across the liberal world. Broader institutional delay and half-measures illustrate these problems. Australia was late to develop universal health insurance, NZ still has some way to go in this respect, and the US is yet to create a national public scheme. Unemployment assistance falls short of high replacement rate universal social protection for wage-earners. Benefits across the liberal world have low replacement rates. They variously combine severance pay for better-off workers, time-limited unemployment insurance, or flat rate benefits now subject to welfare paternalism. Full employment policies across these countries were still limited compared to Europe, and constrained by weak or discontinuous labour institutions and, moreover, the refusal of capitalist power to allow state capacity to develop in the interests of coordinated economic change.

Still, in the decade leading up to the COVID-19 pandemic, the liberal countries achieved low official employment and mostly high employment rates. But the 'truncated repertoire' has continued to weaken and complicate responses to the socioeconomic problems of the neoliberal era. Rising earnings and income inequality in the liberal countries are the most serious consequences. Building system-wide responses to inequalities in the liberal states has been further limited by the declining power resources of the challengers: weakened unions and the electoral retreat of centre-left parties. Chapter 3 covers some key moves in the centre-left accommodation of a new pro-market consensus. In doing so, those parties appealed to new middle-class electorates while endorsing market-driven employment and features of the neoconservative welfare paradigm (see, for example, Deeming 2015; Gingrich and Häusermann 2015, p 61; Wilson and Spies-Butcher 2016). Similar trends – weakness in the European social democratic parties, for example – can be found elsewhere. But European systems of social protection and collective bargaining remain mostly intact, and have proved durable sources of stability during the COVID-19 crisis.

Living wage mobilisations and policies directed at higher wage floors over the past decade highlight the stress points building up on Anglo-American politics and institutions. As argued in Chapter 3, the intellectual disruption to the low-wage policy monopoly has added to these opportunities, a prompt to policy experimentation that has sometimes coincided with wider efforts to regulate low-wage labour markets. However, pressures from below – through union activism and civil associational responses – have been critical.

This chapter considers the new politics of the living wage in three parts. The first part demonstrates the extent of liberal structural inequalities by adding to labour market comparisons highlighted in Chapter 1. The problem of earnings inequality – measured by the share of workers on low wages – emerges as the central feature since 2000. In the post-COVID 2020s, Anglo-American labour markets will be tested further, especially if they depend on private sector investment and deregulation to confront severe unemployment that accompanies poor wages.

The second part chronicles specific developments in living wage politics and policy at two levels. The first focuses on the Fight for $15 movement in the US. The US model has resulted in the worst opportunity structure for worker mobilisation. Worker tactics and achievements in the difficult to organise and mobilise workplaces and politics carry special significance. The second considers pro-wage-earner institutional reform emerging out of cooperation between the 'old' political alliances of established trade unions and labour parties. The most important examples of this politics come from NZ and the UK; both countries have dramatically improving Kaitz index scores following reforms. Reforms in Canada and Ireland are more recent, responsive to mobilisation and institution-building in their larger neighbours. Australia, oddly, has been the least responsive – a consequence of its stronger wage-earner institutions and the conservative hiatus in its federal political sphere. Nonetheless, Australia's award system remains relevant for policy learning across the liberal regimes.

The final part looks at the *potentials* emerging from living wage reforms, focusing on three areas. The first outlines the potential for living wages to contribute to a new 'egalitarian coalition', as Piketty (2020) calls it. The second is related, demonstrating the potential for redistribution produced by 'spillover' impacts of higher wage floors on better-off workers. The third identifies the potential for living wage policies to provide one way around clear signs of electoral and fiscal limits on traditional tax-and-spend redistribution. Here, the data is clear: liberal countries spend less on 'wage-earner welfare'. If fiscally austere times follow in the 2020s, pressure for a predistributive strategy will only rise.

Structural inequalities behind minimum wage claims

A central claim of this book is that mobilisations for higher minimum wages across the six English-speaking democracies have structural foundations in unresponsive employment and welfare institutions. In social policy terms, these states have adjusted to the postindustrial employment realities through the markets and low-wage service sectors (see Esping-Andersen 1999; Esping-Andersen and Regini 2000). Wage-earner and fiscal institutions accommodated these transitions and further limited the opportunity structure for addressing inequalities.

The large share of low-income households and small middle class was presented as key evidence of this problem in Chapter 1. Here, I go further, looking at the structural problems of Anglo-American labour markets in more detail. This evidence advances my claim that structural inequalities left reformist forces with few places to go. Worker mobilisation and experimentation with higher minimums is the result.

Liberal jobs machine: pre-COVID-19 overall employment trends

The pre-COVID-19 decade of the 2010s provided cause for liberal optimism. In 2019, *The Economist* devoted attention to the 'jobs boom' under way across high-income countries.[1] The article observes that

> the rich-world jobs boom is partly cyclical … But it also reflects structural shifts. Populations are becoming more educated. Websites are efficient at matching vacancies and qualified applicants. And ever more women work. In fact, women account for almost all the growth in the rich-world employment rate since 2007. That has something to do with pro-family policies in Europe, but since 2015 the trend is found in America, too.

The article also recognises the impact of harsher welfare policies, concluding: 'Last, reforms to welfare programmes, both to make them less generous and to toughen eligibility tests, seem to have encouraged people to seek work.'

Given that liberal politics has been the strongest ideological source of the pro-work and anti-social welfare compact, we need to know whether liberal countries have actually performed better on employment. Table 4.1 compares a range of welfare states on three separate measures of employment performance using OECD data covering the period up to 2019, just prior to when the pandemic began. These are official unemployment rates, employment rates, and a measure of labour market 'slack' called labour underutilisation. The latter combines underemployment, unemployment, and an estimate of those 'marginally attached' to employment (OECD 2015). Comparisons are made of the jobs performance since 2000 for the six liberal countries, four Nordic countries, four Southern European (Greece, Italy, Portugal and Spain), four or five Continental European countries (Austria, Belgium, France, Germany, and the Netherlands), and two high-income Asian democracies (Japan and South Korea).

Table 4.1: Employment performance of the liberal countries compared, %

	Unemployment rate		Employment rate		Labour underutilisation
	2000	2019	2000	2019 Q4	2016
Australia	6.3	5.2	69.1	74.4	28.5
Canada	6.8	5.7	70.9	74.4	26.0
Ireland	4.3	5.0	65.2	70.0	33.5
New Zealand	6.2	4.1	70.3	77.3	21.4
United Kingdom	5.6	3.8	71.2	75.4	23.5
United States	4.0	3.7	74.1	71.5	25.7
Liberal average (6)	5.5	4.5	70.1	73.8	26.4
Nordic countries (4)	5.7	5.6	73.7	75.4	21.6
Southern European (4)	10.0	13.1	58.7	62.6	39.2
Continental Europe (3/5)	6.4	5.0	67.3	72.3	26.4
Japan and South Korea	4.6	3.1	65.3	72.6	–

Notes: Employment rate excludes France and Germany, but labour underutilisation includes both countries. Sweden's unemployment data for 2000 is actually from 2001.

Sources: Unemployment data: OECD (2020e); Employment rate data: OECD (2020d); Labour underutilisation rates: OECD (2018b, p 54, Table 3.1)

Official unemployment in the six liberal countries trended down from 2000 to the end of the 2010s. However, improvements were not markedly better than performances in the two East Asian countries or the Continental European countries with more regulated labour markets. The Continental European average unemployment rate was 6.4% in 2000, declining to 5.0% in 2019. This result compared to 4.5% for the liberal countries, a small difference. Japan and South Korea have very low unemployment, at an average of 3.1%. The worst performance belongs to Southern Europe, which has long-term unemployment problems due to the Eurozone recession (13.1% in 2019). The liberal countries have achieved lower unemployment over the past two decades, but this performance was not exemplary in comparative terms.

A second measure of labour market performance is the employment rate, which the OECD defines as 'the ratio of the employed to the working age population' aged 15–64 years. These employment rates are 'sensitive to the economic cycle, but in the longer term they are significantly affected by governments' higher education and income support policies and by policies that facilitate employment of women and disadvantaged groups' (OECD 2020d). The liberal countries did indeed achieve the second highest of the respective families (73.8%), with NZ recording 77.3% employment in 2019. The Nordic countries maintain the highest average employment rate at 75.4%. The liberal countries have significantly improved overall employment since 2000 (+3.7%) but that performance was bested by large rises in the Continental European countries (+5.0%), as well as dramatic growth in employment in Japan and South Korea (averaging +7.3%). The Continental European trends here only include the three countries of Austria, Belgium, and the Netherlands for which there is sufficient trend data. Trends over a shorter period that include France and Germany produce a similar average rise, with large improvements in Germany. The recession-hit Southern European group also recorded increases (+3.9% on average), but their group-wise employment rate is still very low at 61.4%.

Importantly, the liberal country average is affected by a poor employment performance by the US. This problem was disguised by low headline unemployment rates in the late 2010s and early 2020. Far short of a 'jobs machine', the US has suffered disturbing declines in overall employment over the past two decades. Scholars are connecting the dots between the 'scarring' effects of poor jobs and tough welfare and greater levels of disability, addiction, and withdrawal evident across the American population (see Blanchflower 2019; Bown and Freund 2019). The liberal average *without* the US rises to over 74%, closer to the Nordic average.

A final way of comparing employment performance is the labour underutilisation rate from 2016. These comparisons do a better job at revealing labour market weakness in the liberal countries because of underemployment and discouragement effects among workers. Liberal countries average 26% underutilisation – a result that is no better than the average for six Continental countries. Nordic countries perform considerably better (21%) on this measure. Recession-affected Southern Europe averages a disastrous 39%.

Combining the evidence, we can conclude that liberal countries did achieve overall high employment rates prior to the pandemic. Signs of labour market weakness, however, are more apparent when the problem of underemployment is brought into view. As reported in Chapter 1, low-wage workers in the mid-2010s reported more concern about pay than job security. But even then, the earnings insecurity story concealed the unemployment problem because pay stress is partly a problem of underemployment.

Country-level causes of weak labour market performance vary across the liberal countries. In America's labour market weakness is revealed in its socially destabilising decline in the employment rate. Australia's weakness is revealed through persistently high underemployment (Carney and Stanford 2018; Patty 2018) – a severe problem in some regions. Ireland's employment rate has risen as the country's economy and gender institutions have modernised. But it has the highest level of underutilisation of the six liberal countries, a result of the twin impacts of the global financial crisis and decade-long austerity policies. NZ and the UK moved closer to full employment on this underutilisation measure and emerge as the two liberal countries that rank in the top third of OECD nations on this measure (OECD 2018b, p 54).

As the obvious contrast, Nordic employment successes derive from historical commitments to full employment achieved through strong export economies, active labour market policies, and large public sectors. High work participation has emerged over time and can be characterised as a 'supply side' dividend of encompassing welfare. Drawing on Henrik Kleven's research, Naidu (2020) writes that

> public expenditures are so complementary to labor supply. Public and cheap high-quality childcare, elder care, health care (including family planning) not contingent on a particular employer, and education, alongside high quality public transportation, are all things that make working easier for individuals and families, and incentivize work even in the face of otherwise rebellion-inducing taxation.

Naidu contrasts the Nordic approach with that of the US, which places obstacles in the way of sustained high employment. The scarring consequences of severe welfare reform and weak investment in childcare and parental leave entitlements illustrate the tensions between the pro-work liberal ideology and the actual outcomes of reform.

Comparing labour market inequality and jobs quality

Commentators who remain convinced of the 'jobs machine' capacities of Anglo-American employment and social policy often concede the approach comes at a cost to equity. Chapter 1 provides evidence of the combined impact of work and welfare institutions in reducing the size of the middle class. Here, we introduce further comparative labour market inequality indicators in Table 4.2. The first allows us to compare the dispersion of earnings for full-time work. Low wages for a full-time job – defined as below two-thirds of the median full-time wage – carry a broader sociological significance. These workers

Table 4.2: Labour market inequalities of the liberal countries compared, %

	Low-wage full-time employment		Earnings inequality ratio: decile 5/decile 1 (full-time)	
	2000	2018/2019 or nearest	2000	2018 or nearest
Australia	16.4	15.4 (–1.0)	1.67	1.66 (–0.01)
Canada	23.2	19.4 (–3.8)	2.00	1.81 (–0.19)
Ireland	17.8	23.0 (+5.2)	1.70	2.02 (+0.32)
New Zealand	11.7	6.9 (–4.8)	1.55	1.47 (–0.08)
United Kingdom	20.8	18.1 (–2.7)	1.84	1.72 (–0.12)
United States	24.7	23.4 (–1.3)	2.05	2.06 (+0.01)
	Early 2000s	Mid to late 2010s	Early 2000s	Mid to late 2010s
Liberal average (6)	19.1	17.7	1.80	1.79
Nordic average (2/4)	6.0	8.0	1.38	1.48
Southern European average (4)	14.8	12.4	1.61	1.57
Continental Europe average (4/5)	12.6	13.1	1.57	1.59
Japan and South Korea	19.6	14.4	1.82	1.63

Notes: Early 2000s includes the earliest annual data for respective countries, and mid to late 2010s includes latest annual data for respective countries. Low-wage incidence for the Nordic countries includes Denmark and Finland only, and the Continental European average excludes France.

Sources: Low pay incidence (for full-time workers): see OECD (2020g); earnings inequality (decile ratios of gross earnings): see OECD (2020h)

commit large amounts of time at work that leave them in poverty or near-poverty conditions.

Low full-time earnings data from the OECD has patchier availability than other labour statistics. Welfare state group comparisons are therefore made between the early 2000s (with the first available year between 2000 and 2004 selected) and the mid to late 2010s (with the last available year between 2015 and 2019 selected). These figures are more indicative, rather than precise, guides to patterns. Still, a high incidence of low-paid full-time workers is evident for the liberal countries. On average, 17.7% of full-time earners across the liberal cluster are low paid, with recent improvements in Canada, NZ, the UK, and the US starting to pull the average down in 2019. Irish data does not reflect recent wage movements, so it still records – along with the US – over one in five full-time workers in low wages. NZ's ambitious policies are significantly reducing the share of low-wage full-time workers – down to 6.9% in 2019. As already noted, NZ also has the lowest median earnings of the six liberal countries, so improvements compensate the lowest paid for their reduced purchasing power. What is clear is that the liberal countries still have the highest share of low-wage workers, displacing Japan and South Korea at the top of the list. Only two Nordic countries are included in the data for the low-wage share in Table 4.2. But, as expected, these figures confirm low shares of low-wage employment.

Table 4.2 reports another way of tracking earnings inequality: the ratio of decile 5 (middle) and decile 1 (very low) earnings for full-time workers, expressed as D5/D1 ratios hereafter. Comparisons are again constrained by data availability, so I compare the early 2000s data with mid to late 2010s data to get a sense of approximate trends. At the start of the period, Japan and South Korea had the worst earnings inequality on this measure. But improvements in South Korea since leave the liberal countries with the worst performance on the D5/D1 measure. Data for all four Nordic countries is available on this measure. Again, they emerge as the best performing – the impact of high wage floors achieved through collective bargaining. Southern and Continental Europe record D5/D1 ratios of around 1.6. Ireland and the US are worst performing on these measures.

Despite important, recent improvements, the liberal countries still perform poorly on full-time earnings inequality and that affects workers at the bottom of the income distribution. One further comparison from the OECD helps make an overall assessment of poor-quality jobs. I have already discussed several measures of new research about trends in good and bad jobs (for the UK, Williams et al 2020; for the US, Ross and Bateman 2020). Clearly, the range of measures highlights different features of work and the literature is still developing. Nonetheless, Gallie (2007) highlighted in an earlier study the 'exceptionalism' of Nordic job quality. Table 4.3 presents three OECD indicators mapping to different dimensions of jobs quality, although these measures could be supplemented by others to reflect innovations in the literature. These indicators are inequality-adjusted earnings, job insecurity, and a measure of job strain. Job insecurity is measured by the expected income loss resulting from job losses as a share of earnings. Job strain is a classic construct from the sociology of work. The OECD developed an index score taking into consideration two subjectively derived measures of job *demands* (time pressure and physical health) and two of job *autonomy* (autonomy and 'social support at work') (see OECD 2018b, p 58).

Table 4.3 presents calculations of rank scores for each of 19 high-income OECD welfare states for which the data is available. Rankings are reversed so that a score of 19 is awarded to the country with the best performance on that category. Average scores for each of the three dimensions of jobs quality are then provided for each welfare state group and a simple overall average is provided in the final column. This time, the Continental European country measure includes France as well as data for the other four countries (Austria, Belgium, Germany, and the Netherlands). Most of the data relates to the studies and collections between 2015 and 2017.

Table 4.3: Three types of 'job quality' scores for the liberal countries compared

	Inequality-adjusted earnings score	Expected monetary loss from unemployment score	'Job strain' score	Average score (higher score = high job quality)
Liberal average (5)	7.6	9.0	12.6	9.7
Nordic average (4)	14.3	12.3	16.8	14.4
Southern European average (4)	4.0	2.5	2.8	3.1
Continental Europe average (5)	15.2	13.4	9.0	12.5
Japan	3.0	19.0	4.0	9.0

Notes: A higher score = better performance on that measure. These scores are the author's calculations, based on averaging a reverse rank score of 19 high-income welfare states for which data is available and are included in comparative analysis.

Sources: See OECD (2018b), ch 3 for definitions and data

As expected, the liberal countries rank poorly on inequality-adjusted earnings, consistent with the findings so far in this chapter. But they are ahead of Japan and Southern European countries, where overall earnings are also lower. The liberal countries rank below the Nordic countries, Continental European countries, and Japan on the measure for expected losses from unemployment, and only rank ahead of Southern Europe where high unemployment contributes to losses. Low replacement rate benefits in the liberal countries are likely contributing to higher losses from unemployment. However, the liberal countries rank reasonably well on job strain, leaping ahead of the Continental European countries.

Overall, these rankings suggest that job quality is highest in the Nordic countries, confirming Gallie's (2007) findings. The five Continental European countries come next. The liberal countries are followed by Japan and then the Southern European group. High earnings inequality and weaker social protections continue to drive down liberal performance on these measures.

Worker voice: unions, rights, and collective bargaining

Job quality and justice at work are intimately connected with the power resources of the labour movement. The relationship between unions and wage-earner institutions is central to Nordic success even as those countries have followed their own liberalisation paths. And union weakness is central to the problems of the liberal model. Table 4.4 reports on the most recent OECD data on union density and collective bargaining coverage as well as a measure of union rights produced annually by the International Trade Union Confederation (ITUC).

Union density is much higher in the Nordic countries because of extensive industry bargaining, large public sectors, and, most importantly, the Ghent system of unemployment insurance (which explains high density in Belgium). The Nordic countries, however, have recorded the largest declines in density over time – albeit from world-beating highs. Average liberal country union density was around 19% in the late 2000s – a decline of around 7% from the early 2000s. The liberal country average has fallen below that of the four Southern European countries, and continues to remain below the Continental European average. However, Belgium has a strong influence on the average for Europe. Once that is taken into account, union density in the remaining four Continental European countries is now below the liberal average.

Table 4.4: Worker voice and protections in the liberal countries compared

	Union density, %		Union rights Score (higher = worse)	Collective bargaining coverage, % Mid to late 2010s	Average employment protection Score (higher = more)
	Early 2000s	Late 2010s			
Australia	24.9	13.7 (−11.2)	3	60.0	1.3
Canada	28.2	25.9 (−2.3)	3	28.1	0.6
Ireland	36.0	24.5 (−11.5)	1	32.5	1.0
New Zealand	22.4	17.3 (−5.1)	2	15.9*	1.2
United Kingdom	29.8	23.4 (−6.4)	3	26.0	0.7
United States	12.9	10.1 (−2.8)	4	11.6	0.3
Liberal average (6)	25.7	19.1 (−6.6)	2.7	29.0	0.8
Nordic countries (4)	70.0	60.2 (−9.8)	1.0	83.5	2.0
Southern European (4)	24.3	20.9 (−3.4)	2.8	65.8	2.3
Continental Europe (5)	29.9	23.7 (−6.2)	1.4	85.2	2.2
Japan and South Korea	16.5	13.8 (−2.7)	3.5	14.8	1.7

Notes: Union density data for some countries is reported as administrative and survey data. The most complete series was used for reporting and averages. Employment protection scores are simple averages of dismissal rights and regulation of temporary contracts for 2013. *NZ collective bargaining coverage statistic was obtained from https://ilostat.ilo.org/.

Sources: Trade unions and collective bargaining data: see OECD (2020c); country-level labour rights score: see ITUC (2019)

Australia and the US have the two lowest union densities of the liberal countries. The US has entrenched legislative and corporate hostility to unions. Australia's situation is deteriorating because of the lengthy rules of union-hostile Coalition governments that have undermined the country's once-strong labour movement. Not surprisingly, the ITUC union rights scores for Australia, the US, and the UK are worse than for the other liberal countries. These countries all score a '3', which signifies a 'regular violation of [union] rights'. Again, the Nordic countries have the best average ITUC rating of 1, a score consistent with only 'sporadic violation of rights'. The Continental European countries are next with an average score of 1.4, which signifies a midway point between the 'sporadic' and 'repeated' violation of union rights.

Liberal and Southern European countries average 2.7 and 2.8 respectively, that is, close to a rating of '3' that corresponds to 'regular violation of rights'. Japan and South Korea score poorly. South Korea's union rights remain very poor (a score of '5', 'no guarantee of rights'). Weak union rights do not automatically mean a lack of union-based contention or a lack of worker interest in unions. For example, South Korean unions have proved powerful contentious actors within the country's emerging democratic system. And, in the US – the worst liberal country for denial of union rights – almost half of non-union workers told researchers at the National Opinion Research Center in 2017 that they would vote for union representation (Kochan et al 2018).

European welfare states have broadly kept their high collective bargaining coverage, which remains much higher than union density except in the Nordic countries. One exception is Greece, whose institutions have been severely affected by austerity. The liberal welfare states have much lower coverage, recording an average of just 29%. And that share is 'inflated' by the OECD's inclusion of Australia's award-covered workers, whose wages are commission-determined, in the collective bargaining statistics. When the Australian data is excluded, the remaining five liberal countries have collective bargaining coverage in the low 20% range, closely matching union density. The same pattern is found for Japan and South Korea: density and bargaining coverage are low for both countries and roughly closely related to each other. Weak collective bargaining coverage in the liberal countries is a clear factor in the shrinking middle class and wage inequality problems found in the liberal countries. As noted in Chapter 3, deliberate policy decisions mattered to this weakness. Visser states:

> In the 1980s the United Kingdom had been the first and only European country with a government determined to end the prevailing system of multi-employer bargaining. Its approach had been preceded in the USA and found followers in New Zealand and Australia, but none in Europe. (Visser 2016, p 29)

Table 4.4 also reports on OECD data that scored labour market protection by country. Unfortunately, the last published updates are for 2013 but they provide a useful if incomplete and slightly dated guide to regime patterns. These indicators measure the extent of worker rights in cases of dismissal and the regulation of the use of temporary contracts. They indicate 'liberal exceptionalism', with the US the least protective on these measures. Moreover, the liberal country average (0.8) indicates less protection for workers than in European countries (with scores ranging from 2.0 to 2.3) and Japan. The orthodox consensus has insisted that deregulated labour markets outperform their regulated counterparts because of their greater flexibility. These claims, however, were weakened by poor employment performance of 'flexible' labour markets in the aftermath of the GFC (Cazes et al 2013). The COVID-19 experience will also reveal more about whether flexible labour markets are much more prone to damaging labour shedding.

Political constraints on pro-wage earner reform

Responsiveness to liberal country inequalities depends on revitalised power resources to organise workplaces, to mobilise, and to build what Piketty (2020) calls a new egalitarian coalition. Much will depend on a revitalised capacity for unions to influence wage-earner institutions, particularly in Australia, the UK, and the US – the three liberal countries where the marginalisation of unions has been most aggressive. Union weakness is one of the key problems that labour and progressive liberal parties face when trying to build majority coalitions – and those parties have sometimes participated in undermining labour movements both politically and industrially. The result is a generally poor performance of the centre-left, at a time of falling working-class living standards and rising inequality. Unions and progressive parties need each other: unions produce organised social classes and electorates, while government control by the political left creates an institutional framework for the protection of workers' rights and interests as well as resources of redistribution.

A glance at electoral trends in the liberal countries confirms the problem. Over the past two decades (2000s and 2010s), the US presidency has been held by the Republicans for more than 50% of the time, with deadlock in Congress sufficient to block any major pro-worker reforms. Of course, the situation at the state level in the US tells a quite different and more optimistic story. In the UK, the Conservatives have governed for 50% of the past two decades and that will extend further in the 2020s. However, the Conservatives have been unusually responsive to living wage politics for reasons explored further in this chapter. Canada has had more aggressively neoliberal policies from its Conservatives who led governments between 2005 and 2016 – around 50% of the two decades. Australia's conservative and reliably anti-union Coalition has been the most electorally successful of all, governing for around 70% of the past two decades. And as a reminder of the transformative power of proportional electoral systems, NZ has elected Labour-led governments around 60% of the time. Finally, the Irish case has involved continuous right-of-centre rule but the inclusion of Labour in a five-year Fine Gael government yielded important reforms for minimum wages.

Only NZ has managed a left-of-centre electoral advantage over the past two decades and that has been critical to the rising minimum wage. Conservative-dominated politics in the US and Australia, by contrast, has led to national minimum wage hiatuses, with the states providing the energy in the US, and the Australian Labor government of 2007–13 able to restore critical functions to award wages determination via the Fair Work Act 2009. Still, centre-left parties in the liberal countries have lacked lengthy and encompassing mandates to enact major wage-earner reforms. These efforts are made harder by four further factors. These are:

1. The advantages of the political right where majoritarian electoral systems produce national governments (Iversen and Soskice 2006).
2. The veto points that block major US reform.
3. The weakness of pro-worker forces in North American liberalism.
4. Centre-left party elites steering too close to business interests and/ or pursuing cautious, technocratic policy.

Given these weaknesses, mobilisation for improvements has started where structural pressures are most obvious and the political opportunities seemingly greatest – within low-wage labour markets. The next section looks at grassroots mobilisation for living wage politics and the political movement to push minimums in the direction of living wages.

Mobilisation, reform, and the politics of living wages

Fight for $15 mobilisations

Structural inequalities ultimately make their way in the daily lives and routines of workers. They are absorbed as hardship and show up in personal and social distress. These inequalities have been most marked in the US where many workers have experienced significantly lower living standards in ways not entirely witnessed in the other liberal countries. The attack on wage-earner institutions in the US is not merely a consequence of labour and welfare battles left over from the 1980s and 1990s. They continue, taking in new sectors of the workforce and involve new corporate and political tactics. The right to work movement that has sought legislative bans on union contracts automatically unionising workers has moved beyond the business-controlled American South. It has had recent successes in 'red states' like Kentucky, but also in traditionally union states of Michigan and Wisconsin. Both states voted for Donald Trump in November 2016 and secured his victory. Shermer (2018) writes on the ongoing impact on politics:

> Midwestern states only started to join that impoverished archipelago in the 2010s ... [when] ... governors, like Wisconsin's Scott Walker, in those heavily gerrymandered states quickly passed these laws at the behest of billionaire donors. ... Then, to avoid confronting angry workers, they used redistricting and new voting restrictions, including ID laws to shield themselves from vulnerability.

Confronted with corporate resistance and hostile legislative traffic, America's unions have struggled. They have moved resources, for example, into patchy political defences. At the same time, unions have tried to reignite the activist organising that led to mass unionisation in the 1930s. Critics describe these efforts as too limited (Moody 1997, 2017). How bureaucratised organisations used to different operational logics reignite grassroots energies remains a major and difficult question for the sociology and practice of unionism. There has, however, been sharply rising support for unions (Gallup 2020) as well as interest in joining. Moreover, large states like California are beginning to experience sustained union growth (Roosevelt 2020).

In ultra-liberalised US labour markets, collective agreements without active union representation are very difficult. Not surprisingly, the most affected sectors – where wage levels are lowest – have low union presence and capacity for bargaining. Unions have had to look to time-consuming and often exhausting and unsuccessful tactical experimentation. The Fight for $15 movement is the most important example of recent mobilisation. Its successes have revived labour movement interest outside the US in pushing statutory minimums towards living wages. Fight for $15 is ultimately a creation of the trade union movement, centred on the large and influential Service Employees International Union (SEIU). But its organisational form has features of advocacy organisation. It is a broader umbrella force with its core resources in the SEIU but one sustained by networks of community and union organisers and, most importantly, activist workers.

In his *Beaten Down, Worked Up: The Past, Present and Future of American Labor*, Steven Greenhouse (2019) chronicles the SEIU's often failed attempts to organise low-wage fast-food workers before the Fight for $15 breakthroughs. Door-knocking by New York Communities for Change, a community organisation, revealed a high level of frustration about housing insecurity among the city's fast-food workers (Greenhouse 2019, pp 233–4). These contacts led to a series of meetings of fast-food workers, many of them women, migrants, and people from minority backgrounds. These assemblies produced the grassroots demands for a $15 minimum wage and union representation that finally led to New York strike action in 2012 (Greenhouse 2019, pp 235–40).

Fight for $15 strikes broadened to other cities. And they have continued to target large sections of low-wage employers in the fast-food industry and more broadly. In Dreier's (2016) words:

> Beginning in 2012, fast-food workers, big box-chain workers, janitors, and other low-wage employees mobilized ... demanding that their employers provide better pay and working conditions. With allies among unions, community groups, and religious organizations, these campaigns – by groups like OurWalmart and the Fight for 15 – organized strikes and rallies that shamed employers like McDonald's and Walmart to raise wages.

Greenhouse (2019, p 241) further argues that low-wage employers not only impoverish communities but do so with subsidises from US governments and taxpayers, noting that SEIU and academic researchers estimated that 'American taxpayers provided $7 billion in subsidies each year to fast-food workers, and some would say indirectly to the industry'. Bernie Sanders, unsuccessful 2020 presidential contender and now Senate Budget Committee Chair, has consistently attacked fiscal 'welfare' that goes towards subsidising poverty wages.

Fight for $15 has also pressured complacent legislatures, building on established relationships between unions and Democrats. But sometimes it has invoked bolder, disruptive tactics to gain political standing. The focus on cities and particularly state legislatures results from near-permanent blocks on reform generated by a divided national Congress. California legislated for a $15 minimum wage under sustained pressure. Dreier (2016) adds: 'SEIU and the broader California labor movement, in a bold move, threatened to put a $15 minimum-wage ballot measure before the voters.' Ballot measures have proved to be remarkable opportunities, unavailable to voters in other liberal countries. New research finds that 'direct democratic initiatives' like ballots reduce a 'policy bias' among legislators who typically favour *lower* minimum wages than what voters prefer (Simonovits et al 2019, p 401).

Ballot measures have been decisive in other states too. Voters passed substantial minimum wage increases in Arizona, Colorado, Maine, and Washington in 2016 (CNN 2016). And, strikingly, these ballot tactics succeeded in the November 2018 mid-term elections in the red states of Arkansas ($11 in 2021) and Missouri ($12 in 2023, with indexation from 2024). Campbell (2018) notes: 'in both states, workers have been unable to get Republican state lawmakers to raise the minimum wage'. Campbell writes further that, in the right to work states where wages are particularly low, 'the overwhelming approval of both ballot measures is a sign that such a strategy could work in ... [the]... 21 states, mostly in the South, where workers still earn the federal minimum wage of $7.25 an hour'. The swing state of Florida held a ballot measure for $15 in the November 2020 general elections – once again a manoeuvre aimed at overcoming Republican legislative control. That victory, which required a supermajority of 60%, adds large numbers of workers to America's emerging living wage welfare state.

Minimum wage ballots initiated at the city level (Simonovits et al 2019, p 408) have unsettled policy stagnation. Policy indifference has also been destabilised by the re-emergent political left in its championing of living wages. Greenhouse (2019) points out that centrist Democrats like Cuomo, the New York State governor, adopted bolder minimum wages policies when threatened politically by a leftwing challenge. Similarly, the LA mayor responded to direct worker mobilisation coordinated by Fight for $15 (Greenhouse 2019, pp 245–6). In New York State's case, the campaign led to the establishment of a 'wages board' to assist in setting pay and conditions across the fast-food industry (Greenhouse 2019, pp 245–6).

By early 2020, the Fight for $15 movement had begun to achieve a nationwide impact. A report by the National Employment Law Project (NELP) estimated that Fight for $15 has achieved around $68 billion in wage increases – a similar redistributive impact to the EITC (Lathrop 2019). The biggest transfer in resources flows from $15 an hour victories in the populous states of California and New York. Successes have, not surprisingly, led to rapid emulation. The NELP report noted in late 2019:

> On January 1, 2020 … the minimum wage will increase in 21 states and 26 cities and counties. In 17 of those jurisdictions, the minimum wage will reach or surpass $15 per hour. Later in 2020, four more states and 23 additional localities will also raise their minimum wages – 15 of them to $15 or more. This is the greatest number of states and localities ever to raise their wage floors, both in January and for the year as a whole. (Lathrop 2019, p 2)

Fight for $15 combines old and new. The organisation mobilised union resources. But, increasingly, striking workers have pushed a bold and clear goal onto business and unresponsive state legislatures – a minimum wage to end working poverty. Successes thus far may well have encountered more resistance if unemployment was higher or if the policy monopoly protecting low minimums held the same sway over progressive legislatures as it had previously. Post-COVID-19 labour markets will prove yet another test for Fight for $15 in the 2020s.

State Republicans have asserted the same intransigence as their federal counterparts. They have resisted local campaigns to increase minimums, even using state laws to ban higher city-wide ordinances. According to Huizar and Lathrop (2019, p 3), pre-emption laws have emerged because the 'corporate lobby has persuaded state-level lawmakers to revoke the underlying local authority to adopt such policies, in some cases rolling back wage increases'. The authors note further: 'To date, 12 cities and counties in six states (Alabama, Iowa, Florida, Kentucky, Missouri, and Wisconsin) have approved local minimum wage laws only to see them invalidated by state statute' (Huizar and Lathrop 2019, p 3).

Ultimately, Fight for $15 mobilisations result from legislative and executive blocks on a federal living wage caused by Republican control over the presidency and Congress. These interests have recklessly favoured corporate interests at the expense of impoverished workers. Still, in early 2020, worker-led campaigns meant that the 'average' minimum wage worker was earning an hourly rate of $12 – the highest effective minimum in US history (Tedeschi 2019). Moreover, the US is following the UK and Australia in an unusual trend: the lowest wage-earners are getting the largest pay increases (Tedeschi 2020).

Union–party alliances and wage institutions in the UK and NZ

Grassroots action, ballot measures, and union mobilisation have been central to the US battles over the minimum wage. Elsewhere, conventional political processes have dominated the path to reform, which is not to diminish their value or significance. Improvements ground out of 'old' union–party alliances, involving the cautious expansion of institutions, are no less significant. They are a reminder of the ongoing need and capacity of centre-left parties to respond to worker interests through their unions.

Table 4.5 shows that the two sharpest movements in the Kaitz index among the liberal countries have come from the UK and NZ. In both instances, there has been nothing of the scale of associational activity involved with Fight for $15. But voluntary living wage associations in both countries have led visible and influential campaigns against working poverty. Both countries, as already noted, endured brutal periods of neoliberal reform in the 1980s and 1990s, with incoming Labour parties in both NZ and the UK committing to 'humanising' neoliberalism rather than policy revanchism. Key wage-earner and social policy reforms of the late 1990s and early 2000s looked similar. These were modest improvements to union ability to negotiate collective bargains, greater use of minimum wage laws to manage incomes and employment in liberalised labour markets, and tax credits to address working poverty.

Turning first to the UK experience. As noted in the Introduction, UK voters told opinion pollsters that the minimum wage was the most important achievement of the Blair Labour period. The broad outlines of the National Minimum Wage, later the National Living Wage, have already been discussed in Chapter 1. It has five pay rates and changes are formally decided by the responsible secretary of state, a political appointment. But to guide the process, the government instituted the Low Pay Commission in 1997, which makes recommendations about wages based on evidence. Given the damage to wage-earner institutions under Thatcher, the union movement had put 'sustained pressure' on Labour to act, especially given that the last Conservative

Table 4.5: Minimum wage trends in the liberal countries, Kaitz index scores

	2000	2019	Additional estimates/comments on 2019–21 scores
Australia	59	54 (–5)	
Canada	41	51 (+10)	Alberta, British Columbia and Ontario have Kaitz scores in the mid-50% range
Ireland	36*	42 (+6)	
New Zealand	50	66 (+16)	NZ's Kaitz score in the high 60% range by 2021
United Kingdom	41	55 (+14)	UK proposed a 60% Kaitz score by 2020
United States	36	32 (–4)	Nationwide averaged Kaitz score in 2019 is approx. 60%
Six-country average	44	50 (+6)	

Notes: Additional estimates take into account recent minimum wage increases. For Canadian provinces, these estimates are early to mid 2020 approximations using Statistics Canada earnings data at www150.statcan.gc.ca. Calculations for the US nationwide are based on Tedeschi's (2019) estimate ($11.80) and Gould (2020a) on 2019 median hourly wage. Calculations for NZ assume proposed minimum wage increases are legislated in 2021 and make estimates of wage levels for the same year based on NZ stats earnings data at www.stats.govt.nz/. *Ireland's score is from 2002.

Source: OECD (2020a)

government had left the country without a minimum wage (Thornley and Coffee 1999, p 528). Labour's initial decision set the wage conservatively, recording a Kaitz index score in 2000 of 41% (see Table 4.5). Although Labour had distanced itself from the unions, the government responded transactionally in meeting union demands for a minimum wage and pragmatically in setting a broad, modest statutory minimum in an otherwise deregulated labour market.

For the first decade and a half, the Low Pay Commission did not have a living wage mandate even though the Kaitz score was steadily improved. Prowse et al state:

> In reality, the Commission has also differentiated between a minimum and a LW stating: 'a living wage aims to assess needs and to provide enough for an employee and their dependants to live on, whereas the NMW aims to provide a wage floor which is affordable for business' (Low Pay Commission 2014, para. 11). (Prowse et al 2017, p 778)

At least one senior industrial relations expert involved with the Low Pay Commission endorsed its independent *advice-giving* role (Brown 2017). This role distinguishes it from the more powerful *decision-making* role of Australia's Fair Work Commission. The UK approach left the final decision to politics, but the advice was aimed at improving a wages floor that would also ensure employment.

A 'conversion' moment for the National Minimum Wage came with the Conservative-led government's commitment to living wages in 2015 (Prowse et al 2017). There was a policy context. The UK's Labour leader Ed Miliband had started championing predistributive strategies, influenced by US scholar Jacob Hacker's articulation of this approach (Hacker 2015). Although critics have disputed the motives and sincerity of the Conservatives' shift, the UK government legislated to increase the National Living Wage to 60% of median wages by 2020 (Cominetti et al 2019, p 3). The party of Margaret Thatcher – one that had abandoned minimum wages in implementing harsh neoliberalism – embraced the living wage.

Why did the Conservatives undertake this conversion? They had at least three motives – and ones taken up further in the final part of this chapter. Central was an enhanced role for a better wage floor to offset severe welfare cutbacks proposed by then Chancellor of the Exchequer George Osborne. The Conservatives further needed to address widening inequalities without compromising the Coalition government's austerity-driven goal of a balanced budget. They were also looking to expand their electoral coalition to encompass more wage-earners. Labour's leader Jeremy Corbyn was ultimately unable to win a majority in the 2017 general election but, with a more radical manifesto, came closer to government than pundits had expected. The Conservatives had to deal with a continuing 'threat' from the political left by moving their policy positions accordingly.

One of the architects of the original minimum wages policy has criticised this political intervention. Brown (2017) rejects the Conservatives' national living wage targets in another way. A *normative* living wage commitment, he argues, has 'politicised' and distorted the intention of a minimum wage as well as the role of the Low Pay Commission. Brown preferred the cautious, more technocratic 'partnership' approach – one he thought preserved some the former wage councils' ability to determine appropriate sectoral differences even though the Commission advises on a single minimum. Brown notes that the UK government sets the minimum wage with a particular 'wage bite' objective. That, in turn, undermines the Commission's role in advising on wage levels to maintain employment. Moreover, a high National Living Wage would become the effective wage for most low-wage workers in some industries (like hairdressing) and would apply widely in poor, job-starved regions.

Brown (2017) rightly observes that the Low Pay Commission's role was altered through political intervention in setting living wages. But Brown's framework remains cautiously fixed on the goal of moderating wage claims to avoid unemployment. That policy goal has been increasingly challenged, as there is scant evidence that living wage increases worsen employment outcomes overall. Brown's critique also does not see advantages in living wage targets becoming a visible measure of government performance. A minimum wage responsive to evidence about living costs has the potential to discipline government decisions and ensure accountability. The UK has many serious socioeconomic problems. However, the National Living Wage has, over two decades, started to reduce earnings inequality and the share of low-paid full-time workers by boosting the earnings of up to 30% of UK workers.

New Zealand is an equally significant case in the new politics of the minimum wage. Recent reforms are particularly significant, given that the country achieved the world's first statutory minimum wages in 1894 legislation. After NZ's dramatic, unsuccessful turn to neoliberal policies – first under a Labour-led (1984–90) and then National-led governments (1990–99) – major institutional gaps emerged in the industrial relations system. Deregulation left NZ with similar regulatory shortcomings as the UK. Statutory minimum wages were augmented as a 'functional' replacement for the older award system that was abandoned earlier. Wilson et al (2013) explain:

> New Zealand's abolition of award-determined wages has made the minimum wage set by the national Parliament more important ... Although minimum wages had fallen sharply in the 1970s and early 1980s, workers overwhelmingly received award wages above the official minimum. But the ECA [Employment Contracts Act] granted employers greater wage-setting flexibility, making a legislated minimum more important. (Wilson et al 2013, p 628)

The Labour-led governments of Prime Minister Helen Clark (1999–2008) committed to a modest rebuilding of the collective bargaining system. Still, the government produced large relative improvements in the minimum wage over the 2000s. The Kaitz index for NZ rose from 50% in 2000 to 59% in 2008, Clark's last year in office. The centre-right National-led government that won the election in 2008 maintained minimum wage relativities, even improving them slightly by 2017, when they were defeated by a Labour coalition led by Jacinda Ardern. As part of a 2017–20 coalition with nationalist New Zealand First, Ardern's government committed to lifting the minimum to NZ$20 in 2021. If the Labour government succeeds in that ambition, then the NZ minimum wage may reach a Kaitz index score somewhere in the high 60s (see Table 4.5). This is the highest score for a high-income OECD country. At the same time, the NZ government would directly legislate the pay of a significant share of the workforce, potentially eliminating low-paid full-time jobs if the two-thirds of median earnings measure is used.

Reforms in Canada, Ireland, and Australia

Canada and Ireland have followed reform patterns influenced by their larger neighbours. Still, these cases bring further insight. Until the 2000s, Canada's institutions had been less destabilised by neoliberalism. Its 'brokerage' model of politics, the slower decline of moderate Red Tories in rightwing politics (Patten 2013), and powerful provincial governments all slowed neoliberalisation. At the same time, Canada's labour movement is stronger and collective bargaining secured by the Rand formula has been sustained, maintaining bargaining coverage. Despite these favourable differences, North American thinking, preoccupied with the unemployment impact of high minimums, has had an influence in Canada as well. As a result, Canada's share of low-wage full-time workers has been relatively high, finally dropping below 20% in 2019 due to progressive provincial reforms (Table 4.2).

Those provincial reforms are starting to reshape the situation for low-wage Canadians. Developing their own programmes as well as following trends in the US, provincial reforms in Alberta, British Columbia, and Ontario have opened up opportunities for policy experimentation in similar ways to the US states. Two major improvements in minimum wages took place under New Democratic Party (NDP) governments in Alberta and British Columbia respectively and the other one occurred under a Liberal government in Ontario. Although these higher minimum wages have emerged out of the policy shifts of three provincial governments, they have also been responsive to local activism, pressure from Canada's union movement, and of course the challenge under way in the US.

Rachel Notley became the NDP premier of Alberta in 2015, defeating a divided and exhausted Conservative establishment. Premier Notley legislated for a C$15 minimum wage as part of a social democratic platform. The United Conservatives then defeated Notley's administration after four years, even though Notley actually gained votes in her re-election attempt as a result of a higher turnout.[2] Premier Jason Kenney has since exempted farm workers from minimum wage laws, and organised a review of minimum wages across the province (Government of Alberta 2019) that led to reduced youth wage rates (Amato 2020). But the United Conservatives have failed to repeal the province's C$15 for adults. Former Premier Notley has continued to defend her reforms, telling the media that 40,000 children in Alberta had been lifted out of poverty as a result of the C$15 reform (Amato 2020).

Kathleen Wynne of the Ontario Liberal Party, another progressive premier, legislated a series of pro-worker labour reforms in the Fair Workplaces, Better Jobs Act 2017, which included timetabled progress to the same C$15 minimum. But Wynne's government was also defeated at the polls, with Conservatives winning because the progressive vote was divided between Liberals and NDP. The new premier, populist rightwinger Doug Ford, halted the planned increases to C$15 in 2019, leaving the minimum wage at C$14. By contrast, the NDP-led government in British Columbia has legislated for increases in the provincial minimum wage in stages to C$15.20 by 2021. The government also established the Fair Wages Commission to make recommendations about staged improvement on the province's minimum wage. Significantly, the Commission's website notes that its mandate encompasses providing advice on 'the discrepancy between the minimum wage and a living wage'. This is an important commitment to monitor wage rates for their basic liveability.

Provincial reforms, combined with heightened campaigning activity by Fight for $15 in Canada, as well as greater labour movement pressure for bolder reforms, suggest a federal legislative response from the federal Liberals at some point in the future. A federal hourly wage of C$15, reformers claim, would act to harmonise provincial minimums at the same level (Canadian Labour Congress n.d.).

Like Canada, Ireland's political system has not endured the institutional upheaval involved with harsher neoliberal experiments elsewhere. Still, it has a small welfare state and the population has endured financial austerity since the early 2010s. Over recent decades, Irish incomes have risen sharply with incoming corporate investment. Even so, Ireland has a high incidence of low-wage workers and widening earnings inequality in recent years (Table 4.2) – indications that rapid income growth has not been shared. Moreover, post-GFC employment has only recovered slowly, with Fine Gael's austerity no doubt a drag on progress. OECD labour underutilisation measures

(Table 4.1) suggest that Ireland had the largest problem with joblessness of all the comparison countries in the 2010s.

Still, these problems do not suggest that Ireland's right-leaning, multiparty politics have avoided alliances with working-class interests. Fianna Fáil managed these through social partnership and Fine Gael governed for some time in coalition with Labour. These arrangements moderated the impact of the neoliberal turn on employment policies (O'Sullivan and Wallace 2011). For example, as the low-wage service economy expanded, the joint labour committee (JLC) system – effectively Ireland's wage councils – expanded to cover low-wage service work. Ireland later followed the UK in introducing a national minimum wage in 2000 to act as a universal wage floor below the wage decisions of the JLCs.

The near-collapse of Ireland's economy produced a Fine Gael-led government that included Labour between 2011 and 2016. Labour's participation in that austerity-focused administration certainly damaged it electorally. But it did gain agreement to reverse Fianna Fáil's minimum wage cut and to establish a UK-style advisory Low Pay Commission. The political response of Fine Gael – combining a programme of austerity with improvements in minimum wages – followed the path followed by UK Conservatives. Still, the Low Pay Commission of Ireland (2019, p 10) has recommended a total of 13% nominal increases in minimum wages since 2015. This includes a further increase to €10.10 per hour in 2020, which the Commission notes will be the second highest in Europe and the sixth highest adjusted for purchasing power (p 11). It further notes that these increases have reduced pay differentials (Low Pay Commission of Ireland 2019, pp 14–15).

Finally, to the Australian experience. Historically, Australia and NZ have had a more even distribution of full-time earnings, closer to Nordic and European averages than to those of North America, Ireland or the UK. Australia's combination of award wages, covering over 20% of workers, and enterprise-level bargaining directly sets the pay of around 60% of workers. These institutions give unions enough influence over wage decisions to weaken unilateral employer control over pay. The country's high minimum wage – the wage floor is effectively A$20 or better – and low taxes boost the spending power of low-wage workers to the highest in the world. In this respect, Australia remains a wage-earners' welfare state, at least in one sense that Castles (1985) originally intended. However, the country's chronic underemployment problems mean that high minimums are insufficient to compensate some low-wage workers for short hours.

Political developments, however, suggest a stagnation in reformist energies, with consequences for Australia's historically strong wage-earner institutions. This problem is directly linked to the political dominance of the conservative Coalition government. Over time, the Coalition has moved closer to US Republican-style politics, bolstered by the pervasive media presence of ultra-conservative News Corporation. As mentioned in Chapter 1, the Coalition government of Prime Minister John Howard (1996–2007) eventually gained a Senate majority, allowing for a major pro-employer neoliberalisation in the 2005 WorkChoices legislation. The combination of faster earnings growth in the 2000s and deliberately constrained wage decisions reduced Australia's Kaitz index score (Table 4.5). Although Labor in government strengthened minimum wage-setting powers, reassigning them to the new Fair Work Commission from 2009, the trend in the Kaitz index for Australia has reflected a more conservative tendency in annual wage reviews. Still, recent minimum wage decisions have driven wages growth (Marin-Guzman 2019), reflecting the Australian Council of Trade Unions' campaign to reinstate a living wage as part of its 'Change the Rules' agenda as well as the probable impact of bolder policy actions elsewhere in the liberal world.

Politically, the labour movement suffered a setback in May 2019 when the opposition Labor Party, promising improvements to collective bargaining and stagnant minimum wages, failed in its election bid. The result, returning the Coalition for a third term, has seen an intensification of a Trump-style focus on low taxes, hostility to unions, and neoconservative welfare. It also ensures there is little progress in Australia's once high Kaitz index, which has fallen behind the UK and is now noticeably behind NZ.

Associational action and business interests

The story thus far points to the role of unions, activist movements, and governments in capitalising on limited opportunities for predistributive reform. The civil sphere has played an important campaigning role in living wage politics that goes back to early efforts to stop sweating industries and improve the plight of single women. Those efforts continue and take many forms that are too expansive for proper discussion here; they range from grassroots union activism and community anti-poverty campaigns tied to churches to the organised interventions of foundations and think-tanks linked to parties and politics. Occasionally, associational-level campaigns have worked in coalition with unions, with various levels of cooperation and success (Nissen 2000; Luce 2005; Prowse et al 2017). At the same time, business organisations have strategic and commercial interests in accommodating living wage claims, even when capitalist organisations have class interests in resisting a larger wages bill. Some central features of both types of contributions are discussed below.

In the US, voluntary associations have added to community organising and advocacy pressure for local living wages in cities with high living costs. The Baltimore living wage of 1994 is the frequently cited example of such localised living wage campaigning (Luce 2004; Reynolds 2001). US research suggests that local campaigns are scalable. They provide the resources for larger mobilisations aimed at state-level minimums. No doubt this is one reason why Republicans have successfully used legislation at the state level to prevent metropolitan-based living wages, achieved either through city contracting agreements or local ordinances. Other prominent examples of localised living wage campaigns include actions focused on Auckland and Vancouver. Local and national activism has also led to greater efforts to calculate and disseminate estimates of living wages for a range of cities, states, and households. This publicity continues to highlight to engaged publics the gap between hourly minimums and living wages.

The UK's Living Wage Foundation has been successful in efforts at accrediting businesses that pay living wages at rates that it calculates (Johnson et al 2019). Accreditation processes involve obtaining commitments to altering procurement policies to promote other businesses paying living wages (Johnson et al 2019, pp 328–30). Commitments to living wages have reputational value to participating businesses. Activist campaigns, by contrast, operate in the opposite fashion, embarrassing those companies paying poor wages in a shame repertoire increasingly adapted to highlighting wage theft.

Observers of UK associational activism argue that persistent campaigning has increased the visibility of living wages as an anti-poverty strategy. This is obviously highlighted by the Conservative government's national living wage policy conversion. Johnson et al (2019) point out, however, that voluntary campaigns have only made a small difference to worker pay. The authors claim this is due to insufficient take-up and the separation of voluntary efforts from union struggles or measures to reduce earnings inequality like revived wages councils or collective bargaining. Johnson et al conclude from the UK case that:

> where social partners do not have the resources or the political capital to engage in effective 'institution building',

progressive wage policies such as the Living Wage, however innovative and disruptive they may be at the level of the organisation, are unlikely to develop beyond non-binding and relatively disorganised forms of private or 'soft' regulation. (Johnson et al 2019, p 330)

By contrast, the capacity to influence local wage policies in the US may mean that voluntary campaigns can produce change. In any case, localised activism has made a major difference to the visibility of low wages as a social justice issue in big cities with diffuse benefits for long-term agenda-setting.

Business organisations gain reputational benefits from paying living wages, as scholars have shown (Johnson et al 2019, citing Wright and Brown 2013). But powerful business organisations may have other reasons to pay higher minimums than those publicly stated. Where businesses are able to exercise various kinds of monopoly power in production and extract higher surpluses, there are at least three benefits to paying higher minimums. The first is that powerful employers in retail, restaurant, and care industries, for example, have been successful in halting unionisation efforts, especially in the US. Paying higher minimums is insurance against the 'threat' of unionisation and even collective bargaining. The second is consistent with the interests of powerful oligopolistic employers in maintaining market dominance: higher hourly pay rates are more likely to exert pressure on the margins of less profitable businesses. The third reason relates to productivity. As evidence in Chapter 1 suggests, employees with low earnings more frequently change jobs. Job turnover affects productivity, even constraining production when employers face tighter competition for workers. COVID-19 will alter these dynamics for the first part of the 2020s but these labour market pressures are likely to return.

The potential of living wages: workers, voters, and budgets

The successes of the living wage movement and improvements to minimum wages over the past two decades are not the product of political altruism. They result from a weakened policy monopoly, one that had scared policymakers away from predistributive policies, and concerted activist and union pressure on politics and legislatures. In this last part, the potentials of the living wage movement for the future of liberal welfare states are discussed. In the absence of trade union power in low-wage sectors, governments have used minimum wages as the least interventionist labour market tool to staunch inequality.

In turn, these developments will generate a political constituency for statutorily shaped living wages. At the same time, progressive reformers have run into major constraints on redistributive tax-and-spend opportunities that will persist through the COVID-19 recovery period. Although higher unemployment creates a significant challenge for the living wage movement, predistributive policies will inevitably play a larger role in class-based and political strategies in austerity-hit liberal countries. Both consequences are addressed before concluding.

Constituencies for living wages

Over the postwar period, low- to middle-income workers had access to the benefit of unions, directly through membership and indirectly through free rider gains from egalitarian wage-earner institutions. Survey evidence presented in Chapter 1, however, confirms what the respective national data shows: that union density is low among low-paid workers. Writing about the UK, Dromey points to the general dilemma here:

> While all workers could benefit from membership of a trade union and collective bargaining coverage, workers who individually lack bargaining power have the most to gain. So it should be a cause for concern that currently it is these workers who are least likely to be members. (Dromey 2018, p 14)

Even though unions have been central to their emergence, higher minimum wages are a compensation for declining working-class power resources. Momentum for higher wage floors today resembles pressure for state intervention over a century ago: the inability and occasional reluctance of unions to organise low-wage sectors. As is now clear, the share of workers earning *literally* minimum hourly wages has not been high in recent history. But this share has the potential to expand where wage floors are pushed higher. Indirect spillover effects resulting from higher floors and larger adjustments also matter. Combined, direct and indirect adjustments paths form a powerful predistributive mechanism. Spillover effects occur when employers 'maintain pay differentials' between minimum wage staff and higher skilled, higher paid workers, or where they employ more of the latter because higher skilled staff have become relatively less expensive (Campolieti 2015, p 16). These adjustments often take place administratively within firms when statutory wage increases are a prompt to revise other wages, to maintain relativities.

Like the employment effects of minimum wages, the size of spillovers is subject to disagreements among economists, albeit quieter ones. The impact of spillovers diminishes as worker earnings rise towards the middle of the earnings distribution. No doubt the impact of large improvements in Kaitz index scores in recent years is an opportunity to gather evidence and assess the total impact of these increases. In the meantime, Table 4.6 provides a brief assessment of the direct and indirect 'spillover' impact of higher minimum wages, which is expanded on as follows:

- Over 20% of Australia's workforce *directly* benefit from graduated award wage floors determined by the Fair Work Commission (Australian Bureau of Statistics 2019). Additionally, the Reserve Bank of Australia estimates that, depending on method, another 6–10% of non-award jobs are indirectly affected by award wages (Bishop and Cassidy 2019, pp 80–3). In total, up to one-third of employees may be gaining benefits from Australia's centralised minimum wage increases.
- Canada's minimum wage workers, by contrast, accounted for over 10% of the workforce in 2019. This doubling in two decades is due to wage rises in Alberta, British Columbia and Ontario (Dionne-Simard and Miller 2019). An earlier study of spillover effects in Canada suggested only weak impact – less than those reported for the US – affecting up to the 10th percentile of female wages (Campolieti 2015). This estimate predated the likely greater distributional reach of higher province minimums.
- Ireland's rising minimum wage is likely to mean that more than the current 8% of workers will earn the minimum. Relying on older data, one study detected some spillover impact of the minimum wage up to the 25th percentile of earnings (Redmond et al 2019).
- New Zealand has around 11% of its workforce earning minimum wages. But there have been no recent estimates of a spillover impact on wages. The small share of low-wage full-time workers in NZ does provide evidence, however, of the *direct* impact of NZ's high Kaitz score on the wages distribution.
- Around 11% of UK workers earned within 20 pence of the National Minimum Wage in 2019 (ONS 2019). And, as reported, the UK Low Pay Commission (2019, p 17) finds spillover effects up to the 30th percentile of hourly earnings, suggesting a stronger influence than earlier findings (Campolieti 2015, p 17).
- In the US, where the situation is changing, around 7 million workers or 4% of the workforce earn the city-wide, state or federal

minimum wage. However, the Economic Policy Institute estimates that the direct and indirect benefits of a national $15 wage would reach around 27% of workers (Cooper 2019). In 2019, as the Democratic House of Representatives was considering national $15 legislation (the Raise the Wage Act), the Congressional Budget Office (2019) arrived at a different estimate of around 27 million or 18% of the workforce.

Table 4.6: Potential reach of higher minimum wages across the liberal countries

Country	Share of workers on minimum wage, %	Potential spillover across the workforce
Australia	23	A further indirect impact on 6–10% of non-award jobs
Canada	10	No recent estimates
Ireland	8	Effects up to 25th hourly pay percentile
New Zealand	4	No recent estimates but likely wider benefit
United Kingdom	11	Effects up to 30th hourly pay percentile
United States	4	A federal $15 minimum could benefit up to 18–27% of the workforce

Sources: Australia: Australian Bureau of Statistics (2019); Bishop and Cassidy (2019, pp 80–3); Canada: Dionne-Simard and Miller (2019); Ireland: Redmond et al (2019); NZ: Ministry of Business, Innovation & Employment (2019); UK: ONS (2019); Low Pay Commission (2019, p 17); US: Cooper (2019); Congressional Budget Office (2019)

The combined direct and spillover impact varies by country and inquiry. Crudely averaging across national contexts, minimum–wage institutions may be influencing the pay of 20–30% of workers.

Low-wage workers as voters and union members

A wider reach of minimum wages has other kinds of spillover effects – to politics. Low-wage earners are voters as well as workers. Not surprisingly, low-income households are stronger supporters of high minimum wages. One 2014 YouGov poll of 1,904 voters across Great Britain found that 72% of C2DE (manual workers) voters supported a 'substantial increase in the minimum wage'. This compares with 61% of ABC1 (professional and white–collar voters). Despite an 11% class difference in support, the results indicate the breadth of popular support for higher minimum wages (Dahlgreen 2014). In the US, analysis of the American National Election Study 2016, undertaken by the pro–Democratic Center for American Progress, indicates strong working-class support for raising minimum wages. It also finds lower but still solid support for higher wages among the electorally significant white working class (Rowell and Madland 2018). Similarly, in Canada, polling conducted in 2018 among Ontario voters about that province's government's decision to increase minimum wages suggested stronger support from low- and middle-income earners (Angus Reid Institute 2017). It was also more popular among women who are more greatly affected by minimum wage reforms.

Cautious centre-left parties have shown greater preparedness to propose higher minimums as part of bolder platforms that occasionally extend further, encompassing better labour market protections for vulnerable workers. They face leftwing challengers in several jurisdictions. Support for a higher minimum appeals to leftist and low-income worker communities, but it is far from a maximalist distributional claim that would repel centrists or invite corporate sector attack. The centre-left also faces challenges from the strategic repositioning of the political right that seeks to appeal to similar electorates by emphasising old-style workerist policies promoting private sector jobs. Conservative embrace of living wages has nonetheless been limited but the UK case is an indication of how conservative politics might address unavoidable problems from rising inequality.

For living wages to emerge as a significant political asset to its political champions, the visibility of minimum wage politics needs to be greater than it is presently. Although working-class voters endorse reform, it is unclear how electorally critical these changes are to voters. There is, for example, scepticism about whether voters who endorse these policies actually decide their vote on minimum wages policies as opposed to policies like healthcare. At least in the US, polling taken in marginally held Democratic congressional districts suggested that voters are more inclined to support representatives in favour of higher minimums (Ingraham 2019).

Pierson's (1994) central insight is instructive here: successful policies *make* the politics. The clearest sign of convergence on a new policy consensus came with UK Conservative government efforts to claim much higher minimum wages with its announcement of a National Living Wage in 2015. Less dramatically, NZ's conservative National Party raised the Kaitz index score of the minimum wage during its 2009–17 period in office. Minimum wages continue to inform electoral strategy on the centre-right. Prior to the December 2019 general election in the UK, the Conservatives made a series of National Living Wage announcements in what *The Guardian* reported was 'fresh evidence that Boris Johnson intends to target voters on modest incomes in Conservative-Labour marginals' (Elliott 2019).

Following Pierson, perhaps future threats to higher minimum wage institutions will crystallise political contestation over wages, mobilising constituencies who have started to benefit from these gains. Political opportunities for such a conflict may not be far off. Post-COVID-19 unemployment offers business and the political right opportunities to demand a period of wage deflation. Progressive parties and unions can engage in this conflict where the next generation of working-class voters could side strongly with the political left. Donald Trump's 2016 victory depended in part on an unusually strong defection of white working-class voters from the Democrats, which, in fact, continues a long-term trend in US politics that implicates the Democratic Party as much as the Republicans. However, as pollster Stanley Greenberg (2019) makes clear, socially conservative workers are not a 'guaranteed' electorate for rightwing populism if it delivers falling wages, frayed communities, and damaged social infrastructure in ways that are still democratically contestable.

Living wage politics also ties welfare state building to agendas that appeal to angry and tax-resistant electorates of struggling workers. Harsh welfare politics and tax resistance among working-class voters have emerged from the breakdown of egalitarian institutions – and not their overextension. Conservatives and neoliberals have capitalised on these failures: wedge politics pitting struggling workers against the welfare-dependent widened the electorate for workfare. And the anti-tax workerism of the contemporary right has pushed tax cuts, ones often most generous to high-income earners, as the primary means of protecting living standards.

Working-class support for living wages makes the most of the limited opportunities available to progressives and socialists. Polling from the US Pew Research Center illustrates the claim. Davis and Hartig (2019) note high support for a $15 minimum wage among Democrats across income groups. But there are substantial differences among Republicans. They note:

> lower-income Republicans are more likely than those with higher incomes to support this proposal: 56% of Republicans with annual incomes of less than $40,000 say they favor raising the federal minimum wage to $15 an hour, compared with 34% of Republicans with incomes of $75,000 or more. (Davis and Hartig 2019)

By contrast, low-income Republicans resist social programmes when the Republican side of politics mobilises against them.

The narrative thus far may seem doubtful about the prospects of union organising in low-wage sectors, given that union weakness has contributed to state intervention on low wages. Despite membership declines – ones made worse by union repression – unions have remained central actors in living wage mobilisation and politics. In some countries, unions have extracted political concessions from long-standing movement–party alliances to improve minimum wages and related worker protections. Moreover, it is significant that a new hybrid organisation like Fight for $15 has led to industry-level and political breakthroughs in the most repressive of low-wage work environments. Still, statutory living wages do not produce automatic and close linkages between higher wages and union membership (Luce 2005). The payoff in higher membership may be small. Unions do, however, indirectly benefit from the 'efficiency wage' implications of living wages. Reduced jobs turnover, higher job satisfaction, and greater reward for productivity build workers' commitment to their employment, reducing anomic conditions in the workplace. That stability, in turn, provides structural resources and environments for union organising to build on.

Higher minimums as austerity compensation

This book argues that the pro-work ideology of Anglo-American social policy means that low-wage labour markets have wider functional significance for social protection. Mead (1997) highlighted this fact in his advocacy of the paternalistic turn in social policy. The pressure for predistributive wage floors has arisen out of political and fiscal blocks to greater tax-and-spend redistribution. Two crises over the space of a decade or so – the global financial crisis and the COVID-19 pandemic – have revealed vulnerabilities in the liberal welfare model. In both cases, liberal countries have either been exposed to the costs of speculative bubbles and overborrowing (the UK, the US, and Ireland) or had to build emergency scaffolding around their inadequate social protection systems to cope with the downturn caused by the pandemic.

Certainly, austerity politics in the decade between the GFC and the COVID-19 crisis was hardly confined to the liberal countries. However, given the smaller welfare capacity of the liberal countries, these states have had diminished fiscal resources to respond to crisis-driven inequality. Table 4.7 demonstrates this, comparing country-level fiscal positions over the past two decades before the massive disruption of COVID-19-related expenditure. Ireland's budget position deteriorated most. But it did so by going from a strong surplus position in 2000 to balanced finances forged out of lengthy austerity. The US

Table 4.7: Fiscal deterioration and spending on wage-earners since 2000, %

	General budget deficit % of GDP		Public social expenditures benefiting working-age households % of GDP	
	2000	2018	2000	2017
Australia	−1.2	−0.6 (+0.6)	7.2	5.7 (−1.5)
Canada	2.6	0.3 (−2.3)	5.9	5.7 (−0.2)
Ireland	4.9	0.1 (−4.8)	5.2	5.2 (nc)
New Zealand	1.9	1.2 (−0.7)	7.7	6.6 (−1.1)
United Kingdom	1.4	−2.2 (−3.6)	6.3	6.8 (+0.5)
United States	0.3	−6.2 (−6.5)	2.8	3.0 (+0.2)
Liberal countries (6)	1.7	−1.2 (−2.9)	5.9	5.5 (−0.4)
Nordic countries (4)	6.8	2.1 (−4.7)	10.5	10.7 (+0.2)
Southern European (4)	−2.7	−1.0 (+1.7)	4.3	5.1 (+0.8)
Continental Europe (5)	−0.8	0.1 (+0.9)	8.1	8.1 (nc)
Japan and South Korea	−	0.4	1.4	3.3 (+1.9)

Note: Public expenditures benefiting working households combines 2000 and 2016 (or latest) expenditure shares of GDP for the following OECD categories: housing, unemployment, active labour market programmes, incapacity and 'other' social spending. These categories either mainly focus on working-age households or benefit this group in part.

Source: For general budget deficits: OECD (2020i); for social expenditures, see OECD (2020f)

followed closely behind Ireland, with a weakening budget position since 2000. The US government has been effectively stimulating its troubled domestic economy for several decades. Australia and NZ were less affected, with the former successfully pursuing fiscal stimulus under a Labor government.

Overall, the liberal countries drifted towards larger deficits since 2000. This was the result of deteriorations in Ireland, the US, Canada, and the UK as well as ongoing deficits in the UK and the US. These deficits, taken together, suggest that the liberal countries have a similar deficit position to the Southern European countries, noting significant variation within the country-level clusters here. Larger deficits are not necessarily a sign of poorer economic performance. In fact, they bolster weak domestic economies. But they are powerful constraints on welfare state expansion especially in countries where efforts to expand social protection create opportunities for the politics of tax resistance. A bleak budgetary situation in the 2020s as economies respond to COVID-19 suggests that the long-term constraints on fiscal expansion for wage-earners will be considerable, even if the fiscal mood is more expansive.

Welfare budgets come under pressure from two sources. The first comes from an erosion of the tax base produced by unsustainable tax cuts to business and high-income earners. The second comes from the social costs of ageing populations involving greater health and care expenditures as well as higher pension costs. To illustrate, OECD data indicates that social expenditures in the US rose by an impressive 4.4% of GDP between 2000 and 2018 but most of this expansion was related to Obamacare.

A clearer sense of the limited fiscal commitment to wage-earners comes from further analysis of OECD social expenditure data. Table 4.7 provides an aggregation of OECD expenditure areas mostly or solely focused on the working-age population (OECD 2020f). These budget items include family expenditures, unemployment spending, active labour market expenditures, resources dedicated to 'incapacity' or disability, and 'other' social expenditures. This estimate is approximate because some expenditure items occasionally provide support for the older population outside the workforce.

The liberal countries devote significantly less to working-age households than the Nordic and continental groups (5.5% of GDP compared to 10.7% and 8.1% respectively). However, the liberal countries are slightly more generous in overall terms than the Southern European ones (5.1%), with the latter focused on pension costs. The outlier cases of the low-spending US and the high-spending UK provide clues about why there are ongoing pressures for predistribution. Consistent with all other evidence, the US has the lowest wage-earner expenditure, dedicating 3% of GDP to this effort. Given limited prospects for a major expansion of working-class welfare through Congress, pressures for greater living wage reforms will remain a vital alternative.

At the other end of the liberal cluster, the UK spends a large 6.8% of GDP on working-age households. But this high spending helps explains why Conservative governments since 2010 have been so focused on austerity: workers gained out of a lengthy period of Labour government. It is for this reason that the Conservatives had clear motives to use the National Living Wage in 2015 to shift the burden of redistribution from the state to employers – and this has come at a significant cost to non-working beneficiaries of the austere universal credit policy. This predistributive strategy 'has been criticised as being a means of justifying austerity' (Grover 2016, p 695). Drawing on Lansley (2014), Grover (2016, p 695) characterises the Conservative policy shift as 'weak predistribution' and argues that the tradeoff limits the benefit from higher minimums by cutting benefits, disproportionately affecting women who have greater reliance on social security.

Conclusion

This chapter has demonstrated that the liberal countries have clear problems with low-wage employment. Understood broadly, the jobs-first approach has weakened the wage-earner and welfare institutions necessary to humanise such a reliance on low-wage labour markets. On a range of measures, the liberal countries perform worse than countries that have pursued the 'jobs with equality' approach, as Kenworthy (2008) calls it. Despite high employment rates overall, labour market underutilisation underlines the weakness of liberal markets to deliver genuinely high employment that the model promotes ideologically through a pro-business wages policy and lean welfare. Critics of this interpretation might point to, for example, severe unemployment problems in Southern Europe to suggest that the problems of high unemployment elsewhere exceed those of 'jobs with inequality' liberal approach. It is true – these countries have serious problems, reinforced by the deflationary consequences of Eurozone membership and painful austerity. Socialist-led governments in the Iberian Peninsula led by Prime Ministers Costa and Sánchez have made significant improvements to wage-earner institutions, particularly so in Portugal.

At the beginning of the 2020s, improvements to minimum wages emerged as a bright spot in efforts to restore redistributive justice in the liberal world. In Chapter 5, I argue that two possible versions of a living wage welfare state can be discerned from these developments. The first is a 'thin' policy approach (Grusky et al 2018) that seeks to humanise a high-employment, low-welfare economy by moderating earnings inequality and contributing to small improvements in job quality in low-wage labour markets. The second involves more significant policy transformation, one that returns us to possible reforms outlined in Table I.1 in the Introduction. Accordingly, improved wage floors emerge as part of a greater policy effort to improve the living standards of low-wage workers. Inevitably, such a model of progress must confront difficult questions and potential obstacles that we have already foreshadowed. Will high minimums lead to greater informalisation and evasion of wage standards? Can higher minimums become a sustainable foundation for broader reform? Will employers respond to higher wages with broader and faster efforts at automation? Is a universal basic income a better response to the inequalities of liberalised labour markets? Further consideration of these questions is taken up in Chapter 5.

Challenges to living wage welfare states

To move in the direction of a fair wage, we have to re-think a whole set of institutions and policies which interact with each other: these include public services, and in particular, education, labour law and organisations and the tax system. (Thomas Piketty 2016)

The minimum wage cannot do all the work on its own. (A.B. Atkinson 2015)

Chapter 4 has shown that minimum wage developments in the six liberal countries are de facto welfare state-building initiatives. They are predictable but important responses to ongoing crises of overburdened labour markets that have been driven by mobilisation as well as institution-building within established politics. Both forms of pressure have been helped by a weakening of a policy monopoly that once dominated policymaker decisions, stalling living wage initiatives. While these reforms can be characterised as only partial solutions to the larger injustices of poor wages, the evidence is clear: higher minimum wage floors have provided one of the few forms of stimulus to an otherwise depressed wages outlook.

Higher minimum wages have also emerged as more vital policy response outside the liberal world. The South Korean example is the most spectacular, underlining the tactical use of minimum wage floors as predistribution where social policy is weak. My claim that these reforms have a particular significance to the reform trajectories of the liberal world rests on three premises. First, liberal labour markets have, by design, fewer institutional levers to correct for rising inequality. Second, the policy monopoly in favour of low minimums has been more 'hegemonic' in states like the US and the UK, with these policy networks dominating liberal policymaking. And, third, welfare austerity across the liberal world has increased dependence on low-wage labour markets more than in similarly affluent countries.

This chapter takes a necessarily more speculative path, looking at prospects for a further development of living wage policies. At the same time, it considers the threats and alternatives to stronger minimum wage institutions. The obvious threat to more encompassing policies is a serious and protracted recession with a major impact on low-wage employment. That has now happened with the COVID-19 pandemic. A slow and politically fraught path to recovery looms in the 2020s that points to significant discontinuities with the politics of the previous decade. There is little doubt that the political right and employer groups will seize on the employment and fiscal crisis to remind us that 'water cannot flow uphill', to use Buchanan's phrase. The battle of the econometricians may well start over again, with policy caution or even policy hiatus convenient to the power resources that have defended liberal institutions. The focus of this chapter, however, is deliberately loftier. It considers questions and problems that matter to the long-term potentials of the living wages movement to contribute to the social democratisation of the liberal regime.

The three sections relate to pathways, threats, and alternatives respectively. The first section contrasts two paths for higher minimum wage institutions and draws on a policy distinction made by Grusky et al (2018). One sees virtue in a narrow or thin version of the reform as self-limiting. By this I mean that the thin approach is ultimately protective of liberalised labour markets, positioned as either an enhancement or replacement for fiscally centred welfare support. The other path is more speculative and ambitious. Thicker reforms build a living wage welfare state proper. Returning to problems encountered in Chapter 2, I highlight the creation of public goods in housing and childcare as central to the architecture of any living wages compact. What is clear is this: money wages cannot do the redistributive work alone. The cost of living in a privatised world needs to be addressed. Moreover, improvements in employment levels over the 2010s have been brought to an abrupt halt. The 2020s will intensify debates about the future of low-wage employment at a time of mass joblessness. It is not realistic to write about living wage welfare policies without saying more about joblessness. Indeed, proponents of a job guarantee have emerged as offering new thinking on long-standing problems that are now more severe.

The second section deals with threats from employers to stronger and more encompassing minimum wage institutions. Sceptics point to many vulnerabilities. Two can be highlighted: the much speculated-on intensification of automation in the face of higher wages that accelerate the 'end of work', and the potential for the wage theft problem to grow with higher wages. I shall argue that neither of these scenarios should be seen as 'terminal' to high wage floors, as protagonists claim. The best counterclaims are briefly set out.

The last section deals with the most academically popular alternative to creating higher wage and better quality jobs. The proponents of basic income see this broad remedy as the only durable solution to problems of deregulated and unequal labour markets. The basic income debate is now so vast that only those features of this discussion that invite a direct challenge to a living wage welfare model are highlighted. Discussion focuses on the contestable premises of basic income proposals: weak or patchy voter coalitions for reform as well as difficulties already apparent in the implementation phase. One likely outcome of basic income politics in the liberal world will be an expanded negative income tax, the consequences of which are addressed at the end.

Two paths from minimum wages

A distinction that helps frame discussion about the range of long-term transitions beyond a higher minimum wage is the difference between 'thin' and 'thick' policy reforms. Grusky et al (2018, p 2) explain that '"thick reform" is all about building new and innovative welfare-preserving institutions, while "thin reform" is all about daring to think about institution-free approaches to poverty'. Although minimum wage policies do not entirely meet the definition of 'thin' reform, the *narrow* version of a high minimum floor is similar to 'institution-free' reform in that it deliberately constrains its scope to improving hourly money wages.

The thin version of minimum wage reform can be characterised as meeting some or all of the following five characteristics:

1. Reforms do not attempt to meet an objectively measured threshold of a living wage. They nonetheless improve living standards.
2. Higher minimums are not indexed to shifts in the cost of living (let alone earnings growth or productivity) and remain subject to uncertain legislative or ballot approvals over time.
3. Reforms are not necessarily the basis for an expansion of low-wage workers' rights – for example, tied to minimum hours' guarantees, legal, industrial, and safety protections for gig workers, or access to either union-based collective or sectoral bargaining.
4. Higher minimum wages are integrated with low-income fiscal support (tax credit policies) but are not accompanied by major reform to the social provision of housing and childcare available for low-income working families.

5. Wage reforms are promoted in the spirit of electoral expediency, policy caution, and/or compensation for cutbacks to social welfare.

A thin reform agenda has one significant advantage. Its limited scope potentially maximises the policy coalition, drawing in elite policymakers, improving chances of success. Indeed, long-term stability of a minimum wage maintained at 60% of median full-time earnings would be an achievement even if broader labour market and welfare institution-building was resisted.

Still, even narrow reforms will face challenges and threats – and on their own territory. Economists will continue to highlight even a limited policy's weaknesses. Apart from likely fierce debates over the long-term employment impact on vulnerable workers, data-focused commentators will underline the poorly targeted nature of high wage floors as an anti-poverty tool, especially compared to targeted tax credits tailored to families with in-built employment incentives.

These claims can be refuted. The distributional crisis in the labour market allows us to broaden the debate, shifting focus from disputes about the anti-poverty impact of higher minimum wages to one that recognises its potential predistributive impact for low- to middle-income households. At the same time, moderate supporters of higher minimums have good reasons to improve the social safety net to enhance more targeted anti-poverty benefits of improved minimum wages. Such commitments would ensure that schemes like the Earned Income Tax Credit in the US or family tax credits in other liberal countries are protected from austerity or expanded, as some states like California have done recently. As highlighted earlier, improvements in minimum wages *and* targeted income support are combining to make significant differences to the earnings of low-income households (Rothstein and Zipperer 2020), with likely greater impact in reducing social stress and income inequality.

Equally, objections to setting a *single* living wage to cover all household contingencies are overstated. Methods for calculating a living wage have always been deliberately conservative. For example, Australia's Justice Higgins made tactical reference to 'frugal comfort' in determining an acceptable living standard for unskilled male breadwinners. There is a degree of principled calculation here. Employers and politicians cannot easily refute minimum income assessments that establish 'the very fine line between the financial independence of the working poor and the need to seek out public assistance' (Glasmeier/MIT 2020). Most living wage formulas do not, for instance, include items like restaurant meals in their calculations or a budget for an annual holiday. Moreover, as Bryan (2008) points out, they were not designed to reflect or improve workers' share of prosperity resulting from productivity growth. For low-wage earners to share fully in capitalist prosperity, they need opportunities for social mobility, the security of public goods, and access to rewards from productivity growth through more generous indexation of wages. The fact that living wages cannot cover all household contingencies is not an argument against them. Nor can they or should they replace the calibrations of household income made possible by the fiscal tools of welfare.

A thin, money wage focus on higher minimum wages would still leave reforms vulnerable to the inequalities and high costs associated with the privatised markets for housing and childcare, as well as to downturns in employment. In the decade preceding the COVID-19 crisis of 2020, employment conditions in the liberal countries had been generally improving or stable. But those circumstances have changed, exposing policy institutions to a worse employment environment.

Where would a 'thicker' set of reforms, ones that build a living wage welfare state, focus? Such an exercise in welfare state-building would require a policy and voter coalition committed to wider social reforms. These reforms would necessarily focus on low- to middle-income households, and particularly their housing and childcare needs. And, in some jurisdictions, massive investments in health and education are also needed. Such institution-building would also need to address serious structural weaknesses in employment across low-wage labour markets. Let's consider these two goals in turn.

One central observation is that the high money wages needed to survive at the bottom end of the labour market are a consequence of inadequate 'public good' provision in housing and childcare. Welfare states that treat the building blocks of social security as public goods (such as the non-market provision of housing) can produce good living conditions for workers on lower money wages. Reforms to housing policy and free or low-cost childcare are particularly important in this respect. Hegewisch and Gornick (2011, p 128) note that 'evaluations by both the OECD and the European Union suggest that inadequate childcare and long-term care have become critical barriers to further expansion of labor force participation in many countries'. The authors draw out the class consequences of inadequate childcare policies. They say: 'Disincentives to work for pay due to childcare costs are significantly higher for less educated women, while the higher earnings capacity of highly educated women makes this group less negatively affected by childcare costs' (Hegewisch and Gornick 2011, p 128).

Given that most low-wage workers are women, a combination of living wages and low-cost childcare would improve gender equality for working-class women (see Krugman 2020).

Just as critical to broader reforms are policies that address the quality and security of employment at the bottom end of the labour market. For higher minimum wage floors to approximate living wages, institutions for maintaining the living cost and relative value of minimum wages need to be made permanent. This arrangement is more or less in place in Australia, given its independent annual wage reviews, but this capacity is compromised elsewhere when wage rises entirely depend on political discretion and/or emerge out of ad hoc political and social bargaining processes that do not necessarily reflect regular and factual assessments of living costs. Reforms in several US states now achieve automatic adjustments for inflation; and so do those now in place in British Columbia. One further consideration in maintaining the value of minimum wage floors is the extent to which they pass on productivity improvements across the economy to low-wage workers; that would mean using an adjustment formula incorporating the broader gains of wage-earners, similar to what can be gained through collective bargaining.

Equally central to higher minimum wage floors is the steady maintenance of living wage jobs. One convincing proposal suited to the liberal context is the job guarantee (Wray 2018; Tcherneva 2018, 2020). A job guarantee, as a mechanism to edge closer to full employment, is not new policy. It can be traced back to Roosevelt's unfinished New Deal project in the US and to more recent initiatives such as *Plan Jefes y Jefas de Hogar Desocupados* (Program for Unemployed Male and Female Heads of Households) in Argentina, which employed 13% of the workforce at the height of Argentina's economic crisis (Tcherneva 2018, p 9). Functionally equivalent roles are played by large public sectors in the Nordic social democracies, although these settings do not represent 'guarantees' of paid work.

Writing in the US context, Tcherneva (2018, p 12) proposes a federal job guarantee administered by the Department of Labor that funds local projects – ranked by employment and social need – that would cost up to a modest 2% of GDP. COVID-19 recovery will involve much greater spending but the fiscal mood is now much more expansive. Employment would pay 'living wages' ($15 an hour) and would be a public job creation scheme with some private sector involvement with training, and so on (Tcherneva 2018, p 39). The great potential for an effective job guarantee would be to 'establish a "labor standard" for the economy as a whole' (Tcherneva 2018, p 6). The combination of near-living wages employment and a job guarantee would place powerful foundations at the base of liberalised labour markets – even if wage-earner institutions for the bulk of the workforce required major reform.

The COVID-19 employment crisis has disproportionately affected low-paid workers (Gardiner and Slaughter 2020; Gould 2020b). The primary impacts have been exposure to immediate health risks in maintaining essential functions, shorter working hours, and job losses. These experiences solidify the case for interventionist labour market policies that the liberal world has resisted. The 2020s will involve a recovery from an extremely severe and sharp shock to employment. The job guarantee offers a distinct and affordable path to reorganising low-wage employment with greater guarantees of stable employment for workers at living wages. And, like higher minimum wages, it is likely to garner considerable voter support because of its clear focus on employment and the type of public sector jobs associated with environmental reconstruction, social care, and local community building. But the social democratisation of the liberal model over the 2020s will likely demand broader experimentation and investment. The expansion of 'traditional' public sector roles and the use of wage subsidies to stimulate private sector employment remain rival forms of labour market interventions available to socialists and progressive liberals. Still, the job guarantee idea is likely to expand the policy and voter coalition for intervention in labour markets badly needed in the 2020s. However, protecting the Keynesian and social democratic features of such an approach from strong paradigmatic and policy incorporation from the right seems imperative (see Sligar and Sturgess 2020). Workfare advocates may well see the job guarantee as a way of transforming hopes of public employment guarantees into enhanced workfare schemes. The risks here would be threefold: a strong element of compulsion relating to job participation; work being paid below minimum wages; and easy private sector access to a cheap, publicly subsidised labour force.

This book also makes clear that opportunities for union-based collective or industry bargaining are necessary and harder challenges in halting labour market inequalities (see Johnson et al 2019). Still, the combined success of a living wage floor and greater guarantees of employment would underwrite wages and job security in the liberalised labour market in ways that are inexpensive, do not crowd out private sector activity, or expand bureaucracy, or add much to inflation (see Wray 2018). These improvements would offer workers greater security to act out their class interests, as Pixley (1993) puts it.

Here, I have tilted the 'provisional utopia'[1] of high minimum wages and a job guarantee to a design suited to a US employer-dominated labour market with a weak redistributive coalition. In other liberal countries, a return of a mix of wages boards or sectoral bargaining that set wage floors and secure conditions for low-wage workers might be more politically realistic, and, in turn, present better ways of integrating minimum wages into pro-worker industrial relations.

Employer responses: technology and evasion

Except in unusual circumstances, employers hold the power in capitalist labour markets. Business power is not only exercised through managerial control over the workplace, that is, through wage negotiations over labour contracts and in the organisation of the workforce and technology. It is also exercised through business influence in the media (agenda-setting, expert analysis, and so on), and through forms of control over public policy that span from regulatory capture to indirect influence produced through donations and networks involving political decision-makers. These channels influence how voters and policymakers assess the impact of higher minimum wages and how these improvements shape future corporate strategy. Here, I focus on the two 'threats' to living wage policies that emerge from business strategy. These are the threat of automation and the risks associated with greater avoidance or evasion of higher wages bills.

The threat of automation

Full employment advocates on the political left and enthusiasts for free markets unite in their objections to predictions about the demise of paid work brought on by technology. Although these opposing camps see labour markets operating differently, they accept that human societies – working through markets or other forms of organisation – continuously generate new forms of work. They also agree that disruptions to full employment are linked to business cycles. The former sees full employment as unlikely to be achieved outside booms, requiring activist government; the latter sees deviations from full employment as problems related to allocative inefficiencies in markets.

However, a large and vocal group of CEOs, futurists, researchers, and politicians are sounding the alarm about prospects that affluent postindustrial societies are nearing an 'end of work' scenario. Logically, higher minimum wage floors add incentives for business to not only outsource and reorganise their workforces to maintain profits, but also accelerate automation, machine learning, and artificial intelligence to replace jobs within the reach of new technologies. Here, it is useful to distinguish between those technologies that reduce the overall need for jobs in production[2] – changes that receive considerable public and media attention – and the combination of law and technology assisting employers to reorganise their workforces. Some technologies do both, but the latter include the use of digital platforms that entrench insecure gig-type labour markets. Labour market regulation, in the liberal world and beyond, must rapidly come to terms with how law and technology combine to undermine worker security and access to rights.

However, the main focus in debates on the future of work concerns the nearing and drastic reach of automation. As it turns out, empirical assessments of the impact of automation vary considerably (OECD 2019e). Recent empirical research by the consulting firm McKinsey creates a context for understanding the complexity of actual changes to work. They argue: 'Technical feasibility of automation is only the first influencing factor. Other factors include the cost of deployment; labor-market dynamics, including labor supply quantity, quality, and the associated wages; the benefits beyond labor substitution that contribute to business cases for adoption; and, finally, social norms and acceptance' (Manyika and Sneader 2018, p 3).

McKinsey analysis has also ranked employment tasks according to the sophistication and predictability (just as others have), concluding that, based on current technology around '50 percent of current work activities are technically automatable by adapting currently demonstrated technologies' (Manyika et al 2017, p 27) and that '60 percent of all occupations have at least 30 percent technically automatable activities' (Manyika et al 2017, p 27). These predictions seem daunting. But the report notes less than 5% of current occupations are completely automatable (Manyika et al 2017, p 27). At the same time, other research estimates 'that 14% of jobs are at high risk of automation – significantly fewer than some researchers have argued' (OECD 2019e, p 13). Based on their empirical analysis, McKinsey's researchers are also sceptical about the prospect of mass technologically driven unemployment, noting scholarly evidence about the job-creating effects of technical change over time, as well as population ageing trends that are slowing labour force growth (Manyika et al 2017, pp 4–5, 12).

The projected impact of automation throws up a few surprises. Some high-paid tasks, such as those associated with the jobs of senior managers, turn out to be highly automatable, while some tasks performed by low-wage workers are much less so. The obvious example is social care employment, now a large and expanding industry and relevant to any discussion of minimum wage employment. Still, the job- and industry-level risks of automation follow patterns of specialist skill and occupational hierarchies, along with the gendered dimensions of both. Predictable physical and mental work tasks (like collecting and processing data) can be automated. And that means that some 'routine' medium- and low-skilled work is especially vulnerable to automation (Manyika et al 2017, p 9). At an industry level, this impact will be realised in industries like accommodation and food services as well as in manufacturing where its effects are already well known. However, manual employment that involves 'unpredictable physical activities' is more difficult to automate (Manyika et al 2017, p 27) and will not contract nearly as quickly and may even grow (Manyika et al 2017, p 9). More generally, there are plenty of jobs that involve social interaction, care, or unpredictable mental and physical tasks that will continue to expand and many will be located in the bottom half of the wage distribution (Manyika et al 2017, p 87).

Generations of workers have already felt the impact of technological change, and that impact won't change. But growing attention to greater automation may be having another impact. A quick search of reported news stories (tracked via Google Trends) between 2008 and 2018 confirms falling mentions of unemployment after 2010 (the immediate aftermath of the global financial crisis) before mentions rose again with the COVID-19 recession in 2020. Over the decade or so before COVID-19, however, there was a reasonably steady rise in news mentions of 'automation', 'artificial intelligence', and 'robots'. One possible impact of the automation threat may not be directly related to its immediate job impact, but rather the *threat* of its impact. Leduc and Liu (2019, p 1) have shown that for the US

> the threat of automating a job weakens workers' bargaining positions and thus restrains wage growth in a tight labor market. Although automation boosts labor productivity, the productivity gains do not fully translate into wage gains. We find that automation has contributed to a signification portion of the decline in the labor share over the past two decades.

The implication is that employers can keep a lid on wage demands if workers are constantly reminded that the robots are after their jobs.

Business and pro-business media have an economic interest in amplifying the threats of automation because they effectively influence what economists call the 'reservation wage', that is, the wage at which workers accept employment. Although direct automation threats can be quantified for industries and occupations, there are few, if any, studies of the impact of media reporting on the technological impacts of unemployment that may also contribute to worker insecurity. Certainly, employers have used the media in the US to signal to workers that their efforts to promote a $15 minimum wage only accelerate the technological replacement of workers (Lee 2016). My claim, admittedly speculative, is that singular media attention to the risks of automation contributes to distorted public perceptions of employment transitions – not unlike the likely impact that publication biases in the economic literature have had on the conventional wisdom about the negative employment consequences of higher minimum wages.

Does the prospect of greater automation make the struggles and agenda of the living wage movement self-defeating? The answer is no, but this conclusion depends on several assumptions. First, forecasts for the growth in low-skilled work in high-income countries do vary but they are not particularly pessimistic. It is likely that low-wage employment will continue to expand over time, even if researchers are finding that the prospects for 'routine' medium-skilled workers are deteriorating. Second, as I have argued, higher minimum wages policies are not only relevant to low-skilled workers who earn low hourly pay. Greater earnings polarisation produced by changing work organisation will mean more relatively skilled workers will enter low or modestly paid employment. A McKinsey report acknowledges this reality, noting that the 'polarization of wages is not due solely to skill gaps; some of the additional demand for middle-skill jobs are in those that are currently paid low wages in countries such as the United States' (Manyika et al 2017, p 87). This earnings polarisation has a greater impact on younger workers, and looms as a major intergenerational equity problem.

Third, pessimistic projections about low-wage employment tend to focus on only one destructive side of the dynamics of capitalist employment. Human societies are creative organisms, and capitalist organisations constantly find ways to develop uses for and derive surplus from human labour. Moreover, technological change itself is a messy, uneven, and complex process. Clunky and poorly coordinated processes of change continuously fail to anticipate their technical and social limitations – and these resulting adjustments are then typically labour intensive. Human organisations generate vast numbers of complex and routine problems, many of which are inadequately addressed under conditions of cost-cutting and managerialism. Some of these tasks do not require advanced training but still require human ingenuity, sociability, and creativity – and some of these types of jobs will continue to be relatively poorly paid.

Fourth, anxiety about the impact of technological change on jobs appears to be greater in countries where labour markets are poorly coordinated by state institutions. Journalist Peter Goodman (2017) observes a dramatic difference in the perceptions of automation in the high employment Nordic countries and the liberal world:

> Eighty percent of Swedes express positive views about robots and artificial intelligence, according to a survey this year by the European Commission. By contrast, a survey by the Pew Research Center found that 72 percent of Americans were 'worried' about a future in which robots and computers substitute for humans.

The reasons for this difference seem clear. Where governments are trusted to promote equality and employment at the same time through their welfare state and industry policies, the public trusts change. One modest step the liberal countries could take to both protect employment and reassure voters would be to implement a job guarantee and/or publicly subsidised employment that gives unemployed workers opportunities to undertake a vast number of unmet environmental, infrastructural, and community needs.

The problem of wages evasion

Higher minimum wage floors prompt employers to think about automation to reduce their wages bill. In the same way, the threat of higher wages prompts employers to think about reorganising their workforces to avoid higher costs, or to be more evasive about their responsibilities. These risks are noted in high-level assessments by the IMF in its cool reception to the idea of a European minimum wage (Detragiache et al 2020). Numerous strategies are available including work intensification, trimming weekly hours for workers, or outright underpayment. Employers can exploit perfectly legal arrangements to avoid rising pay obligations. The gig economy depends on the strategic redefinition of employees (as contractors or suppliers, and so on) to avoid paying higher wages and ensuring many basic employment conditions. Unions, industrial commissions, and responsive legislatures must, in turn, grapple with the consequences of the legal and technological effects of the gig economy on low-wage and precariously employed workers. Legal and policy responses have involved a range of mechanisms, from outright bans on gig-like arrangements (for example, ride-sharing services in the city of London), to fining corporations for evasive tactics (such as in New Jersey), and modernised definitions of employees that minimise the exploitation of legal loopholes (such as changes attempted in California).

However, one significant problem is the deliberate evasion of minimum wages by employers. Good quality survey data from the UK (the Annual Survey of Hours and Earnings) suggests that underpayment of wages is actually low overall. Still, it is a considerably more serious problem in low-wage employment and thus affects part-time working women more than others (Low Pay Commission 2017, pp 9–10, 19). And, higher minimum wage floors *are* producing greater noncompliance, but given the widening coverage of the higher national minimum wage, this growth is not disproportionate and cannot be interpreted as a sign of the policy's unenforceability (Low Pay Commission 2017, p 12). As noted previously, in Australia, where enforcement by government is lagging, the underpayment of workers generates continuous media scandals. This problem has surfaced in minimum and low-wage industries such as retail and restaurants. But it occasionally emerges in higher-wage industries and in the public sector and universities as well. Systematic underpayment of wages involves not only underpaying workers on an hourly basis. It also involves more subtle forms – for instance, when working hours for low-paid staff are improperly calculated and do not reflect true working time. A Resolution Foundation report from the UK illustrates this problem in social care workers:

> unpaid time included time spent travelling between clients in domiciliary care, and unpaid training and 'on call' hours across domiciliary and residential care settings. While calculating total working time can be complex, the law is clear that these activities are in scope for the purposes of the NMW. (Gardiner 2015, p 2)

Rising minimum wage floors deliberately add to the wages bill of business and, logically, raise the incentives for evasion. Weak union membership levels in low-wage sectors reduce the capacity to maintain local oversight and empower staff to resist these. Evasive practices under such conditions, especially when they are reinforced by weak sanctions and limited surveillance, can produce industry-wide norms of wage-setting that institutionalise underpayment. Still, greater public attention to minimum and low-wage employment puts pressure on legislatures and government agencies to act. This pressure to act is compounded by 'shaming mechanisms' available to workers and unions where the mass media continuously highlights individual examples of underpayment. Equally, enforcement in the UK also uses 'naming' strategies to promote compliance across industries (Low Pay Commission 2017, pp 27–30).

Without union oversight and an industry-wide compliance 'culture', responses to wage theft and systematic underpayment fall on enforcement agencies. Brown and Wright (2018, p 488) note that: 'Lack of resources for government inspectorates is generally a major challenge for labour standards enforcement, particularly given the decline of unions, which once played an important *de facto* role in this process.' But this area of regulation is also an area of considerable innovation. UK enforcement entails softer and harder forms of compliance measures, ranging from widespread education of employers about changes to hourly pay to publicly naming underpaying corporations and court action (Low Pay Commission 2017).

Still, weak regulation is a major problem and staffing shortages are critical. Investigative journalism from the US noted that

> a nine-month investigation by POLITICO ... found that workers are so lightly protected that six states have no investigators to handle minimum-wage violations, while 26 additional states have fewer than 10 investigators. Given the widespread nature of wage theft and the dearth of resources to combat it, most cases go unreported. Thus, an estimated $15 billion in desperately needed income for workers with lowest wages goes instead into the pockets of shady bosses. (Levine 2018)

Aggrieved workers acting alone must weigh up the risk involved in tolerating underpayment and the risk of losing their jobs. Levine (2018) quotes Victor Narro of the UCLA Labor Center: 'Low-income workers are already in this fragile balance ... One paycheck of not being able to get the wages they're owed can cause them to lose everything.' Satisfactory resolution is limited not only by a lack of enforcement but by the industries and operators involved: 'states lack the tools to go after the landscaping firms, restaurants, cleaning companies and other employers that shed one corporate skin for another, changing names while essentially continuing the same businesses – often to evade orders to pay back their workers' (Levine 2018).

One promising avenue for better regulation by resource-stretched agencies may emerge as they gain greater insight about prevailing market structures. Brown and Wright (2018, p 488) note the tactical possibilities:

> The 'strategic enforcement' model developed by David Weil … [in the US] … is one way for underfunded enforcement agencies to make the most of limited resources. In the US, as in Britain, breaches of labour standards are most likely to occur among employers situated at the lower tiers of supply chains, who are large in number and difficult to monitor. Under Weil's leadership, the Wages and Hours Directorate … focused on 'lead firms' such as supermarket retailers and major brand names, situated at the apex of supply chains, and made them accountable for the standards of their suppliers and labour contractors. Such strategies are most effective among lead firms which are protective of their brand image, whose commercial reputation gives them a large incentive to maintain decent standards in their supply chains.

Consistent with more strategic oversight, one UK Low Pay Commission report into the National Living Wage notes that a larger national enforcement budget has enabled a focus on deeper investigations of larger employers where the payoff for workers is highest: 'In large part their success in 2016/17 has come from targeted enforcement of a small number of large and complex cases, particularly in the retail sector' (Low Pay Commission 2017, p 30).

The structure of employment in low-wage labour markets – high industry and job turnover, low unionisation, the tactical, legal and industrial advantages held by employers, and the social exclusion of workers – looms as a problem for living wage approaches. But these problems should not be portrayed as hopeless, even when political systems fail to deliver resources for compliance. Employer evasion of lawful wages is hardly a reason to argue that raising the wages of low-wage workers is self-defeating. Even if legal enforcement is patchy or only ever strategically undertaken, higher statutory pay rates still have an impact on the pay rates that evaders can get away with. Improving the capacity for surveillance and penalties for evasion are essential, but the task of enforcing better local and industry adherence ultimately requires stronger unions.

Basic income versus a living wage welfare state

The twin threats of automation and wage evasion by cost-cutting employers discussed so far in this chapter add to the scepticism encountered in Chapter 3 about the likely success of higher wage floors as effective policy. Not surprisingly, these arguments also add to what is, by now, an enormous literature advocating universal basic income. Although there is a rightwing libertarian case for a universal basic income, such as the one advanced by Charles Murray, the main case for this reform has been made by the postindustrial left. Its arguments and premises form the most relevant broad-ranging alternatives to the ones advanced in this book. They are that:

- labour markets face irreversible technological unemployment;
- the maintenance of high levels of employment in capitalist labour markets requires increasingly repressive social policies built around workfare;
- pro-jobs social organisation and public policy implicitly devalue other uses of time and a wider conception of human freedom; and
- the climate crisis requires a socioeconomic system that is decoupled from ecologically destructive growth.

Relying on the overall distribution of money between people and sectors as its key policy resource, the basic income is a prime example of what Grusky et al (2018, p 2) refer to as *thin* public policy: 'it lets money itself do all the poverty-abating work'. Universal basic income is no longer a 'pie in the sky' proposal. Various pilot and economy-wide schemes are now either under consideration or being implemented. As such, basic income represents an advanced rival set of arguments and tools to those developed for employment-focused social democracy. Moreover, the successful implementation of a generous basic income would make living wages combined with a job guarantee as regulatory mechanisms in low-wage labour markets look comparatively modest.

When compared with current low-wage and poverty problems prevailing under liberal institutions, even a partial basic income scheme – that is, one implemented as a more generous negative income tax – would offer advantages. But even this achievement would depend on what sort of political bargain such a reform depended on. If it was implemented as a 'grand compromise' emanating from the centres of organised politics, with the corporate sector demanding even fewer employment rules in return for higher taxes, then the distributional dynamics of a partial scheme may be unpredictable. My reservations, set out below, highlight three weaknesses. All of these feature in a well-developed public debate, but they are introduced here to draw out the comparative advantages of rival approaches. The first addresses whether capitalist labour markets can still generate both the social movements as well as the structural foundations for 21st-century economic justice. The second queries whether the 'thin' form of the basic income would ultimately address the problems of low-wage workers. And the third draws attention to the weak electoral coalition for a universal basic income as well as to signs that actual basic income reform encounters difficulties in implementation.

First, basic income proposals are mostly but not exclusively pessimistic about the capacity of employment systems to produce 'quality jobs with equality'. Generations of basic income scholars and utopians (for example, Andre Gorz, Claus Offe, Jürgen Habermas, Jeremy Rifkin, and Kathi Weeks) have presented an assortment of facts and prognostications that point to a near-jobless future and the need to transcend the cultural emphasis on paid work. However, as presented earlier, sophisticated empirical work in this area is not forecasting a jobless future. Rather, it predicts growth in both skilled and unskilled employment, with the impact of technology most affecting medium-skilled jobs that involve 'predictable' or routine tasks. The problems confronting the labour markets of rich countries in the 21st century are more significantly about the polarisation of jobs and pay, rather than an inevitable lack of work.

Basic income critics are, however, on stronger ground when they point to weak union density and falling pay. They conclude that, even if employment still dominates social life, then the mobilising structures that can make jobs meaningful and equal are disappearing. This assumption can be questioned. At the very least, the Fight for $15 movement in the US, as well as pro-worker minimum wage reforms elsewhere, are reminders of the capacity to revitalise wage-earner institutions. The longer-term challenge for predistributive justice is to discover what fusion of class mobilisation, political coalition-building, and policy redesign could guarantee living wage employment for the most disadvantaged jobseekers, especially through recessions, and build new collective institutions within liberalised labour markets.

Several Marxist sociologists, particularly Erik Olin Wright (2004), see in a universal basic income some potential for a revival of union power. Once a universal minimum income floor is secured, the argument goes, workers have security beyond the labour contract that could well spark greater militancy and risk-taking in their jobs. This is a logical conclusion drawn from a Marxist interpretation of limits on voice that arise from worker reliance on employers for their livelihoods. However, a universal basic income may have unintended consequences, famously described in Polanyi's discussion of the English Poor Laws implemented in 'Speenhamland'.[3] Secured under compromised conditions, basic income could equally undermine minimum wages by guaranteeing a low non-wage income. Workers might well become more apathetic about their jobs, especially if low-wage workforces were less inclined to resist employer tactics to reduce the costs of employing workers (through gig platforms, shorter shifts, piece rates, or noncompliance with labour laws) or to undermine trade unions. Of course, these counterpoints are not reasons to deny the benefit of basic income to workers; rather they highlight the ongoing need to defend quality paid work.

Second, the deliberately 'thin' design of basic income raises serious questions about its capacity to address the structural quality of life issues facing low-wage working households. No doubt this approach appeals to liberal policymakers because it keeps questions of income distribution separate from the organisation of markets. However, an extensive basic income scheme is also expensive, forcing hellish tradeoffs between boosting cash incomes and public goods investment. Other than objecting to higher taxes, supporters of free markets would not see any dilemma here: a generous scheme would finance private welfare consumption. But evidence from plenty of experiments in welfare state quasi-markets continues to highlight problems with cost and quality. Chapter 2 focused in particular on the high costs of housing for low-income working households. Direct government intervention in areas of housing and childcare are extremely cost-effective ways of reducing living costs. For this reason, there is a growing interest in *universal public services* as opposed to a universal basic income (Coote and Yazici 2018, p 37). Universal provision of quality services is central to improved working-class living standards. They help lower the effective money wage that produces a living wage, which in turns contains costs on business. Job guarantee employment would also contribute to jobs in universalised basic services.

Finally, basic income schemes appear to be frustrated by weak electoral coalitions (Vlandas 2020) and significant compromises in the implementation phase. A wide range of countries have already experimented with basic income-type schemes (Coote and Yazici 2018, pp 27–8). The brief focus here is exclusively on rich country experiments with implications for liberal countries. First, in one instance (Switzerland in 2016), where voters had a direct say on a basic income proposal in a referendum, it was resoundingly defeated

(77% voted no). Second, some of the trial results have not been yet been particularly promising. Assessment, of course, depends on what the trials attempted to achieve and to study. The Finnish partial basic income experiment that concluded in 2018, which was provided to 2,000 long-term unemployed participants, produced contrasting assessments of its success. The job search success of recipients (versus the 'control' group) did not suggest major benefits (Martinelli 2019), but not many basic income advocates would accept these as essential. Some research emphasised improved trust but criticised the experiment's highly limited application and the difficulties in evaluating its outcomes, given the absence of baseline data (on trust and wellbeing, for instance) and by changing rules for labour market participation for the unemployed in the 'control group' (Hiilamo 2019). In any case, the new Social Democratic-led government has not pursued the policy (O'Donnell 2019).

The Canadian experiment, sponsored by the Wynne Liberal government in Ontario, was abandoned abruptly by the incoming Progressive Conservatives, with some positive survey results based on its halted phase of implementation (Ferdosi et al 2020). Finally, the Italian and Spanish basic income schemes, like the other two schemes, are far from universal and offer only low replacement benefits. Italy's has been aimed at the unemployed but was introduced at a much lower monthly level than the Five Star Movement coalition government had proposed in the lead-up to the 2017 Italian national elections. The Spanish scheme is available to 850,000 poor families and offers a very modest $1,145 per month (Graham 2020). A $15 minimum wage job for 35 hours per week offers approximately double that.

In all four cases – Finland, Ontario, Italy, and Spain – the eventual design of basic income benefits looked like more liberally administered unemployment benefits aimed at highly disadvantaged jobseekers or families. These practical experiments and policies in the policy field of basic income are a reminder of the difficulties of converting intelligent utopias into practical large-scale reform.

Conclusion: living wages and liberal welfare states in the 21st century

Writing about current events and 'live topics' makes demands on the author, particularly when it comes to discerning what is likely to genuinely matter for the future. This concluding chapter hopes to establish some of the longer-term significance of the current struggle for higher minimum wages in the English-speaking or liberal welfare states. To do this, it makes sense to return to the typology presented in the Introduction (Table I.1) as a basis for evaluating trends and prospects for living wage politics. As elsewhere, English-speaking welfare states have continued to develop and, in some areas, expand as societies age and healthcare needs have grown more expensive. Governments have been reasonably responsive in part because the Anglo-American political right is now highly electorally dependent on older voters, as the UK general election of December 2019 further demonstrated.

Nevertheless, there is a strong sense, supported by equally strong evidence, that the labour market foundations of the liberal welfare states are insufficient to avoid deteriorating living standards for low-income workers and their households and, increasingly, middle-income households. Although the English-speaking countries have developed a more active political 'left' over the past decade, there have not been many major breakthroughs where radical social democratic programmes have produced electoral majorities. The only possible exception is the Ardern Labour government of New Zealand (2017–), which has been the most socially reformist government of the liberal countries in the past decade at least at a national level. Given the strength of the political right in policy and electoral terms, the search for policies that have succeeded in dealing with labour market inequalities takes on even greater importance. Assessed on these pragmatic grounds, the forces promoting a 'thin' version of living wages policies, understood as relatively isolated measures to increase minimum wages, have made significant gains.

A thin policy of minimum wages

The Anglo-American model of deregulated labour markets, tough income support policies, and privatised social services has followed and, indeed, extended the path to post-industrialisation that Gösta

Esping-Andersen (1999) mapped out two decades ago. Liberal economists and conservative politicians can – and do – point to 'headline' improvements that underscore the successes of the neoliberal route out of the dilemmas of rich industrial societies. Before the COVID-19 shock, official unemployment had mostly declined over the past two decades. And official measures of welfare dependency are also lower. Moreover, liberal welfare states have adapted to providing *some* level of social care for ageing and changing communities of need.

The costs of the Anglo-American policy approach to employment and welfare are now considerable and continue to mount, a topic explored in Chapter 4. Too many jobs are now poor quality and do not pay well. In some jurisdictions, income support policies for vulnerable working-age populations are inadequate and increasingly overly policed. Public welfare and care services are often a patchwork that barely cover need. Workers and low-income communities struggle with high housing costs and personal finance debts, combined with the financial stresses of keeping up in expensive, status-driven worlds in which class networks once again determine opportunity and life chances. Moreover, the critical voice for democratisation at work and in politics – the labour movement – has been driven out of many workplaces, and that in turn has damaged the networks and resources for resisting the unfair burdens placed on many. Nonetheless, with a dominant political and voter coalition blocking the fiscal resources to expand welfare-based redistribution, there has been a significant build-up of pressure on labour markets to produce new institutions for justice. Without stronger trade unions in these sectors, this situation has added to pressures for statutory intervention to improve minimum standards at the bottom of the labour market. Such interventions are by no means new: a century ago, statutory minimum wages were recruited to provide minimum standards across low-wage or sweated industries where women worked and where unions struggled to organise.

The weakness of alternative policy coalitions in the liberal countries has become a longer-term problem for greater justice at work. This problem explains why a policy of lifting minimum wage floors has garnered a wide policy coalition, spanning low-wage workplaces, organised politics, unions, activist organisations, some businesses, and community anti-poverty activists. The core reasons for its breakthrough successes involve a mix of new forms of activist mobilisation emerging out of structural opportunities and policy experimentation afforded by the partial weakening of a policy monopoly in favour of low minimum wages. The most important findings of this project are summarised below.

1. **Mobilisation and coalition-building have responded to poverty wages, making the most of limited opportunities.** The Fight for $15 movement in the US has been symbolic of the living wage movement. It has produced activism across America and beyond and encouraged forms of mobilisation adapted to local industrial and political opportunities. The central structural reason for its emergence is that the employer-controlled labour markets of postindustrial America are producing too many low-wage, poor-quality jobs and there are too few institutional paths for addressing this problem. This new workers' movement, built on anger about poverty wages, gained the confidence to strike and organise communities, target local and state government, and has used ballots as tactical threats to force reform or to push past intransigent Republican administrations at state and federal levels. Although Fight for $15 is still centrally dependent on union organisation and mobilisation in the workplace, its organisation has a unique presence in the digital media and politics in raising the profile of minimum wage workers. In this respect, the Fight for $15 movement also exemplifies the 'movementisation' of politics (Meyer and Tarrow 2018), where activist organisations become critical allies for political reformers in a generally similar way that unions have in both the US and other liberal countries.

   Widespread adoption of higher minimum wages across the US in the 2020s is following a process of emulation and adaptation, to borrow Charles Tilly's (1999) terms. These achievements count as the best evidence of the wide progressive coalitions that unions and activists are building. It is possible that, sometime in the 2020s, the US will legislate for a federal minimum wage of $15, which the House of Representatives passed in 2019. But unlike previous national-led welfare state reforms of the 1930s and 1960s, the struggle for a living minimum wage has emerged despite national blocks on reform – literally from cities to states across America. It remains to be seen whether the greater activism across communities, cities, and states on this issue will generate wider demands for the next steps – an indexation of minimum wages to protect living standards from political hiatuses and pressure for a job guarantee to ensure that a modest living wage is more recession proof and extends to more low-wage jobs. The enhanced role of states as 'laboratories of democracy' (Reed, in Gingrich et al 2018, p 7) is itself a significant development.

2. **Old alliances can still build new institutions.** In other liberal countries, working-class political disenfranchisement is less pronounced than it is in the US. Still, the level of responsiveness to wage-earners by centre-left parties has been the subject of a long and drawn-out debate. Rather cautious Labour-led experiments in the UK and New Zealand that began two decades ago, however, illustrate the longer-term impact of institutions built from 'old' alliances between unions and labour parties. In fact, these policies were responses to the ultra-liberal policy reforms in both countries in the 1980s and 1990s. The Blair Labour government exemplified this caution, responding to unions with a modest statutory national minimum wage to be determined by the government in Westminster on the advice of the Low Pay Commission.

As Pierson (1994) has shown convincingly, policy generates politics. Labour in office steadily improved the Kaitz index of the minimum wage. But a spectacular about-face by the Cameron Conservative-led government to rebrand the minimum wage as the National Living Wage proved significant in two ways. It reversed long-standing Tory opposition to minimum wages, guaranteeing a consensus in UK politics in favour of staged improvements in the minimum wage to a Kaitz score of around 60% in 2020. The Conservatives had a series of complex political and fiscal motives. They recruited what Grover (2016) called a 'weak predistributive' strategy to compensate low-income households from the fallout of severe cuts to social expenditures, and to protect the government from accusations of a return to Thatcherism.

New Zealand Labour throughout the 2000s followed the UK in expanding the greater predistributive role for the minimum wage. In NZ's case, this involved an instance of policy *conversion* (Béland 2007), reviving previously dormant minimum wage legislation, which was then recruited to perform a similar function in distributing incomes as the old award system that NZ had abandoned in the early 1990s. The minimum wage formed a central 'headline' in the Labour-led government's coalition agreement with the nationalist New Zealand First. It was a simple and practical way that the centre-left coalition led by NZ Labour could demonstrate commitment to low-paid NZ workers crucial to the party at election time. NZ's minimum wage has by far the highest Kaitz index of the liberal countries – the product of two Labour governments, support from the National Party, and near full-employment conditions. New rounds of OECD data in the early 2020s may well show that NZ has reduced the incidence of low-wage full-time employment to below the levels found in Nordic countries, which rely on industry-level bargaining to drive down the number of low-paid jobs.

Canadian developments also deserve further comment because that country appears to be poised to develop national living wage institutions over the 2020s. Here again, this is a response to subfederal policy experimentation, this time from Canada's powerful provinces that have authority over pay and labour law. Three progressive governments in Alberta, British Columbia, and Ontario (two New Democratic, one Liberal) legislated for C$15 minimum wages and improved protections for wage-earners. These governments have increased low minimum wages in a system with otherwise stable protections for unionised collective bargaining, thereby expanding the direct impact on minimum wages to over 10% of Canadian wage-earners. A confluence of supportive factors has encouraged reforms: strong centre-left party representation in key provinces; union pressure for legislative action; and greater confidence to act, given developments in its influential neighbour.

3. **Living wage reforms have been central to a messy, ongoing repositioning of centre-left politics.** Centre-left political elites have been under considerable pressure, particularly in the US and the UK where democratic socialists Bernie Sanders and Jeremy Corbyn energised younger electorates in unsecure jobs, often saddled with high student debts, as well as migrant and minority workers subsisting on poverty wages. A large group of voters are now frustrated with the inert centrism of centre-left parties. In the case of conservative workers, those frustrations have boosted electoral support for rightwing populists inside and outside mainstream conservative parties. These competing pressures have forced action and repositioning in centre-left politics. In the US, Democratic governors have in part responded to the unions and Fight for $15 on higher minimum wages because of the *threats* emerging on the left in the form of candidates who appeal to voters frustrated by inert politics. Higher minimum wages – in their thin policy version – do not commit to wider revision of labour market institutions likely to provoke fierce business resistance. But they do produce modest redistribution from business to workers. And they represent visible and tactical commitments that appeal to younger, progressive, and poorer voters. The central place of living wage commitments to the governing pact of Prime Minister Ardern in New Zealand is a good illustration of a national leader using a

living wage platform in repositioning her Labour Party to the left of the social liberalism of previous Labour governments.

Centre-left parties need working-class voters and the living wage ambition is a policy that serves that political end. The voter base for living wages is also a solid starting point for what Piketty (2020) identifies as the search for new egalitarian coalitions. While voter support for tax-and-spend redistributive measures remains steady in high-quality surveys, there are recent examples of social democratic platforms from Australia and the UK – ones that made honest commitments to higher taxes – being rebuffed by voters. However, a wider coalition of voters is supportive of higher minimum wages and that has been demonstrated by several developments in the past few years. Perhaps the best evidence of this fact comes from examples in the most difficult of political territories. The political right in the US has failed to dismantle higher minimum wages and conservative electorates have supported ballots for higher minimum wages in red states in the US, such as Arizona in 2016, Missouri in 2018, and the swing state of Florida in 2020. These successes do not prove that red and swing state voters are moving to the left, but they do indicate that living wage campaigns are popular with voters, notably working-class conservatives. Greater policy emphasis and voter mobilisation over clear and achievable wage-earner improvements are likely to remain significant political assets to labour and progressive liberal parties in the 2020s.

4. **The policy monopoly stabilising low minimum wage policies has been disrupted.** So far, I have focused on mostly structural, workplace, and political factors in accounting for the rise of living wage policies and politics. But these have critically depended on *ideational* developments discussed in Chapter 3. Policies exist in stable form for long periods of time because a set of interests, organisations, activists, and networks stabilise and protect them from alternatives. But policy monopolies (Meyer 2003) occasionally undergo major disruption from new evidence or paradigms, or from powerful challengers with different ways of framing policy problems and their solutions. Here, I have argued that the challenge came from methodological innovation and evidence from within the economics profession itself in the 1990s as well as bolder reformers taking risks in raising minimum wages.

The policy monopoly in favour of low minimum wages (and against living wages) has been sustained by orthodox economists who have enjoyed decades-long influence over policymakers on the right as well as the centre-left. Contrarian findings in the 1990s from US economists studying fast-food workers changed that. Since then, economists, freed from dogmatic assumptions, have followed the braver wage experiments around the liberal world, conducting research on the employment impacts of higher minimums. Although there is far from a new consensus, the evidence so far does not support claims of large negative impacts – or even any impact – on aggregate employment due to higher minimums (Dube 2019a, p 50). This conclusion broadly extends to the employment impacts of higher wage floors on marginally positioned workers as well. The loosening of the influence of the orthodox policy monopoly has no doubt been a driving influence on the willingness of politicians to champion living wages. At the same time, it has made it possible for a broader range of sociological evidence to come into public view – evidence slowly mounting over the decades confirming the prosocial impact of higher minimum wages on worker wellbeing, social engagement, and job performance (Desmond 2019). These considerations are ignored in artificially narrow debates focused on often tiny adjustments to employment levels.

5. **Welfare reform and political limits on redistributive budgets are increasing long-term pressure for predistribution.** Liberal welfare states are distinct for their low replacement benefits, inconsistent and frustratingly discontinuous institutions, and deregulated labour markets. Like all welfare states, the liberal countries have responded with greater spending and resources to the health, pension, and care needs of an ageing population. By contrast, evidence in Chapter 4 shows that liberal countries spend comparatively less on their working-age populations, although there is considerable variation between expenditures in the US (very low) and in the UK (higher).

In seeking explanations for the rise of living wage politics, this book has deliberately kept in view those significant, negative developments in welfare policy for the working-age population for a clear reason. As a whole, these developments amount to what Tcherneva (2017) calls 'welfare state sabotage', which one can interpret as further altering the functional role of low-wage labour markets in modern society. Workfare policies are ultimately designed to engineer dependence on low-wage labour markets which in turn these markets are poorly equipped to handle. Policy directions in three countries – the US, Australia, and the UK – have been particularly influenced by harsh benefit reform, encouraged by the 1990s neoconservative push for workfare in the US. These policies, like low minimum wages, have achieved paradigmatic status in policy terms because of their popularity with voters, politicians, and administrators looking to reduce spending on welfare dependence. Their supporters claim reduced dependency rates and improved work participation. Dependency rates have certainly fallen. But it has been difficult to isolate the impact of welfare reform from general improvements in employment. What seems more certain is that inadequate and overly regulated benefit systems have contributed to more low-income Americans dropping out of work and welfare institutions altogether. Moreover, at a macro level, there is little or no evidence of improved working-age poverty rates in the three countries pursuing workfare furthest.

Still, there are unknowns: Are harsh benefit systems deterring legitimate claimants who avoid benefits, drop out of institutions, or stay in jobs they do not like? The absence of a social safety net outside a paid job may well contribute to increased pressure on workers to keep a job – even a low paid or unpleasant one – at any price. The clear implication is that improved minimum wages become an even more critical policy response to harsh welfare reforms, especially if the policy and voter coalitions required to humanise workfare policies are weak and still forming. The more workers depend on minimum wage jobs in these environments, the more they need to be secure and able to cover living costs.

Living wage welfare states in the 2020s

This book ends by sketching out – perhaps optimistically – where a living wage welfare state might sit in a revised welfare state typology for the 2020s. It depends on ongoing voter and worker mobilisation but also growing awareness from elites about the damaging direction that the Anglo-American model of capitalism and ultra-liberalised labour markets has taken (Cass 2018; Naidu 2020). A model promoting profits by defeating organised labour and entrenching managerial control in the workplace furthers low productivity and worker insecurity in overextended labour markets, ones unchecked by responsive social security and labour market policy. Low replacement rate benefits and tightly policed welfare contribute to the problems of low-wage labour markets: too often, workers are forced into income-losing transitions or poorly matched job opportunities. Public subsidies through the social security system also contribute to the proliferation of low-wage jobs. Further developments in capitalist work organisation using technology and legal power threaten to entrench insecure employment for the next generation, with profound implications for opportunities for younger generations and the design of social security systems. Societies are producing skilled workers but too many jobs without career paths, security, and fair pay.

Table C.1 compares three 'ideal types' of welfare approaches primarily to situate a living wage welfare state between what I shall call a conservative liberal model and the social democratic model exemplified by the Nordic approach. My intention is to avoid proposing a raft of ways of building a 'living wage welfare state' that are really only a wish list for social democracy. The conservative liberal model is familiar by now. It combines an unchecked managerial capitalist model of work organisation that is buttressed by workfare and a limited social safety net. Employment is subject to the economic cycle, with the costs of downturns realised in rising inequality and the scarring of low-paid, insecure, and indebted workforces.

The living wage welfare model nonetheless builds on the structural foundations and weaknesses of the Anglo-American social model and the political opportunities for reform that are present. This model must necessarily exceed the limits set by the conservative liberal approach or even a 'thin' adaptation to higher minimum wages – even if a living wage model falls short of a recognisable social democratic transformation. In sketching the living wage model, there is an assumption that the power resources of the labour movement in liberal countries will remain insufficient to reinstitutionalise widespread

Table C.1: Comparing liberal, living wage, and social democratic welfare states

	Conservative liberal	Living wage liberal	Social democratic
Minimum wages	Low	Higher wage floors, adjusted for living costs	High wage floors achieved by industry bargaining
Welfare support	Time limited and/or low replacement rate; workfare focused	EITC-style tax credit or partial basic income	Universalism/social insurance
Social services	Mix of public and private	Universal basic services (housing and childcare)	Universal with some privatisation
Collective wage-earner institutions	Weak with an enterprise focus	Similar to liberal model or wages boards	Union-coordinated industry bargaining
Employment policies	Economic cycle	Job guarantee and/ or expanded labour market policies	Large public sector and active labour market policies

wage-earner institutions for the foreseeable future. Higher wage floors must additionally address living costs and wage floors must be sustained through regular, expert-informed adjustment processes and adequate monitoring and enforcement of labour standards. Related to this will be the development of a pro-worker response to the damaging downsides of the reorganisation of employment in the gig economy and pervasive underpayment of workers. Some countries and subnational jurisdictions (such as California) have attempted important steps in this direction already.

Minimum wages that approximate living wages may provide improvements in the pay and living standards of up to a third of the workforce. However, as Dube (2019c) notes, the broader crisis in wage levels will require even greater public intervention. One ambitious development would be to legislate for industry bargaining (where the minimum wage would be set sectorally by industry negotiations) but this is politically unlikely in liberal countries like the US. Dube (2019c; Dube et al 2020) sees the Australian model of 'wages boards' (industrial awards set and adjusted by a national commission) as one way of setting pay and conditions for above-minimum wage workers who have lost out from the decline of collective bargaining across the liberal countries. Ireland also maintains wages councils with less extensive powers and functions. Dube (2019c) further notes that, for the US to adopt this wages board approach, 'federal law would need to be changed' – and that would require unlikely Congressional action. But he adds that 'at least five states (Arizona, Colorado, California, New Jersey, and New York) already have legislation on the books that allows for constituting wage boards by industry or occupation'.

Based on the discoveries of this book, three further living wage welfare reforms must be seen as essential. The first two point to the need for greater intervention in housing and childcare markets to reduce costs for working-class families and to put women's employment opportunities on an equal footing to men's. Here, the movement for universal basic services treats housing and childcare as public goods. Ironically, the overextension of markets in both areas is adding considerably to the money wages required to avoid working poverty. A combination of living wage employment, massive investment in social housing, and universal childcare provide a stronger and more gender-equal foundation for working-class living standards than a basic income, especially one likely to be achieved through compromises. The evidence of the productivity, tax, and employment benefits of universal high-quality childcare services is overwhelming (Esping-Andersen 2009).

One further set of commitments is imperative. The global downturn that came in 2020 with the COVID-19 pandemic has severely damaged low-wage labour markets, forcing the extension of social security payments in countries like Australia and the US. No doubt the 2020s will bring renewed calls to respond to the crisis through a return to market-clearing wage austerity and even greater deregulation of labour conditions. This platform will once again gather a powerful coalition of supporters. However, if the pro-work rhetoric of the liberal welfare model is to be realised with greater equality, it makes sense that experimentation with high wage floors is matched with effective 'floors' for job security in low-wage labour markets. Proposals for a job guarantee are emerging as a cost-effective way of ensuring countercyclical employment stability by ensuring adequate living wage jobs for unemployed or underemployed workers. These proposals would be more expensive than Tcherneva's (2018) earlier estimates, given the extent of current unemployment, but such a 'public option' would reinforce living wages. Still, job guarantees need to be weighed against other progressive labour market options such as wage subsidies – and progressives would need to safeguard such programmes from a conservative 'conversion' into sub-minimum wage workfare.

Living wage reforms protected by limited public job guarantees, buttressed by greater public investment in housing and childcare, aim at protecting minimum standards of work and dignity in the liberal-style labour market. They do not deal with the broader problems of inequality at work. Restoring the rights of unions to organise, take industrial action, and bargain collectively is consistent with a progressive version of liberal freedom and would help address the crisis of predistribution. These proposals are ultimately aimed at taking the realities of the liberal model that is now in clear transition, and suggesting how they might be encouraged in a social democratic and pro-worker direction.

Notes

Introduction

[1] *The Economist* (2015) 'The new Conservatism', 11 July. Available from: www. economist.com/leaders/2015/07/11/the-new-conservatism.

[2] Kaitz index scores express the ratio or percentage of hourly minimum wages to the median (or average) full-time hourly earnings. They can be interpreted as a measure of generosity to the lowest-paid workers in the formal labour market, but high Kaitz indexes can be produced by falling median wages as well. They can be interpreted in a similar way to relative poverty measures and do not take into consideration the purchasing power of wages.

Chapter 1

[1] The Wikipedia page updates for Canadian minimum wage changes and variations, including concessional rates and indexation formulas (where they apply). See: https://en.wikipedia.org/wiki/Minimum_wage_in_Canada.

Chapter 2

[1] I am grateful to Professor Peter Saunders of the University of New South Wales Social Policy Research Centre for pointing to some features of living cost calculations, particularly the distinction between normative and behavioural approaches to these calculations.

[2] Mead, however, is clear about the limits of his version of paternalism: 'unlike the work issue they [the public] are not impatient and moralistic with marriage breakdown' (Mead, cited in Ramesh 2010).

[3] Recent studies of unemployment insurance suggest that more generous schemes improve job matches because workers have the option of waiting for better matches to come along (Tatsimaros 2020). One implication of this finding is that the incentive structure of time-limited and/or low replacement rate benefits reinforces a low-wage employment regime with a weak focus on improving job matching.

[4] Rickard (1984, pp 175–7) observes that Higgins' motivations about male breadwinner wages indirectly dealt with the situation of women in the family. At the same time, Higgins deals with the issue of equal pay for women, in part because of the threat that low-paid women might pose to the jobs of male breadwinners.

[5] Even the most enlightened early defences of living wages did not deal with the structural inequalities inherent in the income shares between labour and capital. Bryan (2008) argues, for instance, in the Australian case that Justice Higgins framed worker entitlements to fair wages as entirely about adequately covering the costs of living. However, the arbitration system in Australia and New Zealand did institutionalise the capacity for unions to push for higher award wages that shared in the economic surplus.

Chapter 4

[1] *The Economist* (2019) 'Across the rich world, an extraordinary jobs boom is under way', 23 May. Available from: www.economist.com/briefing/2019/05/23/across-the-rich-world-an-extraordinary-jobsboom-is-under-way.

[2] The Wikipedia entry for the 2019 Alberta general election reports a 15,000 vote gain for Alberta's New Democratic Party, which was nonetheless easily defeated by a reunited Conservative Party that also benefited from a higher turnout. Notley's period in office has, however, created a more even left–right competition in that province.

Chapter 5

[1] This term derives from the combination of practical, obtainable politics, and the utopian vision laid out in the political vision of reformist Swedish socialist Ernst Wigforss. See Higgins and Dow (2013).

[2] Following Autor and Salomons (2018, pp 1–2), this reduction ultimately involves the 'wages bill' and can come from cuts to hours, wages, or total staffing.

[3] Here, I am referring to Polanyi's observations in *The Great Transformation* about the 'pauperisation' of employment produced by outdoor relief in the Speenhamland system.

References

Abbott, T. (2000) 'Renewing the social fabric: Mutual obligation and work for the dole', *Policy*, Spring, pp 38–42.

ACTU (Australian Council of Trade Unions) (2016) *ACTU Submission: Annual Wage Review 2016–17*. Available from: www.actu.org.au/media/1033223/actu-submission-2016-17-annual-wage-review-initial-submission.pdf.

Adams-Prassi, A. (2020) 'Welfare policy & alternative work arrangements', The IFS Deaton Review workshop: Welfare and the low-wage labour market, 1 October, Institute of Fiscal Studies. Available from: www.ifs.org.uk/inequality/wp-content/uploads/2020/10/Adams-Prassl.pdf.

Alvaredo, F., Atkinson, A.B., Piketty, T. and Saez, E. (2013) 'The top 1 percent in international and historical perspective', *Journal of Economic Perspectives*, 27(3): 3–20.

Alsos, K., Nergaard, K. and van den Heuvel, A. (2019) 'Collective bargaining as a tool to ensure a living wage: Experiences from the Nordic countries', *Transfer: European Review of Labour and Research*, 25(3): 351–65.

Amable, B., Gatti, D. and Schumacher, J. (2006) 'Welfare-state retrenchment: The partisan effect revisited', *Oxford Review of Economic Policy*, 22(3): 426–44.

Amato, S. (2020) 'Minimum wage increase was wrong but UCP platform committed to keep it: Kenney', CTV News. Available from: https://edmonton.ctvnews.ca/minimum-wage-increase-was-wrong-but-ucp-platform-committed-to-keep-it-kenney-1.4990861.

Andriotis, A., Brown, K. and Shifflett, S. (2019) 'Families go deep in debt to stay in the middle class', *The Wall Street Journal*, 1 August. Available from: www.wsj.com/articles/families-go-deep-in-debt-to-stay-in-the-middle-class-11564673734.

Angus Reid Institute (2017) 'Six-in-ten Ontario residents support legislation to raise minimum wage to $15 per hour'. Available from: http://angusreid.org/ontario-minimum-wage/.

Anker, R. (2006) 'Living wages around the world: A new methodology and internationally comparable estimates', *International Labour Review*, 145(4): 309–38.

APHA (American Public Health Association) (2016) 'Improving health by increasing the minimum wage', 1 November. Available from: www.apha.org/policies-and-advocacy/public-health-policy-statements/policy-database/2017/01/18/improving-health-by-increasing-minimum-wage.

Arendt, H. ([1958] 1998) *The Human Condition*, 2nd edn, Chicago: University of Chicago Press.

Atkinson, A.B. (2015) *Inequality: What Can Be Done?*, Harvard, MA: Harvard University Press.

Australian Bureau of Statistics (2019) *6306.0 Employee Earnings and Hours*, May 2018. Available from: www.abs.gov.au/statistics/labour/earnings-and-work-hours/employee-earnings-and-hours-australia/latest-release.

Autor, D. and Salomons, A. (2018) 'Is automation labor-displacing? Productivity growth, employment, and the labor share', Brookings Papers on Economic Activity, BPEA Conference Drafts, 8–9 March.

Bavel, J.J., Baicker, K., Boggio, P.S. et al (2020) 'Using social and behavioural science to support COVID-19 pandemic response', *Nature Human Behavior*, 4(5): 460–71.

Bean, C. and McAllister, I. (2009) 'The Australian election survey: The tale of the rabbit-less hat: Voting behaviour in 2007', *Australian Cultural History*, 27(2): 205–18.

Beatty, C. and Fothergill, S. (2017) 'The impact on welfare and public finances of job loss in industrial Britain', *Regional Studies, Regional Science*, 4(1): 161–80.

Beatty, C. and Fothergill, S. (2018) 'Welfare reform in the UK 2010-16: Expectations, outcomes and local impacts', *Social Policy & Administration*, 52(5): 950–68.

Beckfield, J. (2020) 'Rising inequality is not balanced by intergenerational mobility', *Proceedings of the National Academy of Sciences*, 117(1): 23–5.

Béland, D. (2007) 'Ideas and institutional change in social security: Conversion, layering, and policy drift', *Social Science Quarterly*, 88(1): 20–38.

Bignall, M. (2019) 'Average UK household debt now stands at record £15,400', *The Guardian*, 7 January. Available from www.theguardian.com/business/2019/jan/07/average-uk-household-debt-now-stands-at-record-15400.

Bishop, J. and Cassidy, N. (2019) 'Wages growth by pay-setting method', Reserve Bank of Australia Bulletin, June. Available from: www.rba.gov.au/publications/bulletin/2019/jun/wages-growth-by-pay-setting-method.html.

Blanchflower, D.G. (2019) *Not Working: Where Have All the Good Jobs Gone?*, Princeton: Princeton University Press.

Bluestone, B. and Harrison, B. (1988) 'The growth of low-wage employment: 1963-86', *American Economic Review*, 78(2): 124–8.

Boeri, T. (2012) 'Setting the minimum wage', *Labour Economics*, 19(3): 281–90.

Bonoli, G. (2003) 'Social policy through labor markets: Understanding national differences in the provision of economic security to wage earners', *Comparative Political Studies*, 36(9): 1007–30.

Borland, J. and Tseng, Y. (2004) 'Does "work for the dole" work?', Melbourne Institute Working Paper 14/4, July. Available from: https://minerva-access.unimelb.edu.au/bitstream/handle/11343/33797/66032_00000576_01_wp2004n14.pdf?sequence=1&isAllowed=y.

Borland, J. and Tseng, Y. (2011) 'Does "work for the dole" work? An Australian perspective on work experience programmes', *Applied Economics*, 43(28): 4353–68.

Bosch, G. (2009) 'Low-wage work in five European countries and the United States', *International Labour Review*, 148(4): 337–56.

Bosch, G. (2018) 'The making of the German minimum wage: A case study of institutional change', *Industrial Relations Journal*, 49(1): 19–33.

Boushey, H. (2002) 'Staying employed after welfare', Economic Policy Institute Briefing Paper #128. Available from: www.epi.org/publication/briefingpapers_bp128/.

Bown, C.P. and Freund, C. (2019) *The Problem of US Labor Force Participation*, Petersen Institute of International Economics, Working Paper 19.1. Available from: www.piie.com/research/economic-issues/labor.

Brady, D. and Lee, H.Y. (2014) 'The rise and fall of government spending in affluent democracies, 1971–2008', *Journal of European Social Policy*, 24(1): 56–79.

Brown, W. (2017) 'The toxic politicising of the national minimum wage', *Employee Relations*, 39(6): 785–9.

Brown, W. and Wright, C.F. (2018) 'Policies for decent labour standards in Britain', *The Political Quarterly*, 89(3): 482–9.

Bryan, D. (2008) 'Minimum living standards and the working-class surplus: Higgins, Henderson and housing', *Labour History*, 95: 213–21.

Buchanan, J. and Oliver, D. (2014) 'Choice and fairness: The hollow core of industrial relations policy', in C. Miller and L. Orchard (eds) *Australian Public Policy: Progressive Ideas in the Neoliberal Ascendency*, Bristol: Policy Press, pp 97–113.

Buddelmeyer, H., Lee, W.S. and Wooden, M. (2010) 'Low-paid employment and unemployment dynamics in Australia', *Economic Record*, 86(272): 28–48.

Burawoy, M. (2018) 'Michael Burawoy on sociology and the workplace', Sage Research Methods. Available from: https://methods.sagepub.com/podcast/michael-burawoy-on-sociology-and-the-workplace.

Bureau of Labor Statistics (2018) 'Characteristics of minimum wage workers, 2018', Bureau of Labor Statistics Report 1078. Available from: www.bls.gov/opub/reports/minimum-wage/2018/home.htm.

Campbell, A.F. (2018) 'Voters just gave nearly 1 million workers a raise in 2 red states', *Vox*, 7 November. Available from: www.vox.com/2018/11/7/18071804/minimum-wage-arkansas-missouri-election-ballot-measure.

Campolieti, M. (2015) 'Minimum wages and wage spillovers in Canada', *Canadian Public Policy*, 41(1): 15–34.

Canadian Labour Congress (n.d.) 'Canadians deserve decent pay'. Available from: https://minimumwage.canadianlabour.ca/.

Card, D. and Krueger, A.B. (1993) 'Minimum wages and employment: A case study of the fast-food industry in New Jersey and Pennsylvania', NBER Working Paper No. 4509, October.

Card, D. and Krueger, A.B. ([1995] 2015) *Myth and Measurement: The New Economics of the Minimum Wage: Twentieth-Anniversary Edition*, Princeton, NJ: Princeton University Press.

Carney, T. and Stanford, J. (2018) *Dimensions of Insecure Work: A Factbook*, Centre for Future Work. Available from: www.futurework.org.au/the_dimensions_of_insecure_work.

Cass, O. (2018) *The Once and Future Worker: A Vision for the Renewal of Work in America*, New York: Encounter Books.

Cassidy, J. (2014) 'Piketty's inequality story in six charts', *The New Yorker*, 26 March. Available from: www.newyorker.com/news/john-cassidy/pikettys-inequality-story-in-six-charts.

Castles, F.G. (1985) *The Working Class and Welfare: Reflections on the Political Development of the Welfare State in Australia and New Zealand, 1890–1980*, Sydney: Allen & Unwin.

Castles, F.G. (2010) 'The English-speaking countries', in F.G. Castles, S. Leibfried, J. Lewis, H. Obinger and C. Pierson (eds) *The Oxford Handbook of the Welfare State*, Oxford: Oxford University Press, pp 630–42.

Castles, F.G. and Mitchell, D. (1993) 'Worlds of welfare and families of nations', in F.G. Castles (ed.) *Families of Nations: Patterns of Public Policy in Western Democracies*, Aldershot: Dartmouth, pp 93–128.

Cazes, S., Garnero, A. and Martin, S. (2017) 'The state of trade unions, employer organisations, and collective bargaining in OECD countries', *Vox: CEPR Policy Portal*. Available at: https://voxeu.org/article/trade-unions-employer-organisations-and-collective-bargaining-oecd-countries.

Cazes, S., Hijzen, A. and Saint-Martin, A. (2015) *Measuring and Assessing Job Quality: The OECD Job Quality Framework*, OECD Social, Employment and Migration Working Papers. Available from: http://dx.doi.org/10.1787/5jrp02kjw1mr-en.

Cazes, S., Verick, S. and Al Hussami, F. (2013) 'Why did unemployment respond so differently to the global financial crisis across countries? Insights from Okun's Law', *IZA Journal of Labor Policy*, 2(10): 1–18.

Center on Budget and Policy Priorities (2019) 'Policy basics: The earned income tax credit'. Available from: www.cbpp.org/sites/default/files/atoms/files/policybasics-eitc.pdf.

Charlton, E. (2018) 'These countries have the highest minimum wages', World Economic Forum: Agenda. Available from: www.weforum.org/agenda/2018/12/these-countries-have-the-highest-minimum-wages/.

CNN (2016) 'Ballot measures'. Available from: https://edition.cnn.com/election/2016/results/ballot-measures.

Coletta, M., de Bonis, R. and Piermattei, S. (2019) 'Household debt in OECD countries: The role of supply-side and demand-side factors', *Social Indicators Research*, 143(3): 1185–217.

Collinson, A. (2019) 'Record household debt levels show why works need a new deal', Trades Union Congress blog, 5 September. Available from: www.tuc.org.uk/blogs/record-household-debt-levels-show-why-workers-need-new-deal.

Cominetti, N. (2019) *Calculating a Living Wage for London and the Rest of the UK: 2019–20, Resolution*, November. Available from: www.livingwage.org.uk/sites/default/files/Living-wage-calculation-2019-20.pdf.

Cominetti, N., Henehan, K. and Clarke, S. (2019) *Low Pay Britain 2019*, Resolution Foundation Report. Available from: www.resolutionfoundation.org/publications/low-pay-britain-2019/.

Conger, K. and Scheiber, N. (2019) 'California bill makes app-based companies treat workers as employees', *The New York Times*, 11 September. Available from: www.nytimes.com/2019/09/11/technology/california-gig-economy-bill.html.

Congressional Budget Office (2019) 'The effects on employment and family income of increasing the federal minimum wage'. Available from: www.cbo.gov/publication/55410.

Cooper, D. (2019) 'Raising the federal minimum wage to $15 by 2024 would lift pay for nearly 40 million workers', Economic Policy Institute, 5 February. Available from: www.epi.org/publication/raising-the-federal-minimum-wage-to-15-by-2024-would-lift-pay-for-nearly-40-million-workers/.

Coote, A. and Yazici, E. (2018) *Universal Basic Income: A Report for Unions*, New Economics Foundation. Available from: www.world-psi.org/sites/default/files/documents/research/en_ubi_full_report_2019.pdf.

Corder, L. (2019) *Survey of US Economists on a $15 Federal Minimum Wage*, Employment Policies Institute. Available from: www.epionline.org/studies/survey-of-us-economists-on-a-15-federal-minimum-wage-2/.

Cranston, M. (2019) 'Lowest paid are in richest 20pc of households, survey shows', *Australian Financial Review*, 13 March. Available from: www.afr.com/policy/economy/lowest-paid-are-in-richest-20pc-of-households-survey-shows-20190311-h1c8zl.

Dahlgreen, W. (2014) 'Cross-party support for raising minimum wage', YouGov, 12 January. Available from: https://yougov.co.uk/topics/politics/articles-reports/2014/01/12/cross-party-support-raising-minimum-wage.

Davidson, P., Saunders, P., Bradbury, B. and Wong, M. (2018) *Poverty in Australia, 2018*. ACOSS/UNSW Poverty and Inequality Partnership Report No. 2, Sydney: Australian Council of Social Service.

Davis, L. and Hartig, H. (2019) 'Two-thirds of Americans favor raising federal minimum wage to $15 an hour', Pew Research Center, 30 July. Available from: www.pewresearch.org/fact-tank/2019/07/30/two-thirds-of-americans-favor-raising-federal-minimum-wage-to-15-an-hour/.

Deeming, C. (2015) 'Foundations of the workfare state: Reflections on the political transformation of the welfare state in Britain', *Social Policy & Administration*, 49(7): 862–86.

Derry, K. and Douglas, P.H. (1922) 'The minimum wage in Canada', *Journal of Political Economy*, 1(30): 155–88.

Desmond, M. (2019) 'The future of work: Dollars on the margin', *The New York Times Magazine*, 21 February. Available at: www.nytimes.com/interactive/2019/02/21/magazine/minimum-wage-saving-lives.html.

Detragiache, E., Ebeke, C., Jirasavetakul, L.F., Kirabaeva, K., Malacrino, D., Misch, F. Park, H.W. and Shi, Y. (2020) 'A European minimum wage: Implications for poverty and macroeconomic imbalances', IMF Working Paper, no. 59, May. Available from: www.imf.org/en/Publications/WP/Issues/2020/05/22/A-European-Minimum-Wage-Implications-for-Poverty-and-Macroeconomic-Imbalances-49453.

Dionne-Simard, D. and Miller, J. (2019) 'Maximum insights on minimum wage workers: 20 years of data', Statistics Canada, 11 September. Available from: www150.statcan.gc.ca/n1/pub/75-004-m/75-004-m2019003-eng.htm.

Doucouliagos, H. and Stanley, T.D. (2009) 'Publication selection bias in minimum-wage research? A meta-regression analysis', *British Journal of Industrial Relations*, 47(2): 406–28.

Dow, W.H., Godøy A., Lowenstein, C.A. and Reich, M. (2019) 'Can economic policies reduce deaths of despair?', IRLE Working Paper No. 104-19. Available from: http://irle.berkeley.edu/files/2019/04/Can-Economic-Policies-Reduce-Deaths-of-Despair.pdf.

Dreier, P. (2016) 'How the Fight for 15 won', *The American Prospect*, 4 April. Available from: https://prospect.org/article/how-fight-15-won.

Dromey, J. (2018) 'Power to the people: How stronger unions can deliver economic justice', Institute for Public Policy Discussion Paper, May. Available at: www.ippr.org/files/2018-06/cej-trade-unions-may18-.pdf.

Dube, A. (2019a) *Impacts of Minimum Wages: Review of the International Evidence*. Available at: www.gov.uk/government/publications.

Dube, A. (2019b) 'Minimum wages and the distribution of family incomes', *American Economic Journal: Applied Economics*, 11(4): 268–304.

Dube, A. (2019c) 'Wages boards can mitigate market failures on inequality', *The Hill*, 13 March. Available at: https://thehill.com/opinion/finance/433915-wage-boards-can-mitigate-market-failures-on-inequality.

Dube, A., Amherst, U. and NBER (2020) 'The future of minimum wages, and complementary policies', Welfare and the low wage labour market, IFS/CEP conference. Available from: www.ifs.org.uk/inequality/wp-content/uploads/2020/10/Dube.pdf.

Economic Policy Institute (2019) 'Why America needs a $15 minimum wage', 5 February. Available from: www.epi.org/publication/why-america-needs-a-15-minimum-wage/.

Edin, K. and Shaefer, L. (2016) *$2.00 a Day: Living on Almost Nothing in America*, New York: Houghton Mifflin Harcourt.

Eichel, L. (2020) 'How Philadelphia's minimum wage compares with other U.S. cities', Pew Trusts. Available from: www.pewtrusts.org/en/research-and-analysis/issue-briefs/2020/05/how-philadelphias-minimum-wage-compares-with-other-us-cities.

Elliott, L. (2019) 'Tories try to woo low-paid with vow to raise national living wage', *The Guardian*, 1 October. Available from: www.theguardian.com/uk-news/2019/sep/30/conservatives-pledge-raise-national-living-wage-by-2024.

Employment and Social Development Canada (2019) *Federal Minimum Wage: Issue Paper*, January. Available from: www.canada.ca/content/dam/esdc-edsc/documents/services/reports/SPAWID-SPLR-IssuePaper-MinWage-FINAL-EN.pdf.

Esping-Andersen, G. (1985) *Politics against Markets: The Social Democratic Road to Power*, Princeton, NJ: Princeton University Press.

Esping-Andersen, G. (1990) *The Three Worlds of Welfare Capitalism*, Princeton, NJ: Princeton University Press.

Esping-Andersen, G. (1999) *Social Foundations of Postindustrial Economies*, Oxford: Oxford University Press.

Esping-Andersen, G. (2009) *The Incomplete Revolution: Adapting Welfare States to Women's New Roles*, Cambridge: Polity.

Esping-Andersen, G. and Regini, M. (2000) *Why Deregulate Labour Markets?*, Oxford: Oxford University Press.

Faraday, F. (2019) 'We can no longer ignore the exploitation of migrant workers in Canada', *The Globe and Mail*, 8 April. Available from: www.theglobeandmail.com/opinion/article-we-can-no-longer-ignore-the-exploitation-of-migrant-workers-in-canada/.

Fawcett, E. (2014) *Liberalism: The Life of An Idea*, Princeton, NJ: Princeton University Press.

Ferdosi, M., McDowell, T., Lewchuk, W. and Ross, S. (2020) *Southern Ontario's Basic Income Experience*, McMaster University Labour Studies, March. Available from: https://labourstudies.mcmaster.ca/documents/southern-ontarios-basic-income-experience.pdf.

Ford, M. (2015) *The Rise of the Robots: Technology and the Threat of a Jobless Future*, New York: Basic Books.

Foster, J.B. (2006) 'The household debt bubble', *Monthly Review*, 58(1): 1–11.

Freeman, S.R. (2007) *Rawls*, London: Routledge.

Freeman, R., Boxall, P. and Haynes, P. (eds) (2007) *What Workers Say: Employee Voice in the Anglo-American Workplace*, Ithaca: Cornell University/ILR Press.

Frey, C.B., Berger, T. and Chen, C. (2018) 'Political machinery: Did robots swing the 2016 US presidential election?', *Oxford Review of Economic Policy*, 34(3): 418–42.

Friedman, M. (1966) 'The case for a negative income tax: A view from the right', in *Proceedings of the National Symposium on Guaranteed Income*, 9 December. Washington, DC: U.S. Chamber of Commerce. Available from: https://miltonfriedman.hoover.org/objects/57681/the-case-for-the-negative-income-tax-a-view-from-the-right.

Gallie, D. (2007) 'Production regimes and the quality of employment in Europe', *Annual Review of Sociology*, 33(1): 85–104.

Gallup (2020) 'At 65%, approval of labor unions in U.S. remains high'. Available from: https://news.gallup.com/poll/318980/approval-labor-unions-remains-high.aspx.

Gardiner, L. (2015) 'The scale of minimum wage underpayment in social care', Resolution Foundation Briefing. Available from: www.resolutionfoundation.org/app/uploads/2015/02/NMW-social-care-note1.pdf.

Gardiner, L. and Slaughter, H. (2020) 'The effects of the coronavirus crisis on workers', *Spotlight*, Resolution Foundation, 16 May. Available from: www.resolutionfoundation.org/app/uploads/2020/05/The-effect-of-the-coronavirus-crisis-on-workers.pdf.

Gartrell, A. (2017) 'Even coalition voters believe the minimum wage is too low, polling finds', *The Sydney Morning Herald*, 16 April. Available from: www.smh.com.au/politics/federal/even-coalition-voters-believe-the-minimum-wage-is-too-low-polling-finds-20170416-gvlpdo.html.

Geary, D. (2015) 'The Moynihan Report: An annotated edition', *The Atlantic*, September. Available from: www.theatlantic.com/politics/archive/2015/09/the-moynihan-report-an-annotated-edition/404632/#Chapter%20IV.

Gertner, A.K., Rotter, J.S. and Shafer, P.R. (2019) 'Association between state minimum wages and suicide rates in the U.S.', *American Journal of Preventive Medicine*, 56: 648–54.

Gingrich, J. and Häusermann, S. (2015) 'The decline of the working-class vote, the reconfiguration of the welfare support coalition and consequences for the welfare state', *Journal of European Social Policy*, 25(1): 50–75.

Gingrich, N., Reed, B. and Schanzenbach, D. (2018) 'The past, present, and future of welfare', *Pathways*, Winter, pp 3–8.

Glasmeier, A./MIT (2020) 'About the living wage calculator'. Available from: https://livingwage.mit.edu/pages/about.

Goodman, P.S. (2017) 'The robots are coming and Sweden is fine', *The New York Times*, 27 December. Available from: www.nytimes. com/2017/12/27/business/the-robots-are-coming-and-sweden-is-fine.html.

Gorz, A. (1982) *Farewell to the Working Class: An Essay on Post-Industrial Socialism*, trans. M. Sonenscher, London: Pluto Press.

Gould, E. (2020a) 'State of working America wages 2019: A story of slow, uneven, and unequal wage growth over the last 40 years', Economic Policy Institute, 20 February. Available from: www.epi. org/publication/swa-wages-2019/.

Gould, E. (2020b) 'Six months into the recession and a 11.5 million jobs deficit remains', Economic Policy Institute, Economic Indicators, 4 September. Available from: www.epi.org/press/six-months-into-the-recession-and-a-11-5-million-jobs-deficit-remains/.

Government of Alberta (2019) Minimum wage expert panel. Available from: www.alberta.ca/minimum-wage-expert-panel.aspx.

Government of British Columbia (n.d.) Fair Wages Commission. Available from: https://engage.gov.bc.ca/fairwagescommission/.

Graeber, D. (2018) *Bullshit Jobs: A Theory*, New York: Simon & Schuster.

Graham, F. (2020) 'Spain's epic economics experiment', *Nature*, 10 July. Available from: www.nature.com/articles/d41586-020-02088-9.

Greenberg, S. (2019) *RIP GOP: How the New America Is Dooming the Republicans*, New York: Thomas Dunne Books.

Greenhouse, S. (2019) *Beaten Down, Worked Up: The Past, Present and Future of American Labor*, New York: Alfred A. Knopf.

Grover, C. (2016) 'From wage supplements to a "living wage"? A commentary on the problems of predistribution in Britain's summer budget of 2015', *Critical Social Policy*, 36(4): 693–703.

Grusky, D.B., Varner, C., Mattingly, M. and Garlow, S. (2018) 'Editors' note', *Pathways: A Magazine on Poverty, Inequality and Social Policy*, Winter, p 2.

Haag, M. and McGeehan, P. (2019) 'Uber fined $649 million for saying drivers aren't employees', *The New York Times*, 14 November. Available from: www.nytimes.com/2019/11/14/nyregion/uber-new-jersey-drivers.html.

Habermas, J. (1986) 'The new obscurity: The crisis of the welfare state and the exhaustion of utopian energies', trans. P. Jacobs, *Philosophy & Social Criticism*, 11(2): 1–18.

Hacker, J. (2015) 'Jacob Hacker: Miliband's not talking about "predistribution" but he has embraced my big idea', *The New Statesman*, 29 April. Available from: www.newstatesman.com/politics/2015/04/jacob-hacker-miliband-s-not-talking-about-predistribution-he-has-embraced-my-big.

Hacker, J. and Pierson, P. (2011) *Winner Take All Politics: How Washington Made the Rich Richer – and Turned Its Back on the Middle Class*, New York: Simon & Schuster.

Hall, P.A. and Soskice, D. (eds) (2001) *Varieties of Capitalism: The Institutional Foundations of Comparative Advantage*, Oxford: Oxford University Press.

Healy, J. and Richardson, S. (2006) *An Updated Profile of the Minimum Wage Workforce in Australia*, National Institute of Labour Studies. Available from: https://melbourneinstitute.unimelb.edu.au/assets/documents/hilda-bibliography/other-publications/pre2010/Healy_etal_AFPC_1_MW_workers.pdf.

Hegewisch, A. and Gornick, J.C. (2011) 'The impact of work-family policies on women's employment: A review of research from OECD countries', *Community, Work & Family*, 14(2): 119–38.

Henriques-Gomes, L. (2020) 'Australia's jobless benefits will be among worst in OECD after Covid supplement cut', *The Guardian*, 8 September. Available from: www.theguardian.com/business/2020/sep/08/australias-jobless-benefits-will-be-among-worst-in-oecd-after-covid-supplement-cut.

Hick, R. and Lanau, A. (2019) 'Tax credits and in-work poverty in the UK: An analysis of income packages and anti-poverty performance', *Social Policy and Society*, 18(2): 219–36.

Higgins, H.B. (1915) 'New province for law and order', *Harvard Law Review*, 29(1): 13–39.

Higgins, W. and Dow, G. (2013) *Politics Against Pessimism: Social Democratic Possibilities Since Ernst Wigforss*, Bern: Peter Lang.

Hiilamo, H. (2019) 'Disappointing results from the Finnish basic income experiment', Nordic Welfare News, University of Helsinki, 2 February. Available from: www.helsinki.fi/en/news/nordic-welfare-news/heikki-hiilamo-disappointing-results-from-the-finnish-basic-income-experiment.

Howard, C. (1997) *The Hidden Welfare State: Tax Expenditures and Social Policy in the United States*, Princeton, NJ: Princeton University Press.

Huizar, L. and Lathrop, Y. (2019) *Fighting Wage Preemption: How Workers Have Lost Billions in Wages and How We Can Restore Local Democracy*, National Employment Law Project Report, 3 July. Available from: www.nelp.org/publication/fighting-wage-preemption/.

Ingraham, C. (2019) 'Voters in battleground districts support $15 minimum wage proposal, survey finds', *The Washington Post*, 28 March. Available from: www.washingtonpost.com/us-policy/2019/03/28/voters-battleground-districts-support-minimum-wage-proposal-survey-finds/.

Ip, G. and Whitehouse, M. (2006) 'How Milton Friedman changed economics, policy and markets', *The Wall Street Journal*, 17 November. Available from: www.wsj.com/articles/SB116369744597625238.

ISSP Research Group (2017) International Social Survey Programme: Work Orientations IV – ISSP 2015. GESIS Data Archive, Cologne. ZA6770 Data file Version 2.1.0, https://doi.org/10.4232/1.12848.

ITUC (International Trade Union Confederation) (2019) *ITUC Global Rights Index 2019*. Available from: www.ituc-csi.org/rights-index-2019.

Iversen, T. and Soskice, D. (2006) 'Electoral institutions and the politics of coalitions: Why some democracies redistribute more than others', *American Political Science Review*, 100(2): 165–81.

Jackson, A. (2019) 'Yes, the best form of welfare is a job. But…', *The Sydney Morning Herald*, 10 September. Available from: www.smh.com.au/politics/federal/yes-the-best-form-of-welfare-is-a-job-but-20190910-p52ptr.html.

Johnson, M., Koukiadaki, A. and Grimshaw, D. (2019) 'The living wage in the UK: Testing the limits of soft regulation?', *Transfer: European Review of Labour and Research*, 25(3): 319–33.

Kaine, S. and Josserand, E. (2019) 'The organisation and experience of work in the gig economy', *Journal of Industrial Relations*, 61(4): 479–501.

Karp, P. (2019) 'Labor vows to change Fair Work Commission rules to lift "unfair" minimum wage', *The Guardian*, 12 March. Available from: www.theguardian.com/australia-news/2019/mar/12/labor-vows-to-change-fair-work-commission-rules-to-lift-unfair-minimum-wage.

Kaufman, J.A., Salas-Hernández, L.K., Komro, K.A. and Livingston, M.D. (2020) 'Effects of increased minimum wages by unemployment rate on suicide in the USA', *Journal of Epidemiology & Community Health*, 74(3): 219–24.

Kelsey, J. (1995) *Economic Fundamentalism: The New Zealand Experiment: A World Model for Structural Adjustment?*, London: Pluto Press.

Kenworthy, L. (2008) *Jobs with Equality*, Oxford: Oxford University Press.

Kenworthy, L. (2015) 'Do employment-conditional earnings subsidies work?', ImPRovE Working Paper No. 15/10, Antwerp: Herman Deleeck Centre for Social Policy, University of Antwerp.

Kim, K.T., Wilmarth, M.J. and Henager, R. (2017) 'Poverty levels and debt indicators among low-income households before and after the Great Recession', *Journal of Financial Counseling and Planning*, 28(2): 196–212.

Klandermans, B. (1988) 'The formation and mobilization of consensus', in B. Klandermans, H. Kriesi and S. Tarrow (eds) *International Social Movement Research*, vol. 1, *From Structure to Action: Comparing Movement Participation Across Cultures*, Greenwich, CT: JAI Press, pp 173–97.

Klein, N. (2007) *The Shock Doctrine: The Rise of Disaster Capitalism*, New York: Allen Lane.

Kochan, T., Yang, D., Kelly, E.L. and Kimball, W. (2018) 'Who wants to join a union? A growing number of Americans', *The Conversation*. Available from: https://theconversation.com/who-wants-to-join-a-union-a-growing-number-of-americans-102374.

Korpi, W. (1980) 'Social policy and distributional conflict in the capitalist democracies: A preliminary comparative framework', *West European Politics*, 3(3): 296–316.

Krugman, P. (2015) 'Liberals and wages', *The New York Times*, 15 July. Available from: www.nytimes.com/2015/07/17/opinion/paul-krugman-liberals-and-wages.html.

Krugman, P. (2016) 'Mind-altering economics', *The New York Times*, 13 January. Available from: https://krugman.blogs.nytimes.com/2016/01/13/mind-altering-economics/.

Krugman, P. (2019) 'Mourning the loss of Alan Krueger', *The New York Times*, 19 March. Available from: www.nytimes.com/2019/03/19/opinion/alan-krueger-dies.html.

Krugman, P. (2020) 'Why does America hate its children?', *The New York Times*, 16 January. Available from: www.nytimes.com/2020/01/16/opinion/children-america.html.

Lake, M. (2019) *Progressive New World: How Settler Colonialism and Transpacific Exchange Shaped American Reform*, Harvard, MA: Harvard University Press.

Lansley, S. (2014) 'Britain's wages crisis: Is "predistribution" or "redistribution" the way forward?', *Political Quarterly*, 85(1): 3–10.

Lathrop, Y. (2019) *Raises From Coast to Coast in 2020: Minimum Wage Will Increase in Record-High 47 States, Cities, and Counties This January*, National Employment Law Project Report, 23 December. Available from: www.nelp.org/publication/raises-coast-coast-2020/.

Leduc, S. and Liu Z. (2019) 'Are workers losing to robots?', *FRBSF Economic Letter*, 30 September. Available from: www.frbsf.org/economic-research/files/el2019-25.pdf.

Lee, D.S. (1999) 'Wage inequality in the United States during the 1980s: Rising dispersion or falling minimum wage?', *Quarterly Journal of Economics*, 114(3): 977–1023.

Lee, T. (2016) '"I told you so": Former McDonald's exec blames Fight for $15 for new touchscreen ordering', *Vox*, 30 November. Available at: www.vox.com/new-money/2016/11/30/13784412/mcdonalds-fight-for-15.

Leonard, T.C. (2000) 'The very idea of applying economics: The modern minimum-wage controversy and its antecedents', *History of Political Economy*, 32(5): 117–44.

Lester, R.A. (1947) 'Marginalism, minimum wages, and labor markets', *American Economic Review*, 37(1): 135–48.

Levine, M. (2018) 'Behind the minimum wage fight, a sweeping failure to enforce the law', Politico, 18 February. Available from: www.politico.com/story/2018/02/18/minimum-wage-not-enforced-investigation-409644.

Levin-Waldman, O. and Whalen, C. (2007) 'The minimum wage is a middle-class issue', *Challenge*, 50(3): 59–71.

Levitz, E. (2019) 'What Andrew Yang gets wrong (and right) about robots', *New York Magazine* (Intelligencer), 2 August. Available from: http://nymag.com/intelligencer/2019/08/what-andrew-yang-gets-wrong-and-right-about-automation.html.

Low Pay Commission (2017) *Non-compliance and Enforcement of the National Minimum Wage*. Available from: https://assets.publishing.service.gov.uk/government/uploads/system/uploads/attachment_data/file/645462/Non-compliance_and_enforcement_with_the_National_Minimum_Wage.pdf.

Low Pay Commission (2018) *National Minimum Wage: Low Pay Commission Report*. Available from: www.gov.uk/government/publications/national-minimum-wage-low-pay-commission-2018-report.

Low Pay Commission (2019) *20 Years of the National Minimum Wage: A History of the UK Minimum Wage and its Effects*. Available from: www.gov.uk/government/publications/20-years-of-the-national-minimum-wage.

Low Pay Commission of Ireland (2019) *Three Year Report (2015–2018)*, LPC no 11, January. Available from: https://assets.gov.ie/40388/2f7092f324644333bf38e3e4799aeea5.pdf.

Low Pay Commission of Ireland (2020) 'The Low Pay Commission'. Available from: www.gov.ie/en/campaigns/6fc06b-low-pay-commission/.

Luce, S. (2004) *Fighting for a Living Wage*, Ithaca, NY: Cornell University Press.

Luce, S. (2005) 'Lessons from living-wage campaigns', *Work and Occupations*, 32(4): 423–40.

Mabbett, D. (2016) 'The minimum wage in Germany: What brought the state in?', *Journal of European Public Policy*, 23(8): 1240–58.

McBride, S. and Williams, R.A. (2001) 'Globalization, the restructuring of labour markets and policy convergence: The OECD 'Jobs Strategy', *Global Social Policy*, 1(3): 281–309.

McCallum, M.E. (1986) 'Keeping women in their place: The minimum wage in Canada, 1910–1925', *Labour/Le Travail*, 1: 29–56.

McKnight, A. (2020) 'Sharp fall in wage inequality', LSE News FAQ. Available from: www.lse.ac.uk/News/Latest-news-from-LSE/2020/c-March-20/Sharp-fall-in-wage-inequality.

MacLeavy, J. (2011) 'A 'new politics' of austerity, workfare and gender? The UK coalition government's welfare reform proposals', *Cambridge Journal of Regions, Economy and Society*, 4: 355–67.

Major, L.E. and Machin, S. (2018) 'Social mobility requires far more than a good education', *The Guardian*, 27 September. Available from: www.theguardian.com/commentisfree/2018/sep/27/social-mobility-good-education.

Mallon, A.J. and Stevens, G.V. (2011) 'Making the 1996 welfare reform work: The promise of a job', *Journal of Poverty*, 15(2): 113–40.

Manning, A. (2020) 'Monopsony in labor markets: A review', *Industrial and Labor Relations Review*, 9(4): 577–88.

Manyika, J. and Sneader, K. (2018) AI, automation, and the future of work: Ten things to solve for, Briefing Note, 1 June, McKinsey Global Institute. Available from: www.mckinsey.com/~/media/McKinsey/Featured%20Insights/Future%20of%20Organizations/AI%20automation%20and%20the%20future%20of%20work%20Ten%20things%20to%20solve%20for/MGI-Briefing-Note-AI-automation-and-the-future-of-work_June2018.pdf

Manyika, J., Lund, S., Chui, M., Bughin, J., Woetzel, J., Batra, P., Ko, R. and Sanghvi, S. (2017) *Jobs Lost, Jobs Gained: Workforce Transitions in an Age of Automation*, Report, McKinsey Global Institute. Available from: www.mckinsey.com/~/media/BAB489A30B724BECB5DEDC41E9BB9FAC.ashx.

Marin-Guzman, D. (2019) 'Australia now has world's highest minimum wage', *The Australian Financial Review*, 12 July. Available from: www.afr.com/work-and-careers/workplace/australia-now-has-world-s-highest-minimum-wage-20190712-p526nv.

Martinelli, L. (2019) 'Basic income: World's first national experiment in Finland shows only modest benefits', *The Conversation*, 22 February. Available at: https://theconversation.com/basic-income-worlds-first-national-experiment-in-finland-shows-only-modest-benefits-111391.

Marx, P. and Starke, P. (2017) 'Dualization as destiny? The political economy of the German minimum wage reform', *Politics & Society*, 45(4): 559–84.

Mason, J.W. (2018) 'Income distribution, household debt, and aggregate demand: A critical assessment', Levy Economics Institute of Bard College Working Paper No. 901. Available from: www.levyinstitute.org/pubs/wp_901.pdf.

Matsakis, L. (2018) 'Why Amazon really raised its minimum wage to $15', *Wired*, 2 October. Available from: www.wired.com/story/why-amazon-really-raised-minimum-wage/.

Mayor of London/London Assembly (2020) 'London living wage'. Available from: www.london.gov.uk/what-we-do/business-and-economy/london-living-wage.

Mead, L. (1997) *The New Paternalism: Supervisory Approaches to Poverty*, Washington, DC: Brookings Institution Press.

Meagher, G. and Szebehely, M. (2019) 'The politics of profit in Swedish welfare services: Four decades of Social Democratic ambivalence', *Critical Social Policy*, 39(3): 455–76.

Meagher, G. and Wilson, S. (2015) 'The politics of market encroachment: Policy maker rationales and voter responses', in G. Meagher and S. Goodwin (eds) *Markets, Rights and Power in Australian Social Policy*, Sydney: Sydney University Press, pp 29–96.

Meyer, D.S. (2003) 'Social movements and public policy: Eggs, chicken and theory'. Available at: https://escholarship.org/uc/item/2m62b74d.

Meyer, D. and Tarrow, S. (2018) 'Introduction', in D. Meyer and S. Tarrow (eds) *The Resistance: The Dawn of the Anti-Trump Opposition Movement*, Oxford: Oxford University Press, pp 1–24.

Milanovic, B. (2016) *Global Inequality: A New Approach for the Age of Globalization*, Cambridge, MA: Belknap Press of Harvard University Press.

Ministry of Business, Innovation & Employment (2018) *Minimum Wage Review 2018*. Available from: www.mbie.govt.nz/business-and-employment/employment-and-skills/employment-legislation-reviews/minimum-wage-reviews/.

Ministry of Business, Innovation & Employment (2019) *Minimum Wage Review 2019*. Available from: www.mbie.govt.nz/business-and-employment/employment-and-skills/employment-legislation-reviews/minimum-wage-reviews/.

Mishel, L. (2012) 'The decline of collective bargaining and the erosion of middle-class incomes in Michigan', EPI Briefing Paper #347. Available from: www.epi.org/publication/bp347-collective-bargaining/.

Mishel, L. and Schmitt, J. (eds) (1995) *Beware the US Model: Jobs and Wages in a Deregulated Economy*, Washington, DC: Economic Policy Institute.

Moffitt, R.A. and Garlow, S. (2018) 'Did welfare reform increase employment and reduce poverty?', *Pathways*, Winter, pp 17–21.

Moody, K. (1997) *Workers in a Lean World: Unions in the International Economy*, New York: Verso.

Moody, K. (2017) *On New Terrain: How Capital is Reshaping the Battleground of Class War*, Chicago: Haymarket Books.

Morath, E. (2019) 'The federal minimum wage really doesn't matter anymore', *The Wall Street Journal*, 11 August. Available from www.wsj.com/articles/the-federal-minimum-wage-doesnt-really-matter-anymore-11565515801.

Morris, A. and Wilson, S. (2014) 'Struggling on the Newstart unemployment benefit in Australia: The experience of a neoliberal form of employment assistance', *The Economic and Labour Relations Review*, 25(2): 202–21.

Morris, A., Wilson, S. and Soldatic, K. (2015) 'Doing the "hard yakka": Implications of Australia's workfare policies for disabled people', in C. Grover and L. Piggott (eds) *Disabled People, Work and Welfare: Is Employment Really the Answer?*, Bristol: Policy Press, pp 43–65.

Murray, C. (1980) *Losing Ground: American Social Policy, 1950–1980*, New York: Basic Books.

Myles, J. and Pierson, P. (1997) 'Friedman's revenge: The reform of "liberal" welfare states in Canada and the United States', *Politics & Society*, 25(4): 443–72.

Naidu, S. (2020) 'Conservatives' newfound interest in dignified work', *Boston Review*, 23 January. Available from: https://bostonreview.net/.

Neumark, D. (2015) 'Reducing poverty via minimum wages, alternatives', *FRBSF Economic Letter*, 38: 1–5.

Neumark, D. (2018a) 'The econometrics and economics of the employment effects of minimum wages: Getting from known unknowns to known knowns', CESifo Working Paper, No. 7386, Center for Economic Studies and Ifo Institute, Munich.

Neumark, D. (2018b) 'Employment effects of minimum wages', *IZA World of Labor*, 6(2): 1–10.

Neumark, D. and Shupe, C. (2019) 'Declining teen employment: Minimum wages, returns to schooling, and immigration', *Labour Economics*, 59: 49–68.

Nissen, B. (2000) 'Living wage campaigns from a "social movement" perspective: The Miami case', *Labor Studies Journal*, 25(3): 29–50.

Nolan, B. and Valenzuela, L. (2019) 'Inequality and its discontents', *Oxford Review of Economic Policy*, 35(3): 396–430.

O'Donnell, J. (2019) 'Why basic income in Finland failed', *Jacobin*, 1 December. Available from: www.jacobinmag.com/2019/12/basic-income-finland-experiment-kela.

OECD (Organisation for Economic Co-operation and Development) (1994) *The OECD Jobs Study: Facts, Analysis, Strategies*, Paris: OECD.

OECD (2014) *United States: Tackling High Inequalities, Creating Opportunities for All.* Available from: www.oecd.org/unitedstates/Tackling-high-inequalities.pdf.

OECD (2015) 'Labour underutilisation rate'. Available from: http://oecdinsights.org/glossary/labour-underutilisation-rate/.

OECD (2016) 'Social spending stays at historically high levels in many OECD countries', Social Expenditure Update, October. Available from: www.oecd.org/els/soc/OECD2016-Social-Expenditure-Update.pdf.

OECD (2018a) *A Broken Social Elevator? How to Promote Social Mobility.* Available from: www.oecd.org/social/broken-elevator-how-to-promote-social-mobility-9789264301085-en.htm.

OECD (2018b) *Good Jobs for All in a Changing World of Work: The OECD Jobs Strategy.* Available from: www.oecd.org/publications/good-jobs-for-all-in-a-changing-world-of-work-9789264308817-en.htm.

OECD (2019a) *Under Pressure: The Squeezed Middle Class.* Available from: www.oecd.org/social/under-pressure-the-squeezed-middle-class-689afed1-en.htm.

OECD (2019b) *Under Pressure: The Squeezed Middle Class: Overview and Main Findings.* Available from: www.oecd.org/els/soc/OECD-middle-class-2019-main-findings.pdf.

OECD (2019c) *Better Life Index: Housing.* Available from: www.oecdbetterlifeindex.org/topics/housing/.

OECD (2019d) 'HC1.2 Housing costs over income'. Available from: www.oecd.org/els/family/HC1-2-Housing-costs-over-income.pdf.

OECD (2019e) *The Future of Work: OECD Employment Outlook 2019: Highlights.* Available from: www.oecd.org/employment/ Employment-Outlook-2019-Highlight-EN.pdf.

OECD (2020a) 'Labour: Earnings: Minimum relative to average wages of full-time workers'. Available from: https://stats.oecd.org/.

OECD (2020b) 'Social protection: Income distribution and poverty: By country – poverty'. Available from: https://data.oecd.org/ inequality/poverty-rate.htm.

OECD (2020c) 'Trade unions and collective bargaining: Collective bargaining coverage'. Available from: https://stats.oecd.org/.

OECD (2020d) 'Employment rate'. Available from: https://data.oecd. org/emp/employment-rate.htm.

OECD (2020e) 'Unemployment rate'. Available from: https://data. oecd.org/unemp/unemployment-rate.htm.

OECD (2020f) 'Social protection and well-being: Social protection: Social expenditure – aggregated data'. Available from: https://stats. oecd.org/.

OECD (2020g) 'Labour: Earnings: Decile ratios of gross earnings: Low pay incidence'. Available from: https://stats.oecd.org.

OECD (2020h) 'Labour: Earnings: Decile ratios of gross earnings'. Available from: https://stats.oecd.org.

OECD (2020i) 'General government deficit'. Available from: https:// data.oecd.org/gga/general-government-deficit.htm.

O'Neill, S. (1993) 'Labour market deregulation: The New Zealand experience', Background Paper no 5, Parliamentary Research Service, Department of the Parliamentary Library, Parliament of the Commonwealth of Australia.

ONS (Office for National Statistics) (2019) *Low and High Pay in the UK: 2019: The Distribution of Earnings of High- and Low-paid Jobs and Jobs Paid below the National Minimum Wage*, 29 August. Available from www.ons.gov.uk/employmentandlabourmarket/peopleinwork/ earningsandworkinghours/bulletins/lowandhighpayuk/2019.

O'Sullivan, M. and Wallace, J. (2011) 'Minimum labour standards in a social partnership system: The persistence of the Irish variant of wages councils', *Industrial Relations Journal*, 42(1): 18–35.

Partington, R. (2019) 'Gig economy in Britain doubles, accounting for 4.7 million workers', *The Guardian*, 28 June. Available from: www. theguardian.com/business/2019/jun/28/gig-economy-in-britain-doubles-accounting-for-47-million-workers.

Patten, S. (2013) 'The triumph of neoliberalism within partisan conservatism in Canada', in J. Farney and D. Rayside (eds) *Conservatism in Canada*, Toronto: University of Toronto Press, pp 59–76.

Patty, A. (2018) 'Australia's underemployment rate and gender pay gap worse than OECD average', *The Sydney Morning Herald*, 10 December. Available from: www.smh.com.au/business/workplace/australia-s-underemployment-and-gender-pay-gap-worse-than-oecd-average-20181206-p50kni.html.

Peetz, D. (2010) 'Are individualistic attitudes killing collectivism?', *Transfer: European Review of Labour and Research*, 16(3): 383–98.

Pickert, R. (2019) 'For 53 million Americans in low-wage jobs, a difficult road out', Bloomberg. Available from: www.bloomberg.com/news/articles/2019-11-07/53-million-in-u-s-have-low-wage-jobs-they-ll-likely-stay-there.

Pierson, P. (1994) *Dismantling the Welfare State? Reagan, Thatcher and the Politics of Retrenchment*, Cambridge: Cambridge University Press.

Piketty, T. (2013) *Capital in the Twenty-First Century*, Cambridge, MA: Harvard University Press.

Piketty, T. (2016) 'Basic income or fair wage?', Le Blog de Thomas Piketty, *Le Monde*, 13 December. Available from: https://www.lemonde.fr/blog/piketty/2016/12/13/basic-income-or-fair-wage/.

Piketty, T. (2020) *Capital and Ideology*, Cambridge, MA: Harvard University Press.

Pixley, J. (1993) *Citizenship and Employment: Investigating Post-industrial Options*, Cambridge: Cambridge University Press.

Polanyi, K. ([1944] 2001) *The Great Transformation: The Political and Economic Origins of our Time*, Boston: Beacon Press.

Powell, D. and Patty, A. (2020) 'Government tells companies to "get house in order" after Coles workers underpaid', *The Sydney Morning Herald*, 18 February. Available at: www.smh.com.au/business/companies/coles-store-managers-underpaid-20-million-over-six-years-20200218-p541ry.html.

Prasch, R.E. (1999) 'American economists in the progressive era on the minimum wage', *Journal of Economic Perspectives*, 13(2): 221–30.

Pressman, S. and Scott, R.H. (2010) 'Consumer debt and poverty measurement', *Focus*, 27(1): 9–12.

Prowse, P., Fells, R., Arrowsmith, J., Parker, J. and Lopes, A. (2017) 'Low pay and the living wage: An international perspective', *Employee Relations*, 39(6): 778–84.

Prowse, P., Lopes, A. and Fells, R. (2017) 'Community and union-led living wage campaigns', *Employee Relations*, 39(6): 825–39.

Ramesh, R. (2010) 'Does getting tough on the unemployed work', *The Guardian*, 16 June. Available from www.theguardian.com/society/2010/jun/16/lawrence-mead-tough-us-welfare-unemployed.

Redmond, P., Doorley, K. and McGuinness, S. (2019) 'The impact of a change in the national minimum wage on the distribution of hourly wages and household income in Ireland', Economic and Social Research Institute Research Series Number 86, March. Available from: www.esri.ie.

Reiakvam, L.K. and Solheim, H. (2013) Staff memo: Comparison of household debt relative to income across four Nordic countries, no 5, Norges Bank. Available from www.norges-bank.no/contentassets/a536086336bd49caa0234d37a6b4d4b8/staff_memo_2013_05_eng.pdf.

Reynolds, D. (2001) 'Living wage campaigns as social movements: Experiences from nine cities', *Labor Studies Journal*, 26(2): 31–64.

Rickard, J. (1984) *HB Higgins: The Rebel as Judge*, Sydney: Allen & Unwin.

Rifkin, J. (2000) *The End of Work: The Decline of the Global Work-force and the Dawn of the Post-market Era*, rev. edn, London: Penguin Books.

Rogers, B. (2019) 'Justice at work: Minimum wage laws and social equality', *Texas Law Review*, 92: 1543–97.

Roosevelt, M. (2020) 'The number of Californians represented by unions grows as national labor organizing stagnates', *The Los Angeles Times*, 23 January. Available from: www.latimes.com/business/story/2020-01-23/california-labor-union-membership.

Rose, M. (2004) *The Mind at Work: Valuing the Intelligence of the American Worker*, London: Penguin.

Ross, M. and Bateman, N. (2019) *Meet the Low-Wage Workforce*, Metropolitan Policy Program at Brookings. Available from: www.brookings.edu/wp-content/uploads/2019/11/201911_Brookings-Metro_low-wage-workforce_Ross-Bateman.pdf#page=9.

Ross, M. and Bateman, N. (2020) 'Low unemployment isn't worth much if the jobs barely pay', Brookings, 8 January. Available from: www.brookings.edu/blog/the-avenue/2020/01/08/low-unemployment-isnt-worth-much-if-the-jobs-barely-pay/.

Rothstein, J. and Zipperer, B. (2020) 'The EITC and minimum wage work together to reduce poverty and raise incomes', Economic Policy Institute. Available from: www.epi.org/publication/eitc-and-minimum-wage-work-together/.

Rothwell, J. and Crabtree, S. (2020) *Not Just a Job: New Evidence on the Quality of Work in the United States*. Available from: www.gallup.com/education/267590/great-jobs-lumina-gates-omidyar-gallup-quality-report-2019.aspx.

Rowell, A. and Madland, D. (2018) 'The working-class push for progressive economic policies', Center for American Progress Action Fund. Available from: www.americanprogressaction.org/issues/economy/reports/2018/04/17/169879/working-class-push-progressive-economic-policies/.

Sachs, J. and Wyplosz, C. (1986) 'The economic consequences of President Mitterrand', *Economic Policy*, 1(2): 261–306.

Sanders, B. (2020) 'Taxpayers subsidize poverty wages at Walmart, McDonald's, other large corporations, GAO finds', 18 November. Available from: www.sanders.senate.gov/newsroom/press-releases/taxpayers-subsidize-poverty-wages-at-walmart-mcdonalds-other-large-corporations-gao-finds.

Saunders, P. and Bedford, M. (2017) *New Minimum Income for Healthy Living Budget Standards for Low-Paid and Unemployed Australians*, SPRC Report 11/17, Sydney: Social Policy Research Centre, UNSW Sydney. Available from: http://doi.org/10.4225/53/5994e0ca804a4.

Sawer, M. (2012) 'Andrew Fisher and the era of liberal reform', *Labour History*, 102: 71–6.

Schmitt, C. and Starke, P. (2011) 'Explaining convergence of OECD welfare states: A conditional approach', *Journal of European Social Policy*, 21(2): 120–35.

Schmitt, J. and Wadsworth, J. (2002) 'Is the OECD jobs strategy behind US and British employment and unemployment success in the 1990s?', CEPA Working Paper 2002–06, April.

Schultz, M.A. (2019) 'The wage mobility of low-wage workers in a changing economy, 1968 to 2014', *RSF: The Russell Sage Foundation Journal of the Social Sciences*, 5(4): 159–89.

Seager, H.R. (1913) 'The minimum wage as part of a program for social reform', *The Annals of the American Academy of Political and Social Science*, 48: 3–12.

Semega, J., Kollar, M., Creamer, J. and Mohanty, A. (2019) *U.S. Census Bureau, Current Population Reports, P60-266, Income and Poverty in the United States: 2018*, Washington, DC: US Government Printing Office.

Semeuls, A. (2016) 'The near impossibility of moving up after welfare', *The Atlantic*, 11 July. Available from: www.theatlantic.com/business/archive/2016/07/life-after-welfare/490586/.

Semeuls, A. and Burnley, M. (2019) 'Low wages, sexual harassment and unreliable tips: This is life in America's booming service industry', *Time*, 22 August. Available from: https://time.com/magazine/us/5658416/september-2nd-2019-vol-194-no-8-u-s/.

Shaefer, L.H. and Edin, K. (2018) 'Welfare reform and the families it left behind', *Pathways*, Winter, pp 22–7.

Shermer, E.T. (2018) 'The right to work really means the right to work for less', *The Washington Post*, 23 April. Available from: www.washingtonpost.com/news/made-by-history/wp/2018/04/24/the-right-to-work-really-means-the-right-to-work-for-less/.

Simonovits, G., Guess, A.M. and Nagler, J. (2019) 'Responsiveness without representation: Evidence from minimum wage laws in US states', *American Journal of Political Science*, 63(2): 401–10.

Sligar, D. and Sturgess, H. (2020) 'Would a job guarantee be work for the dole 2.0?', *Inside Story*, 8 September. Available from: https://insidestory.org.au/would-a-job-guarantee-be-work-for-the-dole-2-0/.

Song, X., Massey, C.G., Rolf, K.A., Ferrie, J.P., Rothbaum, J.L. and Xie, Y. (2020) 'Long-term decline in intergenerational mobility in the United States since the 1850s', *Proceedings of the National Academy of Sciences*, 117(1): 251–8.

Stabile, D. (2016) *The Political Economy of a Living Wage: Progressives, the New Deal, and Social Justice*, London: Palgrave Macmillan.

Standing, G. (2011) *The Precariat: A New Dangerous Class*, London: Bloomsbury.

Standing, G. (2015) *A Basic Income: And How We Can Make It Happen*, London: Penguin Books.

Stansbury, A. and Summers, L. (2020) 'Declining worker power and American economic performance', *Brookings Papers on Economic Activity*. Available from: www.brookings.edu/wp-content/uploads/2020/03/Stansbury-Summers-Conference-Draft.pdf.

Starke, P. (2006) 'The politics of welfare state retrenchment: A literature review, *Social Policy & Administration*, 40(1): 104–20.

Statistics Canada (2020) 'Employee wages by industry, monthly, unadjusted for seasonality'. Available from: www150.statcan.gc.ca/n1/en/type/data?HPA=1.

Stein, J. (2018) 'In expensive cities, rents fall for the rich, but rise for the poor', *The Washington Post*, 6 August. Available from: www.washingtonpost.com/business/economy/in-expensive-cities-rents-fall-for-the-rich--but-rise-for-the-poor/2018/08/05/a16e5962-96a4-11e8-80e1-00e80e1fdf43_story.html.

Stewart, A. and Stanford, J. (2017) 'Regulating work in the gig economy: What are the options?', *Economic and Labour Relations Review*, 28(3): 420–37.

Stigler, G.J. (1946) 'The economics of minimum wage legislation', *American Economic Review*, 36(3): 358–65.

Sturn, S. (2018) 'Do minimum wages lead to job losses? Evidence from OECD countries on low-skilled and youth employment', *Industrial and Labor Relations Review*, 71(3): 647–75.

Tatsimaros, K. (2020) 'Unemployment benefits and job match quality: Do unemployment benefits help those seeking work to obtain better jobs?', *IZA World of Labor*. Available from: https://wol.iza.org/articles/unemployment-benefits-and-job-match-quality/long.

Tcherneva, P.R. (2017) 'Trump's bait and switch: Job creation in the midst of welfare state sabotage', Levy Economics Institute, Working Paper no. 887. Available from: http://www.levyinstitute.org/publications/trumps-bait-and-switch-job-creation-in-the-midst-of-welfare-state-sabotage.

Tcherneva, P.R. (2018) 'The job guarantee: Design, jobs, and implementation', Levy Economics Institute, Working Paper no. 902. Available from: www.levyinstitute.org/publications/the-job-guarantee-design-jobs-and-implementation.

Tcherneva, P.R. (2020) *The Case for a Job Guarantee*, London: Polity Press.

Tedeschi, E. (2019) 'Americans are seeing highest minimum wage in history (without federal help)', *The New York Times*, 24 April. Available from: www.nytimes.com/2019/04/24/upshot/why-america-may-already-have-its-highest-minimum-wage.html.

Tedeschi, E. (2020) 'Pay is rising fastest for low earners. One reason? Minimum wages', *The New York Times*, 3 January. Available from: www.nytimes.com/2020/01/03/upshot/minimum-wage-boost-bottom-earners.html.

Thompson, P. and Pitts, F.H. (2018) 'Is your job bullshit? And if so, is there life beyond it?', The RSA Blog, 9 July. Available from: www.thersa.org/blog/2018/07/bullshit-about-jobs.

Thornley, C. and Coffee, D. (1999) 'The Low Pay Commission in context', *Work, Employment & Society*, 13(3): 525–38.

Tilly, C. (1999) *Durable Inequality*, Berkeley CA: University of California Press.

University of California Berkeley Labor Center (n.d.) *Low Wage Work in California*. Available from: http://laborcenter.berkeley.edu/low-wage-work-in-california/#industries-and-occupations.

Visser, J. (2016) 'What happened to collective bargaining during the great recession?', *IZA Journal of Labor Policy*, 5(1): 1–35.

Vlandas, T. (2020) 'The political economy of individual level support for the basic income in Europe', *Journal of European Social Policy*. DOI: 10.1177/0958928720923596.

Waltman, J. (2008) *Minimum Wage Policy in Great Britain and the United States*, New York: Algora Publishers.

Waltman, J. and Pittman, S. (2002) 'The determinants of state minimum wage rates: A public policy approach', *Journal of Labor Research*, 23(1): 51–6.

Weaver, K.R. (2000) *Ending Welfare As We Know It*, Washington, DC: Brookings Institution Press.

Weir, M. (1992) *Politics and Jobs: The Boundaries of Employment Policy in the United States*, Princeton, NJ: Princeton University Press.

Weissmann, J. (2016) 'The failure of welfare reform', *Slate*, 1 June. Available from: https://slate.com/news-and-politics/2016/06/how-welfare-reform-failed.html.

Weller, C.E. (2018) 'Working-class families are getting hit from all sides', Center for American Progress, 26 July. Available from: www.americanprogress.org/issues/economy/reports/2018/07/26/453841/working-class-families-getting-hit-sides/.

Wilkins, R. and Lass, I. (2018) *The Household, Income and Labour Dynamics in Australia Survey: Selected Findings from Waves 1 to 16*, Melbourne Institute: Applied Economic & Social Research, University of Melbourne.

Wilkinson, R.D. and Pickett, K. (2009) *The Spirit Level: Why More Equal Societies Almost Always Do Better*, London: Allen Lane/Penguin Group.

Williams, L.A. (1997) 'Rethinking low-wage markets and dependency', *Politics and Society*, 25(4): 541–50.

Williams, M., Zhou, Y. and Zou, M. (2020) *Mapping Good Work: The Quality of Working Life Across the Occupational Structure*, Bristol: Policy Press.

Wilson, S. (2018) 'Superdiversity, exploitation, and migrant workers', in J. Pixley and H. Flam (eds) *Critical Junctures in Mobile Capital*, Cambridge: Cambridge University Press, pp 254–67.

Wilson, S. (2020) 'Rising pressures, new scaffolding, uncertain futures: Australia's social policy response to the COVID-19 pandemic', *Journal of Australian Political Economy*, 85: 183–92.

Wilson, S. and Spies-Butcher, B. (2011) 'When Labour makes a difference: Union mobilization and the 2007 federal election in Australia', *British Journal of Industrial Relations*, 49(Supplement 2): s306–31.

Wilson, S. and Spies-Butcher, B. (2016) 'After New Labour: Political and policy consequences of welfare state reforms in the United Kingdom and Australia', *Policy Studies*, 37(5): 408–25.

Wilson, S., Spies-Butcher, B., Stebbing, A. and St John, S. (2013) 'Wage-earners' welfare after economic reform: Refurbishing, retrenching or hollowing out social protection in Australia and New Zealand?', *Social Policy & Administration*, 47(6): 623–46.

Wray, L.R. (2018) 'A consensus strategy for a universal job guarantee program', Policy Note, Levy Economics Institute. Available from: www.levyinstitute.org/pubs/pn_2018_3.pdf.

Wright, E.O. (2000) *Class Counts: Student Edition*, Cambridge: Cambridge University Press.

Wright, E.O. (2004) 'Basic income, stakeholder grants, and class analysis', *Politics & Society*, 32(1): 79–87.

Wright, E.O. (2015) *Understanding Class*, London: Verso.

Yang, K.-C., Varol, O., Davis, C.A., Ferrara, E., Flammini, A. and Menczer, F. (2019) 'Arming the public with artificial intelligence to counter social bots', *Human Behavior and Emerging Technologies*, special issue article, 6 February. Available from: https://onlinelibrary.wiley.com/doi/full/10.1002/hbe2.115.

Yon, H. (2020) 'Employers circumvent minimum wage burdens by reducing hours and benefits, report shows', Hankyoreh (news website). Available from: http://english.hani.co.kr/arti/english_edition/e_business/923344.html.

Index

www.ingramcontent.com/pod-product-compliance
Lightning Source LLC
Chambersburg PA
CBHW070924030426
42336CB00014BA/2520